스파르타 토익 Vol.3

실전 1000제

LISTENING

English&북스

스파르타 토익

실전 1000제

LISTENING Vol.3

1쇄 인쇄 2021년 5월 26일
1쇄 발행 2021년 5월 28일

저 자 잉글리쉬앤 어학연구소
펴낸이 박성호
펴낸곳 잉글리쉬앤 (주)

편 집 박고우니, 박혜리
마케팅 박상신, 정슬기

주 소 서울 특별시 관악구 쑥고개로 67-1
대표전화 (02) 878-1945
출판등록 2002년 3월 3일 제 320-2002-00045호

ISBN 978-89-6715-140-9 13740

* 가격은 뒤표지에 있습니다. 파본은 바꾸어 드립니다.
www.english.co.kr

CONTENTS

■ 토익 소개 4
■ 파트별 출제 경향 6
■ 학습 플랜 13

실전 모의고사

TEST 01 14
TEST 02 28
TEST 03 42
TEST 04 56
TEST 05 70
TEST 06 84
TEST 07 98
TEST 08 112
TEST 09 126
TEST 10 140

정답 및 스크립트 154

온라인 모의고사 이용 방법

books.english.co.kr 접속 ▶ 상단 메뉴 '도서인증받기' 클릭
▶ 인증 내용 입력 ▶ 인증 완료 ▶ 테스트 응시

토익 소개

토익이란?

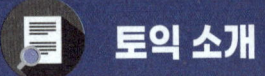

Test Of English for International Communication의 약자로, 영어가 모국어가 아닌 사람들의 일상생활이나 국제 업무 등에 필요한 실용 영어 능력을 평가하는 국제 평가 시험

▶ 시험 구성

구성	Part	유형		문항 수		시간	배점
듣기(LC)	1	사진 묘사		6	100	45분	495점
	2	질의 응답		25			
	3	대화문		39			
	4	담화문		30			
읽기(RC)	5	단문 공란 채우기		30	100	75분	495점
	6	장문 공란 채우기		16			
	7	지문 독해	단일 지문	29			
			복수 지문	25			
TOTAL	7 Parts			200문항		120분	990점

▶ 시험 내용

Part	유형	유형 내용
1	사진 묘사	제시된 사진을 알맞게 설명하는 보기 고르기
2	질의 응답	질문을 듣고 알맞은 대답 고르기
3	대화문	대화를 듣고 질문에 알맞은 내용 고르기
4	담화문	담화를 듣고 질문에 알맞은 내용 고르기
5	단문 공란 채우기	빈칸에 맞는 내용을 골라 단문 완성하기
6	장문 공란 채우기	빈칸에 맞는 내용을 골라 장문 완성하기
7	지문 독해	단일 지문 또는 이중 · 삼중 지문을 읽고 문제에 맞는 내용 고르기

접수 방법은?

▶ 한국 토익 위원회 사이트 혹은 앱으로 접수 ➔ www.toeic.co.kr
▶ 인터넷 접수할 때 시험일, 고사장, 개인 정보 등을 입력 (증명사진 필요)
※ 접수 마감일 이후 추가 접수일에 접수 시 추가 비용 발생

응시 준비물은?

▶ 규정 신분증 (주민등록증, 운전면허증, 기간 만료 전의 여권, 중고등학생만 학생증 인정)
▶ 연필, 지우개 (볼펜이나 사인펜은 사용 금지)
▶ 아날로그 시계 (전자 시계 불가)

시험 진행은?

▶ **시험 시간이 오전일 경우** 오전 9:20까지 입실 (오전 9:50 이후 입실 불가)
▶ **시험 시간이 오후일 경우** 오후 2:20까지 입실 (오후 2:50 이후 입실 불가)

오전 시험	오후 시험	시험 진행
오전 9:30 ~ 9:45 (15분)	오후 2:30 ~ 2:45 (15분)	답안지 작성에 관한 오리엔테이션
오전 9:45 ~ 9:50 (5분)	오후 2:45 ~ 2:50 (5분)	수험자 휴식 시간
오전 9:50 ~ 10:05 (15분)	오후 2:50 ~ 3:05 (15분)	신분 확인
오전 10:05 ~ 10:10 (5분)	오후 3:05 ~ 3:10 (5분)	문제지 배부, 파본 확인
오전 10:10 ~ 10:55 (45분)	오후 3:10 ~ 3:55 (45분)	듣기 평가(LC)
오전 10:55 ~ 12:10 (75분)	오후 3:55 ~ 5:10 (75분)	읽기 평가(RC)

※ 읽기 평가(RC) 시간에 2차 신분 확인 실시

성적 확인은?

▶ 시험일로부터 약 2주 후에 토익 위원회 사이트(www.toeic.co.kr)에서 확인 가능
▶ 온라인 출력과 우편 수령은 1회 무료, 이후에는 유료 발급

PART 1

사진 묘사 6문제

파트 1은 4개의 보기 중에서 사진을 가장 잘 묘사하는 보기를 고르는 유형이다. 총 6문제가 출제되며, 인물 및 사물/풍경 사진 등 다양한 유형의 사진이 등장한다.

| 핵심 전략 |

- 사진 유형별로 자주 출제되는 어휘와 표현을 익힌다.
- 난이도가 높은 경우 주어가 사물인 보기가 자주 등장하므로 수동태, 현재완료 수동태, 수동태 진행형과 같은 문법을 완벽하게 숙지한다.
- 오답 소거법을 통해, 사진을 완벽하게 묘사한 보기가 아닌 정답에 가장 가까운 Best Answer를 고르도록 훈련한다.
- 유사 발음, 연상 어휘 등을 이용하거나, 사람과 사물의 상태 및 동작을 잘못 묘사하는 오답이 자주 등장한다.

| 문제 형태 |

1

Look at the picture marked number one in your test book.

(A) She is cleaning her desk.
(B) She is sharpening a pencil.
(C) She is filing some papers.
(D) She is holding a phone.

PART 2

질의 응답 25문제

파트 2는 3개의 보기 중에서 질문에 가장 적절한 응답을 고르는 유형이다. 문항 수는 총 25개로, 의문사 의문문, Yes/No 의문문 등이 출제된다.

| 핵심 전략 |

- 질문의 앞부분을 집중해서 듣고 질문 유형을 파악하는 연습을 한다.
- 의문사 의문문은 가장 자주 출제되는 유형으로, 답변 패턴이 정해져 있다. 의문사별로 정답 유형을 숙지해 두자.
- 평서문은 답변 패턴이 정해져 있지 않아서 어렵게 느껴질 수 있다. 오답 소거법을 이용하여 보기 중 가장 적절한 응답을 고르는 훈련이 필요하다.
- 유사 발음 어휘, 질문의 단어 반복 등을 이용한 보기가 오답으로 자주 등장하므로 이를 주의하여 정답을 골라야 한다.

| 문제 형태 |

7 Mark your answer on your answer sheet.

How much longer do you need on this project?

(A) About ten pages long.
(B) Roughly half an hour.
(C) The project was successful.

PART 3

대화문 39문제

파트 3는 2~3명이 나누는 대화를 듣고 이와 관련된 3개의 문제를 푸는 유형이다. 총 39문제가 출제되며, 3인 대화가 1~2세트 출제된다. 화자 의도 파악 문제와 시각 자료 연계 문제는 각각 2~3세트 출제된다.

| 핵심 전략 |

- 대화를 듣기 전에 문제를 먼저 읽고, 키워드를 파악한 후 그 부분을 집중적으로 듣는 훈련을 하자.
- 첫 번째 문제는 주로 주제나 장소, 신분에 관한 문제로, 정답의 단서가 대화 초반에 나오므로 처음 부분을 놓치지 않고 들어야 한다.
- 화자 의도 파악 문제는 먼저 제시된 표현을 확인하고, 음성을 들으면서 해당 표현이 나올 때까지 문맥을 정확히 파악해야 한다.
- 시각 자료 문제는 미리 도표를 읽고 지문의 내용을 예측해 본다. 또한, 시각 자료와 음성을 연계하여 정보를 파악하는 능력을 길러야 한다.
- 3인 대화에서 화자는 국적에 따라 발음이 구분되므로, 미국, 영국, 호주 등의 다양한 발음에 익숙해지도록 연습한다.

| 문제 형태 |

32 What does the woman imply when she says, "I got one for my friend"?

(A) She is inviting the man to meet her friend.

(B) Her friend is the same size with his wife.

(C) She is willing to pay for the product.

(D) She is emphasizing it's a good product.

Questions 32 through 34 refer to the following conversation.

M: Hi, I'm looking for a birthday present for my wife. I think she'd like one of these sweaters, but do you have any in a smaller size?

W: I'm pretty sure everything we have is out here on the display table. But I can check the stockroom in the back if you'd like.

M: Thanks, that'll be great. You know they look perfect for early spring. Light, but warm. You can wear them indoors or outdoors.

W: That's right. I got one for my friend who wears it a lot, so I'm sure your wife would love one. And we're selling them for 30% off this week.

M: That's good to know. I hope you have one in my wife's size.

PART 4

담화문 30문제

파트 4는 담화를 듣고 이와 관련된 3개의 문제를 푸는 유형이다. 총 30문항이 출제되며, 녹음 메시지나 공지, 뉴스 등이 주로 출제된다. 파트 3와 마찬가지로, 화자 의도 파악 문제와 시각 자료 연계 문제가 2~3세트씩 출제된다.

| 핵심 전략 |

- 담화를 듣기 전에 문제를 먼저 읽고, 키워드를 파악한 후 그 부분을 집중적으로 듣는 훈련을 하자.
- 첫 번째 문제는 주로 주제나 장소, 신분에 관한 문제로, 정답의 단서가 담화 초반에 나오므로 처음 부분을 놓치지 않고 들어야 한다.
- 화자 의도 파악 문제는 파트 3와 달리 한 사람의 담화이므로 문맥의 흐름을 더 쉽게 파악할 수 있다. 따라서 담화의 전반적인 문맥 흐름을 이해하고, 해당 문장의 앞뒤 상황을 정확히 파악하는 훈련을 하자.
- 시각 자료 문제는 미리 도표를 읽고 지문의 내용을 예측해 본다. 또한, 시각 자료와 음성을 연계하여 정보를 파악하는 능력을 길러야 한다.

| 문제 형태 |

Tour Schedule	
Garden Tour	10:00 A.M.
Lunch	Noon
Museum Visit	1:30 P.M.
Theater Performance	4:00 P.M.

98 Look at the graphic. What time is this talk most likely being given?

(A) At 10:00 A.M.
(B) At noon
(C) At 1:30 P.M.
(D) At 4:00 P.M.

Questions 98 through 100 refer to the following talk and schedule.

Can I have everyone's attention at the front of the bus? I hope you enjoyed your lunch at Restaurant Baron. As I mentioned earlier, it first opened in 1880 and has been operating longer than any other restaurants in Charlestown. Now, if you look out the window on your right, you'll see the National Museum of History and according to our schedule, we're right on time. We'll be spending about 2 hours here. I'll pass out the brochures with the information about the permanent and temporary exhibits you'll be seeing today. We'll meet again at the main entrance at 3:30 for our next schedule. Enjoy yourselves.

PART 5

단문 공란 채우기 30문제

파트 5는 문장 안에 있는 빈칸에 적절한 단어나 어구를 채워 넣는 유형이다. 총 30문항이 출제되며, 문법 문제와 어휘 문제가 등장한다. 문제 유형에 따라 풀이 방식이 다르므로 이를 가장 먼저 파악하는 것이 중요하다.

| 핵심 전략 |

✚ 문제를 풀기 전, 보기를 통해 문제 유형을 파악하는 연습을 한다.

✚ 문법 문제는 문장 구조나 빈칸 주변의 문법을 통해 문제를 풀어야 한다. 문법 문제를 단시간에 풀기 위해서 명사, 동사, 형용사 등의 기본적인 문법 규칙을 확실히 익혀 두자.

✚ 어휘 문제는 해석을 통해 문맥에 가장 적절한 단어를 선택해야 한다. 가능한 한 많은 어휘와 표현을 암기하고, 예문을 통해 어휘가 어떻게 사용되는지까지 익혀 두자.

✚ 자주 함께 쓰이는 단어 및 표현을 숙지하여 빠른 시간 내에 푸는 것이 관건이다.

| 문제 형태 |

101 Sky Motors offers a variety of training programs to help enhance ------- in the workplace.

(A) productivity
(B) produce
(C) productive
(D) productively

102 The fundraising event recorded such high ------- that the proceeds will be higher than expected.

(A) representative
(B) consultation
(C) safety
(D) attendance

PART 6

장문 공란 채우기 16문제

파트 6는 지문 안에 있는 4개의 빈칸에 알맞은 보기를 선택하는 유형이다. 문법, 어휘, 문장을 넣는 문제가 등장하며, 총 16문항이 출제된다. 문맥에 맞는 문장을 고르는 문제는 각 지문마다 1개씩 출제된다.

| 핵심 전략 |

- ✚ 전체 문맥을 이해해야 풀 수 있는 문법 및 어휘 문제가 나오므로 지문의 흐름을 놓치지 않는 것이 중요하다.
- ✚ 빈칸에 알맞은 문장을 넣는 문제는 빈칸 앞뒤와 전체 맥락을 파악하여 정답을 골라야 하므로 독해력을 꾸준히 길러야 한다.
- ✚ 문장 삽입 유형은 지문을 읽으며 앞뒤 흐름상 자연스러운 내용을 예측하면 정답을 쉽게 찾을 수 있다.

| 문제 형태 |

Questions 135-138 refer to the following notice.

Important Notice about Hatter Industries

Please note that the contact information for Hatter Industries changed on March 21. Due to the closure of our Dabbley office and the -------(135) of our operations in Buena, all correspondence concerning our products and services should now be sent to the following address: Hatter Industries, 642 Mandela Lane, Buena, CA. Our employees' e-mail addresses, as well as our Web site's address, www.hatterindustries.com, remain -------(136). However, we are still waiting for our new telephone and fax numbers. -------(137) will be updated on our Web site as soon as the new numbers are assigned as of March 25. -------(138).

135 (A) decision
(B) relocation
(C) suspension
(D) result

136 (A) assigned
(B) even
(C) formal
(D) unchanged

137 (A) Yours
(B) Another
(C) These
(D) Theirs

138 (A) We apologize for any inconvenience and thank you for your understanding.
(B) Refer to the side of the packet for full details of instructions before applying.
(C) Her office location will also remain the same.
(D) For more information about the forthcoming event, visit www.lizard.org.br/events.

PART 7

지문 독해 54문제

파트 7은 지문을 읽고 지문과 관련된 문제 2~5개를 푸는 유형이다. 총 54문항이 출제되며, 편지, 문자 메시지, 광고, 공지문 등 다양한 유형의 지문이 나온다. 단일 지문 10개, 이중 지문 2개, 삼중 지문 3개의 세트가 등장한다.

| 핵심 전략 |

- 지문의 종류와 제목, 키워드를 파악하여 내용을 미리 예측하고 정답 단서를 찾는다.
- 지문의 정답 단서가 보기에서는 다르게 패러프레이징될 수 있으므로, 단어를 암기할 때 동의 표현을 함께 익힌다.
- 복수 지문에서는 2개 이상의 지문을 연계하여 풀어야 하는 문제들이 출제되므로, 지문 간의 관계를 파악하는 연습을 해야 한다.

| 문제 형태 |

Questions 162-164 refer to the following advertisement.

ACCOUNT SERVICE DIRECTOR WANTED

A leading financial service bank is looking for an account services director. —[1]—. He or she will be responsible for reclassifying income payment to ensure the accurate reporting of tax payments. —[2]—. Validating tax related information, determining reclassification amounts, processing reclassifications using various internal systems, and performing quality-control checks relevant to all tax-reporting processes will be some of the other responsibilities. —[3]—. In order to qualify, the candidate must have a college degree and previous tax or brokerage experience along with strong analytical skills. —[4]—.

If you are interested, please send your résumé to:

Rosabeth Moss Kanter / Lawrence Financial, Inc.
985, Andrew Park Avenue / Houston, TX 48954

162 What position is being advertised?

(A) Public official
(B) Real estate agent
(C) Accountant
(D) Financial consultant

163 Which of the following is required for the position?

(A) Communication skills
(B) A license approved by a related organization
(C) Background knowledge of Lawrence Financial, Inc.
(D) A college education

164 In which of the positions marked [1], [2], [3], and [4] does the following sentence best belong?

"They must also be able to work overtime and weekends when required."

(A) [1]
(B) [2]
(C) [3]
(D) [4]

학습 플랜

> 2주 완성

	Day 1	Day 2	Day 3	Day 4	Day 5
1 week	TEST 1 & Review	TEST 2 & Review	TEST 3 & Review	TEST 4 & Review	TEST 5 & Review
2 week	TEST 6 & Review	TEST 7 & Review	TEST 8 & Review	TEST 9 & Review	TEST 10 & Review

> 4주 완성

	Day 1	Day 2	Day 3	Day 4	Day 5
1 week	TEST 1	TEST 1 Review	TEST 2	TEST 2 Review	TEST 3
2 week	TEST 3 Review	TEST 4	TEST 4 Review	TEST 5	TEST 5 Review
3 week	TEST 6	TEST 6 Review	TEST 7	TEST 7 Review	TEST 8
4 week	TEST 8 Review	TEST 9	TEST 9 Review	TEST 10	TEST 10 Review

MP3와 해설 파일은 온라인에서 제공됩니다.

▶▶ **books.english.co.kr**

TEST 01

T1.mp3 | 정답 p.156

LISTENING TEST

In the Listening test, you will be asked to demonstrate how well you understand spoken English. The entire Listening test will last approximately 45 minutes. There are four parts, and directions are given for each part. You must mark your answers on the separate answer sheet.
Do not write your answers in your test book.

PART 1

Directions: For each question in this part, you will hear four statements about a picture in your test book. When you hear the statements, you must select the one statement that best describes what you see in the picture. Then find the number of the question on your answer sheet and mark your answer. The statements will not be printed in your test book and will be spoken only one time.

Statement (B), "They're shaking hands," is the best description of the picture, so you should select answer (B) and mark it on your answer sheet.

1.

2.

GO ON TO THE NEXT PAGE

3.

4.

5.

6.

GO ON TO THE NEXT PAGE

PART 2

Directions: You will hear a question or statement and three responses spoken in English. They will not be printed in your test book and will be spoken only one time. Select the best response to the question or statement and mark the letter (A), (B), or (C) on your answer sheet.

7. Mark your answer on your answer sheet.

8. Mark your answer on your answer sheet.

9. Mark your answer on your answer sheet.

10. Mark your answer on your answer sheet.

11. Mark your answer on your answer sheet.

12. Mark your answer on your answer sheet.

13. Mark your answer on your answer sheet.

14. Mark your answer on your answer sheet.

15. Mark your answer on your answer sheet.

16. Mark your answer on your answer sheet.

17. Mark your answer on your answer sheet.

18. Mark your answer on your answer sheet.

19. Mark your answer on your answer sheet.

20. Mark your answer on your answer sheet.

21. Mark your answer on your answer sheet.

22. Mark your answer on your answer sheet.

23. Mark your answer on your answer sheet.

24. Mark your answer on your answer sheet.

25. Mark your answer on your answer sheet.

26. Mark your answer on your answer sheet.

27. Mark your answer on your answer sheet.

28. Mark your answer on your answer sheet.

29. Mark your answer on your answer sheet.

30. Mark your answer on your answer sheet.

31. Mark your answer on your answer sheet.

PART 3

Directions: You will hear some conversations between two or more people. You will be asked to answer three questions about what the speakers say in each conversation. Select the best response to each question and mark the letter (A), (B), (C), or (D) on your answer sheet. The conversations will not be printed in your test book and will be spoken only one time.

32. What does the woman ask about?
(A) Payment options
(B) The price of a product
(C) The status of an order
(D) A shipping address

33. What products are the speakers discussing?
(A) Office furniture
(B) Telephones
(C) Cameras
(D) Computers

34. What does the man offer to do?
(A) Check a delivery date
(B) Reduce a price
(C) Expedite a shipment
(D) Cancel an order

---

35. What does the man want to do?
(A) Transfer some money
(B) Open a bank account
(C) Deposit some money
(D) Apply for a loan

36. What problem does the man have?
(A) Mr. Jenkins is at lunch.
(B) The bank is closing in 30 minutes.
(C) Mr. Jenkins is busy at the moment.
(D) There is a long line of people.

37. What does the woman suggest the man do?
(A) Sit in a waiting area
(B) Make an appointment
(C) Try another location
(D) Fill out a form

---

38. What does the woman want to do?
(A) Arrange a meeting
(B) Set a sales goal
(C) Revise a report
(D) Upgrade a software

39. What does the woman imply when she says, "I need to do some research online right now"?
(A) She does not want to wait until the technician arrives.
(B) She thinks the man can solve the problem.
(C) She is concerned she will not meet the deadline.
(D) She wants to hire someone with lots of experience.

40. What does the man say he will do?
(A) Call the IT Department
(B) Shop for a new computer
(C) Send an e-mail
(D) Go to another floor

---

41. Why is the woman calling?
(A) To offer a refund
(B) To verify an address
(C) To promote a new product
(D) To collect feedback

42. What does the man say about the service?
(A) The delivery was fast.
(B) Returning merchandise was easy.
(C) The service agents were helpful.
(D) The fees are reasonable.

43. What does the woman want to do?
(A) Postpone a shipping date
(B) Substitute an item
(C) Post some comments
(D) Confirm an order quantity

GO ON TO THE NEXT PAGE

44. What does the man request?

(A) A ticket to Atlanta
(B) A sample of a product
(C) A bus schedule
(D) A ride to an event

45. What will the speakers probably do on Tuesday?

(A) Leave work early
(B) Give a demonstration
(C) Participate in a conference call
(D) Pick up a car from a shop

46. Why does the woman say she will take the bus?

(A) It is less expensive.
(B) Her car is being repaired.
(C) It will save her time.
(D) She cannot find anyone to ride a car with.

---

47. What is the man looking for?

(A) A customer list
(B) A timetable
(C) A questionnaire
(D) A menu

48. Who will the man meet this afternoon?

(A) A client
(B) An employee
(C) A job candidate
(D) A manager

49. What does the man ask the women to do?

(A) Review a file
(B) E-mail a document
(C) Conduct a survey
(D) Print a document

---

50. What are the speakers discussing?

(A) A baseball team
(B) A nearby restaurant
(C) A company-sponsored event
(D) An awards ceremony

51. Why is the man considering not attending the event?

(A) He has somewhere else to be.
(B) He is concerned about the weather.
(C) He doesn't like baseball.
(D) He thinks the tickets are too expensive.

52. According to the woman, what will the company provide?

(A) Transportation to an event
(B) Paid vacation time
(C) A hotel room
(D) Complimentary refreshments

---

53. What are the speakers talking about?

(A) Registering for an online course
(B) Paying with a credit card
(C) Arranging for an appointment
(D) Getting a new card

54. What does the woman give the man?

(A) An application form
(B) A Web site address
(C) A credit card number
(D) A deposit slip

55. Why does the man say, "How long does it usually take to get approval"?

(A) He is eager to get a loan as soon as possible.
(B) He wants to talk to a service agent in person.
(C) He is ready to apply for another position.
(D) He wants to get details about a process.

---

56. What is the conversation mainly about?

(A) Working over the weekend
(B) An overdue report
(C) A change in plans
(D) A marketing plan

57. What is the woman concerned about?

(A) The ticket price
(B) The missing data
(C) The inclement weather
(D) The lack of budget

58. What will the woman do next?

(A) Visit a marketing office
(B) Ask for a deadline extension
(C) Call a travel agency
(D) Contact other departments

---

59. Where most likely are the speakers?

(A) At a community center
(B) At a public library
(C) At a real estate agency
(D) At a university

60. What does the man suggest the woman do?

(A) Meet with a superior
(B) Cancel a class
(C) Teach an additional class
(D) Close enrollment

61. What does the woman ask for?

(A) A phone number
(B) Textbooks
(C) Business hours
(D) A list of students

#	Tasks	Dates
1	Design	March 1
2	Wiring	March 10
3	Flooring	March 15
4	Roofing	March 30

62. What are the speakers talking about?

(A) Budget approval
(B) A construction project
(C) The purchase of property
(D) The distribution of merchandise

63. Look at the graphic. Which job took longer than expected?

(A) Design
(B) Wiring
(C) Flooring
(D) Roofing

64. What does the man ask the woman to do?

(A) Postpone a project deadline
(B) Cancel a product shipment
(C) Revise a construction design
(D) Request a lease extension

GO ON TO THE NEXT PAGE

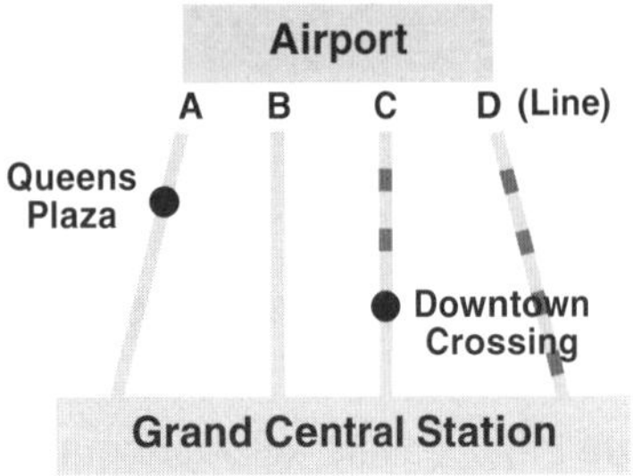

Special Service	Fee
Oversized Item	$10
Fragile Item	$15
International Service	$17
Overnight Service	$20

65. Where does the conversation take place?
(A) At an airport
(B) At a subway station
(C) At a sales seminar
(D) At a restaurant

66. Look at the graphic. Which line does the man suggest the woman take?
(A) Line A
(B) Line B
(C) Line C
(D) Line D

67. What does the man offer to do?
(A) Draw a subway map
(B) Find out a train schedule
(C) Buy the woman some food
(D) Accompany the woman to a platform

68. What does the woman want to sell?
(A) Bottled water
(B) Organic food
(C) Cosmetics
(D) Domestic produce

69. According to the man, what can be done on a Web site?
(A) Ordering products at discounted prices
(B) Purchasing shipping materials
(C) Tracking the locations of delivery trucks
(D) Determining the cost of mailing a package

70. Look at the graphic. Which special fee will the woman most likely pay?
(A) $10
(B) $15
(C) $17
(D) $20

PART 4

Directions: You will hear some talks given by a single speaker. You will be asked to answer three questions about what the speaker says in each talk. Select the best response to each question and mark the letter (A), (B), (C), or (D) on your answer sheet. The talks will not be printed in your test book and will be spoken only one time.

71. What department does the speaker probably work for?
(A) Human Resources
(B) Information Technology
(C) Accounting
(D) Security

72. What are the listeners instructed to do?
(A) Submit a résumé
(B) Present identification
(C) Log into a network
(D) Fill out some forms

73. What will mostly likely happen in 20 minutes?
(A) User IDs will be issued.
(B) A tour of the office will be provided.
(C) Managers will be introduced.
(D) Company benefits will be explained.

---

74. Who most likely is the speaker?
(A) A travel guide
(B) A store manager
(C) A hotel employee
(D) A bus driver

75. What does the speaker imply when she says, "Be sure to take all personal belongings"?
(A) She will discuss a new topic now.
(B) She thinks more items will be needed.
(C) She wants to prevent possible mishaps.
(D) She wants to encourage the listeners to shop more.

76. Where are the listeners asked to return?
(A) To an office
(B) To a hotel
(C) To a dock
(D) To a tour bus

---

77. Where does the speaker most likely work?
(A) At a furniture company
(B) At a delivery service
(C) At a restaurant
(D) At a clothing factory

78. What is the problem?
(A) A delivery truck is not working.
(B) An installer is busy on the scheduled day.
(C) The wrong item was delivered.
(D) An order is not ready.

79. What does the speaker ask the listener to do?
(A) Change her order
(B) Schedule a meeting
(C) Give directions to her home
(D) Confirm a date

---

80. What is the purpose of the talk?
(A) To report some financial figures
(B) To raise funds for charity
(C) To introduce an award winner
(D) To announce an employee's promotion

81. According to the speaker, what was Ms. Nuckols' latest position?
(A) Company president
(B) Head manager
(C) Corporate accountant
(D) Chief financial officer

82. What will Ms. Nuckols do in the future?
(A) Prepare for an upcoming event
(B) Retire from the McNeal Corporation
(C) Be promoted to company president
(D) Join the Accounting Department

GO ON TO THE NEXT PAGE

83. What are the listeners asked to do?

(A) Attend a dinner
(B) Look at a schedule
(C) Give a presentation
(D) Register in the main hall

84. What does the speaker say will happen in 10 minutes?

(A) Coffee and dessert will be served.
(B) Dr. Collier will speak.
(C) Conference registration will begin.
(D) Books and videos will be distributed.

85. What does the speaker imply when she says, "be sure to take a look at them"?

(A) It is important to meet the speaker in person.
(B) The discount rate is the biggest of the year.
(C) Books will be autographed by the author.
(D) It is a good opportunity to purchase some products.

---

86. What is the main purpose of the talk?

(A) To create a training schedule
(B) To discuss quarterly production figures
(C) To announce the launch of a new product
(D) To prepare for a new procedure

87. In which division do the listeners most likely work?

(A) Accounting
(B) Personnel
(C) Manufacturing
(D) Maintenance

88. What are the listeners asked to do?

(A) Meet with their teams
(B) Purchase some equipment
(C) Distribute the training manuals
(D) Submit ideas to improve efficiency

---

89. Why is the speaker leaving the message?

(A) To confirm an appointment
(B) To advertise a new business
(C) To request a service
(D) To make a reservation

90. What does the speaker imply when he says, "I'll highlight the new address"?

(A) He needs to provide a reason for the company's relocation.
(B) He is suggesting that the listener visit his office.
(C) He wants to save the listener the trouble of finding information.
(D) He is pointing out that the office will be closed soon.

91. What does the speaker say about the payment?

(A) He has not received money for previous services.
(B) It should be left with the receptionist.
(C) His company accepts only cash.
(D) The address to mail it has recently changed.

---

92. What is the talk mainly about?

(A) An organization's finances
(B) Some project updates
(C) A new board member
(D) Future projects

93. What is the main goal of the organization?

(A) To organize social events
(B) To help contractors network
(C) To construct homes for the poor
(D) To provide food for the homeless

94. What are the listeners invited to do?

(A) Speak to a project coordinator
(B) Sign up on a list
(C) Attend a separate meeting
(D) Send an e-mail to the group

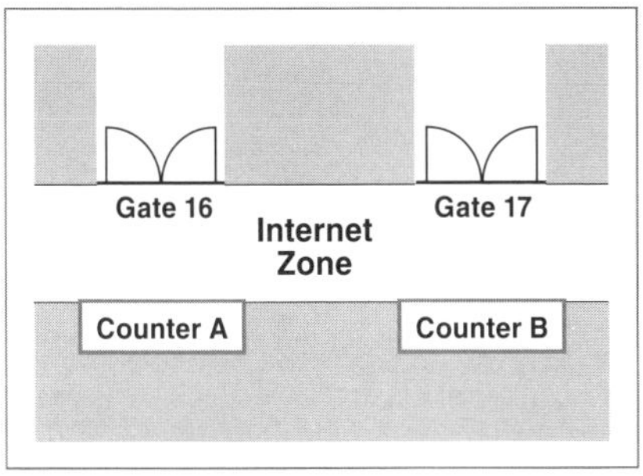

95. What is the purpose of the announcement?
(A) To inform passengers of a departure time change
(B) To get passengers ready for the boarding process
(C) To warn about the mishandling of baggage
(D) To give information about a travel destination

96. What are the passengers asked to get ready?
(A) Their ID cards
(B) Their boarding passes
(C) Their customs forms
(D) Their passports

97. Look at the graphic. Where should the passengers who want to check in their bags go to?
(A) Gate 16
(B) Gate 17
(C) Counter A
(D) Counter B

Friday Schedule	
9:00 A.M.	
10:00 A.M.	Palace Tours
11:00 A.M.	
12:00 P.M.	Lunch
1:00 P.M.	Garden Tours
2:00 P.M.	
3:00 P.M.	Outdoor Performance
4:00 P.M.	

98. Who most likely are the listeners?
(A) Palace guards
(B) Tourists
(C) Gardeners
(D) Tour guides

99. What does the speaker say about the weather?
(A) Some tours must be canceled because of it.
(B) Rain has been predicted for the afternoon.
(C) It is going to be sunny all day.
(D) The weather bureau needs to be contacted to check it.

100. Look at the graphic. What time will the private tour be conducted?
(A) At 9:00 A.M.
(B) At 11:00 A.M.
(C) At 2:00 P.M.
(D) At 4:00 P.M.

MP3와 해설 파일은 온라인에서 제공됩니다.

▸▸ **books.english.co.kr**

TEST 02

T2.mp3 | 정답 p.164

LISTENING TEST

In the Listening test, you will be asked to demonstrate how well you understand spoken English. The entire Listening test will last approximately 45 minutes. There are four parts, and directions are given for each part. You must mark your answers on the separate answer sheet.
Do not write your answers in your test book.

PART 1

Directions: For each question in this part, you will hear four statements about a picture in your test book. When you hear the statements, you must select the one statement that best describes what you see in the picture. Then find the number of the question on your answer sheet and mark your answer. The statements will not be printed in your test book and will be spoken only one time.

Statement (B), "They're shaking hands," is the best description of the picture, so you should select answer (B) and mark it on your answer sheet.

1.

2.

3.

Spice
Key west
Lil' Red
Velvet
Tuxedo
Bombe
Reese's
Cookies
Red Velvet
Cookie

4.

5.

6.

GO ON TO THE NEXT PAGE

PART 2

Directions: You will hear a question or statement and three responses spoken in English. They will not be printed in your test book and will be spoken only one time. Select the best response to the question or statement and mark the letter (A), (B), or (C) on your answer sheet.

7. Mark your answer on your answer sheet.

8. Mark your answer on your answer sheet.

9. Mark your answer on your answer sheet.

10. Mark your answer on your answer sheet.

11. Mark your answer on your answer sheet.

12. Mark your answer on your answer sheet.

13. Mark your answer on your answer sheet.

14. Mark your answer on your answer sheet.

15. Mark your answer on your answer sheet.

16. Mark your answer on your answer sheet.

17. Mark your answer on your answer sheet.

18. Mark your answer on your answer sheet.

19. Mark your answer on your answer sheet.

20. Mark your answer on your answer sheet.

21. Mark your answer on your answer sheet.

22. Mark your answer on your answer sheet.

23. Mark your answer on your answer sheet.

24. Mark your answer on your answer sheet.

25. Mark your answer on your answer sheet.

26. Mark your answer on your answer sheet.

27. Mark your answer on your answer sheet.

28. Mark your answer on your answer sheet.

29. Mark your answer on your answer sheet.

30. Mark your answer on your answer sheet.

31. Mark your answer on your answer sheet.

PART 3

Directions: You will hear some conversations between two or more people. You will be asked to answer three questions about what the speakers say in each conversation. Select the best response to each question and mark the letter (A), (B), (C), or (D) on your answer sheet. The conversations will not be printed in your test book and will be spoken only one time.

32. Where is the conversation probably taking place?
(A) In an airport
(B) In an airplane
(C) In a theater
(D) In a train station

33. What does the woman ask for?
(A) A refund
(B) A meal
(C) A seat change
(D) An updated schedule

34. What will the woman do next?
(A) Book a different flight
(B) Cancel a reservation
(C) Buy something to eat
(D) Talk to her husband

---

35. Why is the woman concerned?
(A) She lost her briefcase.
(B) She cannot find a document.
(C) She missed a presentation.
(D) She is late for a meeting.

36. What is the man asked to do?
(A) Call her secretary
(B) Make another copy
(C) Set up equipment
(D) Postpone a meeting

37. Where will the woman probably go next?
(A) To a store
(B) To her house
(C) To her office
(D) To a conference room

---

38. What are the speakers discussing?
(A) A plan for a workday
(B) A reservation for dinner
(C) An upcoming business trip
(D) A dental procedure

39. What does the woman suggest?
(A) Canceling the dentist's appointment
(B) Undertaking a specific work
(C) Taking a vacation day
(D) Rescheduling a meeting

40. What time will the speakers meet?
(A) At 9:00 A.M.
(B) At 9:30 A.M.
(C) At 10:00 A.M.
(D) At 10:30 A.M.

---

41. Where does the conversation take place?
(A) At a local café
(B) At a magazine company
(C) At a photography gallery
(D) At an awards ceremony

42. What is mentioned about Café a Roma?
(A) It has expanded its menu.
(B) It is hiring new employees.
(C) It was recently awarded a prize.
(D) It is a good location for an event.

43. What is Kevin asked to do?
(A) Take pictures
(B) Edit some articles
(C) Contact the café owner
(D) Prepare some food

GO ON TO THE NEXT PAGE

44. Where most likely are the speakers?

(A) In a bank
(B) In a meeting room
(C) In an office building
(D) In an electronics store

45. What problem are the speakers discussing?

(A) A client missed a meeting.
(B) There is a long wait.
(C) A machine is malfunctioning.
(D) A payment is late.

46. What does the man say he will do?

(A) Use an ATM
(B) Reschedule an appointment
(C) Send another check
(D) Return later

---

47. What is the purpose of the call?

(A) To discuss a defective product
(B) To ask for a receipt
(C) To report a lost item
(D) To inquire about a new model

48. What does the man imply when he says, "that's not going to work for me"?

(A) He is not working tomorrow.
(B) He wants his money back.
(C) He cannot arrive at the place on time.
(D) He cannot visit a store in person.

49. What will the woman probably do next?

(A) Send a package
(B) Call a manufacturer
(C) Provide information
(D) Fix the stereo herself

---

50. Why is Mr. Humphrey upset?

(A) He did not receive a schedule.
(B) He misplaced an important file.
(C) He found an error in a document.
(D) He doesn't like his schedule.

51. What did the woman do on Monday?

(A) She sent an e-mail.
(B) She updated contact information.
(C) She made some copies.
(D) She called Mr. Humphrey.

52. What does the woman say she will do?

(A) Check an e-mail address
(B) Fax a report
(C) Deliver a document
(D) Sign a contract

---

53. What is the conversation mainly about?

(A) Making some investments
(B) Coordinating some schedules
(C) Laying off some employees
(D) Receiving some applications

54. When will the speakers probably conduct the interviews?

(A) On Monday
(B) On Tuesday
(C) On Wednesday
(D) On Thursday

55. Why is the company hiring a new financial analyst?

(A) Someone is retiring soon.
(B) It is opening a new international division.
(C) Customers are complaining about a slow process.
(D) The department has too much work.

---

56. What is the topic of the conversation?

(A) The availability of a special dish
(B) The skill of a new chef
(C) The location of a restaurant
(D) The addition of new ingredients

57. What does the man say will happen?

(A) Some groceries will be delivered.
(B) Some new staffers will be trained.
(C) A group of customers will arrive.
(D) A restaurant will be closed for renovations.

58. What does the woman ask about?

(A) What time she can leave work
(B) Whether she should update the menu
(C) Where they should store the supplies
(D) How many customers are in a party

---

59. What did the man recently do?

(A) He registered for a seminar.
(B) He did some holiday shopping.
(C) He sent out some product brochures.
(D) He reviewed customers' feedback.

60. Why does the woman say, "I've been really busy checking inventory"?

(A) To provide an excuse
(B) To prepare for a change
(C) To ask for help
(D) To confirm a meeting time

61. What will the man suggest at next week's meeting?

(A) Updating some materials
(B) Extending hours of operation
(C) Holding a special sale
(D) Expanding a product line

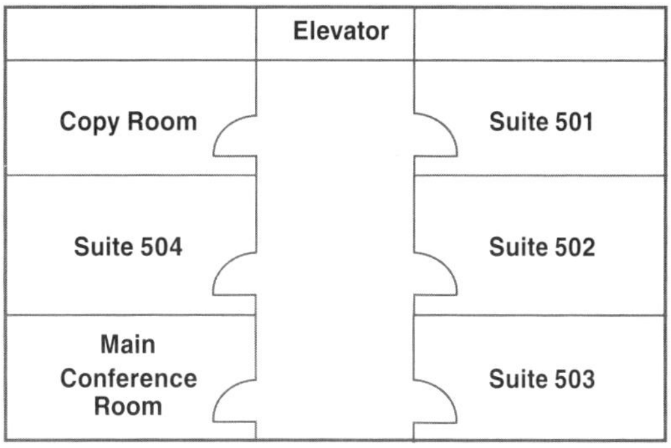

62. What does the man ask the woman to do?

(A) Use a different entrance
(B) Wear an ID badge
(C) Turn off her cell phone
(D) Come back at a later time

63. What did the woman do last week?

(A) She got Mr. Campbell's signature.
(B) She discussed a project plan.
(C) She set up a meeting.
(D) She asked for some advice.

64. Look at the graphic. Which office does the woman need to visit?

(A) Suite 501
(B) Suite 502
(C) Suite 503
(D) Suite 504

Item	Price
Sandwiches	$12
Bagels	$10
Assorted Beverages	$8
Assorted Cookies	$6

65. Why is the man calling the woman?

(A) To organize an event
(B) To make a reservation
(C) To confirm an order
(D) To apologize for a delay

66. What information does the woman provide?

(A) The reason for a gathering
(B) The topic of a meeting
(C) The name of a venue
(D) The number of attendees

67. Look at the graphic. How much is the item the woman wants to add?

(A) $12
(B) $10
(C) $8
(D) $6

Destination	Gate	Time	Status
New York	A3	16:50	Delayed
Boston	B12	17:10	On time
Chicago	A9	16:55	Canceled
Minneapolis	C22	17:30	On time

68. What type of event are the speakers traveling to?

(A) An awards banquet
(B) A sports competition
(C) A cultural festival
(D) A business function

69. Why is the woman staying at her destination for a short time?

(A) She must return for a meeting.
(B) She has to meet some colleagues.
(C) She has a limited budget.
(D) Her flight schedule has changed.

70. Look at the graphic. What city are the speakers flying to?

(A) New York
(B) Boston
(C) Chicago
(D) Minneapolis

PART 4

Directions: You will hear some talks given by a single speaker. You will be asked to answer three questions about what the speaker says in each talk. Select the best response to each question and mark the letter (A), (B), (C), or (D) on your answer sheet. The talks will not be printed in your test book and will be spoken only one time.

71. Where does the announcement take place?
(A) At a food manufacturer
(B) In a grocery store
(C) In a restaurant
(D) At a farmers' market

72. What does the speaker say she will provide this week?
(A) Lower prices
(B) Expedited delivery
(C) Product samples
(D) Gift certificates

73. What should the listeners do to buy products which are not on display?
(A) Ask the supervisor for a special order
(B) Place an order online
(C) Ask for help from a store employee
(D) Visit a manufacturer's Web site

---

74. For whom is the talk intended for?
(A) University students
(B) Company employees
(C) Business managers
(D) Professors

75. What will most likely happen in the morning session?
(A) Some skills will be tested.
(B) Textbooks will be provided.
(C) A video will be shown.
(D) Experts will give a lecture.

76. According to the speaker, what can the listeners do during lunch?
(A) Register for another seminar
(B) Have a group talk
(C) Buy a book
(D) Discuss the course materials

---

77. According to the speaker, what is an advantage of the hotel?
(A) Reasonable rates
(B) Friendly staff
(C) A pleasant environment
(D) A convenient location

78. Why does the speaker say, "make your life easier by booking your next stay online with us"?
(A) To introduce a new online system
(B) To announce further discounts
(C) To promote its renovated facilities
(D) To encourage people to try some services

79. What does the speaker say about *Urban Traveler* magazine?
(A) It offers some useful travel tips.
(B) It introduces a variety of hotel chains.
(C) It highly evaluated the company.
(D) Its subscribers can get special treatment.

---

80. Where most likely are the listeners?
(A) At a retail store
(B) At an employment agency
(C) At a bookstore
(D) At a publisher

81. Who is Tom Welker?
(A) An editor
(B) A job counselor
(C) A bookstore owner
(D) A novelist

82. What will happen at the end of the event?
(A) A new book will be released.
(B) Samples will be distributed.
(C) Books will be signed.
(D) Interviews will be held.

---

83. What is the purpose of the announcement?

(A) To begin a lecture
(B) To introduce an employee
(C) To describe a tour
(D) To cancel an event

84. What are the listeners allowed to do?

(A) Eat lunch early
(B) Buy souvenirs
(C) Take photographs
(D) Carry personal belongings

85. What does the speaker suggest?

(A) Changing into warm clothes
(B) Using the restroom in advance
(C) Buying some food or drinks
(D) Turning off cell phones

---

86. What is the main topic of the talk?

(A) Applications for a construction permit
(B) Design plans for a renovation
(C) Reviewing a proposal
(D) Tips for operating a museum

87. What does the speaker imply when he says, "the museum is almost 50 years old"?

(A) It has a large number of collections.
(B) It needs to be fixed in many places.
(C) He wants to sell the property for a high price.
(D) It is the oldest museum in the area.

88. What will the speaker probably do next?

(A) Turn off the lights for better viewing
(B) Listen to the guest lecturer
(C) Visit the museum himself
(D) Show the listeners some plans

---

89. Who is the speaker talking to?

(A) Customers
(B) Accountants
(C) Managers
(D) Designers

90. What did customers complain about?

(A) Billing services
(B) The voicemail system
(C) Delivery delays
(D) The quality of the products

91. According to the speaker, what will happen next?

(A) Survey results will be discussed.
(B) A group project will be presented.
(C) All customers will be contacted.
(D) Response cards will be distributed.

---

92. What is the purpose of the message?

(A) To inquire about a job
(B) To ask about business hours
(C) To report on the status of a project
(D) To ask for some information

93. What does the speaker mention about the cleaning service?

(A) It is out of business.
(B) It offered high quality work.
(C) It launched a new product.
(D) It changed its location.

94. What does the speaker mean when she says, "I need a crew to come over soon"?

(A) She wants to complain in person.
(B) An emergency has occurred at her home.
(C) She has carpets that need to be cleaned.
(D) She needs help meeting a client.

SCHEDULE

Workshop	Time
Getting Started	10:00 A.M.
Communications	11:00 A.M.
Market Trends	1:00 P.M.
Customer Management	2:00 P.M.

95. Who most likely are the listeners?
(A) Receptionists
(B) Local students
(C) Travel agents
(D) Realtors

96. Look at the graphic. According to the speaker, when will the workshop on Communications start?
(A) At 10:00 A.M.
(B) At 11:00 A.M.
(C) At 1:00 P.M.
(D) At 2:00 P.M.

97. What are some listeners asked to do?
(A) Go to the registration desk
(B) Listen to further instructions
(C) Attend another workshop
(D) Request a different schedule

Survey Results

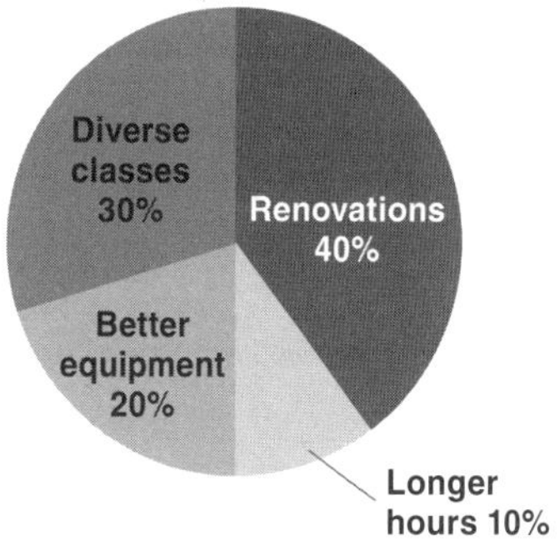

98. According to the speaker, what is the center's main concern?
(A) Observing industry regulations
(B) Satisfying current members
(C) Reducing operating costs
(D) Expanding to a new market

99. Look at the graphic. What item does the speaker want to address?
(A) Renovations
(B) Diverse classes
(C) Better equipment
(D) Longer hours

100. What does the speaker ask the listeners to do?
(A) Tour a facility
(B) Take a certification class
(C) Refer potential employees
(D) Request a transfer

MP3와 해설 파일은 온라인에서 제공됩니다.

▶▶ **books.english.co.kr**

TEST 03

T3.mp3 | 정답 p.172

LISTENING TEST

In the Listening test, you will be asked to demonstrate how well you understand spoken English. The entire Listening test will last approximately 45 minutes. There are four parts, and directions are given for each part. You must mark your answers on the separate answer sheet.
Do not write your answers in your test book.

PART 1

Directions: For each question in this part, you will hear four statements about a picture in your test book. When you hear the statements, you must select the one statement that best describes what you see in the picture. Then find the number of the question on your answer sheet and mark your answer. The statements will not be printed in your test book and will be spoken only one time.

Statement (B), "They're shaking hands," is the best description of the picture, so you should select answer (B) and mark it on your answer sheet.

1.

2.

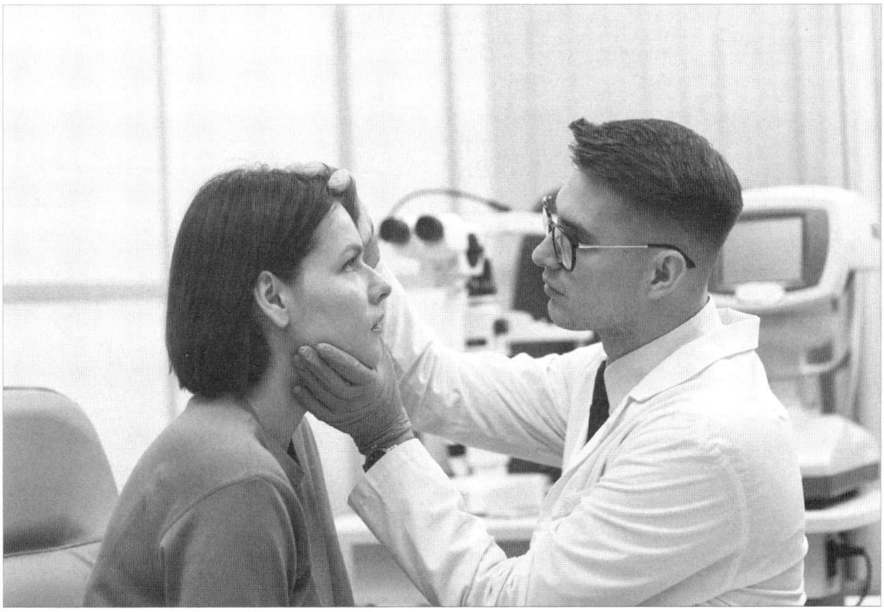

GO ON TO THE NEXT PAGE

3.

Dips Gutt
Dips Jente
VG
Dagbladet
MORGENBLADET
KRENK-O-RAMA

4.

5.

6.

GO ON TO THE NEXT PAGE

PART 2

Directions: You will hear a question or statement and three responses spoken in English. They will not be printed in your test book and will be spoken only one time. Select the best response to the question or statement and mark the letter (A), (B), or (C) on your answer sheet.

7. Mark your answer on your answer sheet.

8. Mark your answer on your answer sheet.

9. Mark your answer on your answer sheet.

10. Mark your answer on your answer sheet.

11. Mark your answer on your answer sheet.

12. Mark your answer on your answer sheet.

13. Mark your answer on your answer sheet.

14. Mark your answer on your answer sheet.

15. Mark your answer on your answer sheet.

16. Mark your answer on your answer sheet.

17. Mark your answer on your answer sheet.

18. Mark your answer on your answer sheet.

19. Mark your answer on your answer sheet.

20. Mark your answer on your answer sheet.

21. Mark your answer on your answer sheet.

22. Mark your answer on your answer sheet.

23. Mark your answer on your answer sheet.

24. Mark your answer on your answer sheet.

25. Mark your answer on your answer sheet.

26. Mark your answer on your answer sheet.

27. Mark your answer on your answer sheet.

28. Mark your answer on your answer sheet.

29. Mark your answer on your answer sheet.

30. Mark your answer on your answer sheet.

31. Mark your answer on your answer sheet.

PART 3

Directions: You will hear some conversations between two or more people. You will be asked to answer three questions about what the speakers say in each conversation. Select the best response to each question and mark the letter (A), (B), (C), or (D) on your answer sheet. The conversations will not be printed in your test book and will be spoken only one time.

32. Who most likely is the man?
(A) A warehouse worker
(B) A restaurant owner
(C) A real estate agent
(D) A building architect

33. What does the man say about his business?
(A) It offers special discounts.
(B) It will be renovated.
(C) It opens every weekend.
(D) It changed its hours.

34. What does the woman offer to do?
(A) Have dinner together
(B) Return his call as soon as possible
(C) Give him some funding
(D) Come to his restaurant

---

35. What does the woman want to do?
(A) Write a children's story
(B) Conduct more research
(C) Find a writer
(D) Publish a book

36. What does the man ask for?
(A) A deposit for a property
(B) A deadline for a report
(C) Product samples
(D) Advice on a project

37. What will the speakers most likely do next?
(A) Sign a contract
(B) Visit a bookstore
(C) Arrange a meeting
(D) Write a new chapter

---

38. Who most likely is the man?
(A) A factory supervisor
(B) A rental agent
(C) An interior designer
(D) A loan officer

39. According to the man, what happened last year?
(A) A building was remodeled.
(B) An employee was hired.
(C) A plant was shut down.
(D) A contract was canceled.

40. What does the woman offer to do?
(A) Purchase some supplies
(B) Apply for a position
(C) Provide a list of references
(D) Make a payment immediately

---

41. Why was the woman unable to hear the news report?
(A) She was visiting another branch.
(B) She was meeting her family.
(C) She got stuck in traffic.
(D) She was with a client.

42. What is the subject of the news report?
(A) A company policy
(B) A council's decision
(C) A marketing plan
(D) A traffic jam

43. Why is the woman pleased?
(A) She can move to Grover City.
(B) Her deadline has been extended.
(C) Her office will be relocated.
(D) Her trip home from work will be faster.

GO ON TO THE NEXT PAGE

44. Where most likely is the conversation taking place?

(A) In a camera store
(B) In a pharmacy
(C) In a laboratory
(D) In an eyeglasses store

45. What does the man want to do?

(A) Change an order
(B) Make an appointment
(C) Fill a prescription
(D) Return a purchase

46. What problem does the woman report?

(A) A product has been discontinued.
(B) An employee is out sick today.
(C) Some test results are not ready.
(D) Some equipment is broken.

---

47. What is the woman asked to do?

(A) Go to a hospital
(B) Arrange a schedule
(C) Meet with some clients
(D) Send out an application

48. Why does the man make the request?

(A) He has to get a diploma.
(B) He is not feeling well.
(C) He is vacationing with his family.
(D) He has a scheduling conflict.

49. What does the man say he will send the woman?

(A) A list of some documents
(B) A cost estimate
(C) A timetable for a process
(D) An application form

---

50. Who most likely are the speakers?

(A) Furniture salespeople
(B) Professional movers
(C) Office workers
(D) Store clerks

51. What does the man mean when he says, "it's about time"?

(A) He is late for the meeting.
(B) A store needs more workers to meet demand.
(C) They need to get off work soon.
(D) Some work has been needed for a long time.

52. What will most likely happen at lunch time?

(A) The speakers will visit a store.
(B) The speakers will purchase some paper.
(C) The speakers will rearrange the office.
(D) The speakers will repair some furniture.

---

53. What is the man's problem?

(A) A library policy has changed.
(B) The book he wants is not available.
(C) He has been overcharged.
(D) He returned a book too late.

54. When did the man receive an e-mail?

(A) Today
(B) Yesterday
(C) Ten days ago
(D) Fourteen days ago

55. What does the woman offer to do?

(A) Send another e-mail
(B) Bring a book from a shelf
(C) Make a new reservation
(D) Provide a copy of the policy

---

56. What position are the candidates applying for?

(A) Board member
(B) Clerical assistant
(C) Personnel manager
(D) Senior editor

57. What does the woman imply when she says, "more doesn't necessarily mean better"?

(A) She wants to hire more people.
(B) She focuses on quality than quantity.
(C) She thinks the company benefits could be improved.
(D) She needs to move to another branch.

58. Why do the speakers mention Wednesday?

(A) The woman is leaving for a business trip on that day.
(B) They need to make a reservation by then.
(C) The woman is available to meet people then.
(D) They need to launch a new magazine on that day.

---

59. What kind of job is being offered?

(A) Marketing assistant
(B) Sales manager
(C) Human Resources director
(D) Delivery person

60. Why should the woman visit the Personnel Department?

(A) To pick up an application
(B) To hand in her résumé
(C) To meet the personnel director
(D) To fill out some paperwork

61. When does the woman say she could start working?

(A) In one week
(B) In two weeks
(C) In four weeks
(D) In two months

---

62. What are the speakers mainly discussing?

(A) Getting ready for an event
(B) Ordering some office supplies
(C) Sending out product catalogues
(D) Having the office painted

63. What does the woman ask the men to decide?

(A) The type of equipment
(B) The size of an order
(C) The method of delivery
(D) The appearance of a document

64. What does the woman mean when she says, "it will be worth every penny"?

(A) They don't have enough money.
(B) They need to postpone the meeting.
(C) The price of the stock has gone up.
(D) They should choose the color option.

GO ON TO THE NEXT PAGE

Northwest Airlines

Luggage Claim Form E-5 (International)

Date:	**Flight Number/Time:**
Mar. 29	NW096 / 1:20 P.M.
Name:	**Contact Info:**
Maria Miller	312-787-4921 (Mayotte Hotel Chicago)

65. What is the woman's concern?

(A) Her arrival time has been changed.
(B) She is unable to locate her bags.
(C) She might miss her connecting flight.
(D) She is late for her appointment.

66. Where does the man suggest the woman go?

(A) To the international terminal
(B) To the customer service desk
(C) To the baggage claim area
(D) To the security office

67. Look at the graphic. Which information should be changed?

(A) Flight number
(B) Flight time
(C) Date of travel
(D) Contact information

Regions	Rate of Increase
The United States	8%
Europe	13%
Middle East	30%
Africa	5%

68. What are the speakers discussing?

(A) The shipment of parts
(B) Overseas sales
(C) Travel destinations
(D) International trade

69. Look at the graphic. Which region will the speakers NOT address?

(A) The United States
(B) Europe
(C) Middle East
(D) Africa

70. What does the man suggest?

(A) Reducing the price by half
(B) Adding some new features
(C) Modifying current designs
(D) Changing marketing plans

PART 4

Directions: You will hear some talks given by a single speaker. You will be asked to answer three questions about what the speaker says in each talk. Select the best response to each question and mark the letter (A), (B), (C), or (D) on your answer sheet. The talks will not be printed in your test book and will be spoken only one time.

71. What is the report about?
(A) Some recent elections
(B) The local weather
(C) The area traffic
(D) A traffic accident

72. Why is there a delay on Burton Avenue?
(A) There is a local festival.
(B) There is some construction work.
(C) There is a stalled car.
(D) There are bad weather conditions.

73. What will the listeners most likely hear next?
(A) Local news
(B) Advertisements
(C) The weather forecast
(D) An event schedule

---

74. What is the purpose of the introduction?
(A) To launch an advertising campaign
(B) To recognize an employee's work
(C) To welcome a new vice president
(D) To announce the retirement of an employee

75. In what department does Ms. Wong work?
(A) The product development team
(B) The overseas marketing team
(C) The accounting team
(D) The sales team

76. What will probably happen next?
(A) A new product will be demonstrated.
(B) A video will be shown.
(C) A speech will be given.
(D) The audience will listen to a book reading.

---

77. Where does the speaker most likely work?
(A) At a pharmaceutical company
(B) At a medical facility
(C) At an employment agency
(D) At a laboratory research center

78. Why did the listener contact the speaker?
(A) To refill a prescription
(B) To change an appointment
(C) To ask about the business hours
(D) To find out the results of a test

79. Why does the Dr. Choi want to see the listener?
(A) To prescribe new medicine
(B) To request payment
(C) To ask him to fill out a form
(D) To examine him

---

80. Why is the speaker making the call?
(A) To order a new projector
(B) To return a product
(C) To reserve a conference room
(D) To report a problem

81. What problem does the speaker mention?
(A) A piece of equipment is out of stock.
(B) An important meeting was canceled.
(C) Some equipment malfunctioned.
(D) There were not enough participants.

82. What does the speaker ask the listener to do?
(A) Send a technician
(B) Book a venue
(C) Review a manual
(D) Prepare a presentation

---

83. What product is being promoted?

(A) Frozen beverages
(B) Fresh fruits
(C) Baked goods
(D) Ice cream

84. What is said about the product packaging?

(A) It is strong and durable.
(B) It is convenient to carry.
(C) It is made from recycled materials.
(D) It keeps the product fresh.

85. What does the speaker mean when she says, "make sure you check them out today"?

(A) Customers should find out about the closing time.
(B) Customers should become members.
(C) Customers should present special coupons.
(D) Customers should purchase the sale items.

---

86. What is the report mainly about?

(A) A famous scientific researcher
(B) The history of a local community
(C) A world-famous exhibit
(D) The construction of a museum

87. Who is Richard Olson?

(A) An architect
(B) A president
(C) A librarian
(D) A reporter

88. What is the next step in the project?

(A) Completing the architectural design
(B) Hiring a consultant for the construction
(C) Selecting a suitable site for the building
(D) Creating a budget to support the project

---

89. What is the purpose of the talk?

(A) To introduce a new plant manager
(B) To promote a new product
(C) To identify problems on the factory floor
(D) To explain a new security policy

90. What does the speaker mean when he says, "It's a must"?

(A) It's mandatory for all employees to wear badges.
(B) The work must be done by the end of the day.
(C) Access to the building is restricted to staff only.
(D) Some employees have to find new jobs.

91. What should the listeners do if they have not received their cards yet?

(A) Contact the personnel office
(B) Go to the employee lounge
(C) Visit the company Web site
(D) Report to their supervisors

Client	Baxter Co.
Date	April 28
Number of People	35 adults
Menu	Standard A
Special Request	Vegetarian option

* 10% security deposit is needed for reservation.

92. What is the message mainly about?

(A) Organizing the committee
(B) Hiring additional staffers
(C) Preparing for a meeting
(D) Making a hotel reservation

93. Look at the graphic. According to the speaker, what information needs to be changed?

(A) Client
(B) Date
(C) Number of People
(D) Special Request

94. Why does the speaker want to meet with the listener?

(A) To change the date of the event
(B) To evaluate some company records
(C) To set up some equipment together
(D) To make some final decisions on details

Program

Presenter	Time
Dr. Randolph	9:30 A.M.
Ms. Nelson	11:00 A.M.
Lunch Break	12:00 P.M.
Workshop	2:00 P.M.
Ms. Connelly	4:00 P.M.

95. What is the purpose of the announcement?

(A) To promote local restaurants
(B) To present an award
(C) To provide an overview of a schedule
(D) To introduce a new presenter

96. Look at the graphic. What program do the participants have to wait 30 minutes for?

(A) Dr. Randolph's
(B) Ms. Nelson's
(C) Workshop
(D) Ms. Connelly's

97. Where can the listeners find a list of restaurants?

(A) On the bulletin board
(B) At the information desk
(C) On a local map
(D) In the conference program

Meeting Schedules	
Assembly Line A	June 20 (Mon.)
Assembly Line B	June 21 (Tue.)
Packing & Shipping	June 22 (Wed.)
Quality Control	June 23 (Thu.)

98. When is the board of directors scheduled to visit?

(A) Before the end of the day
(B) Tomorrow
(C) Next week
(D) In three weeks

99. What will each department discuss at the meetings?

(A) Preparations for a visit
(B) Transfers to a different location
(C) Staff evaluations by the personnel division
(D) The revision of the meeting schedule

100. Look at the graphic. According to the speaker, when will the meeting for Quality Control be held?

(A) On June 21
(B) On June 22
(C) On June 23
(D) On June 24

TEST 03

MP3와 해설 피일은 온라인에서 제공됩니다.

▶▶ **books.english.co.kr**

TEST 04

T4.mp3 | 정답 p.180

LISTENING TEST

In the Listening test, you will be asked to demonstrate how well you understand spoken English. The entire Listening test will last approximately 45 minutes. There are four parts, and directions are given for each part. You must mark your answers on the separate answer sheet.
Do not write your answers in your test book.

PART 1

Directions: For each question in this part, you will hear four statements about a picture in your test book. When you hear the statements, you must select the one statement that best describes what you see in the picture. Then find the number of the question on your answer sheet and mark your answer. The statements will not be printed in your test book and will be spoken only one time.

Statement (B), "They're shaking hands," is the best description of the picture, so you should select answer (B) and mark it on your answer sheet.

1.

2.

GO ON TO THE NEXT PAGE

3.

4.

5.

6.

GO ON TO THE NEXT PAGE

PART 2

Directions: You will hear a question or statement and three responses spoken in English. They will not be printed in your test book and will be spoken only one time. Select the best response to the question or statement and mark the letter (A), (B), or (C) on your answer sheet.

7. Mark your answer on your answer sheet.

8. Mark your answer on your answer sheet.

9. Mark your answer on your answer sheet.

10. Mark your answer on your answer sheet.

11. Mark your answer on your answer sheet.

12. Mark your answer on your answer sheet.

13. Mark your answer on your answer sheet.

14. Mark your answer on your answer sheet.

15. Mark your answer on your answer sheet.

16. Mark your answer on your answer sheet.

17. Mark your answer on your answer sheet.

18. Mark your answer on your answer sheet.

19. Mark your answer on your answer sheet.

20. Mark your answer on your answer sheet.

21. Mark your answer on your answer sheet.

22. Mark your answer on your answer sheet.

23. Mark your answer on your answer sheet.

24. Mark your answer on your answer sheet.

25. Mark your answer on your answer sheet.

26. Mark your answer on your answer sheet.

27. Mark your answer on your answer sheet.

28. Mark your answer on your answer sheet.

29. Mark your answer on your answer sheet.

30. Mark your answer on your answer sheet.

31. Mark your answer on your answer sheet.

PART 3

Directions: You will hear some conversations between two or more people. You will be asked to answer three questions about what the speakers say in each conversation. Select the best response to each question and mark the letter (A), (B), (C), or (D) on your answer sheet. The conversations will not be printed in your test book and will be spoken only one time.

32. Who most likely are the speakers?

(A) Sales representatives
(B) Travel agents
(C) Hotel receptionists
(D) Telephone operators

33. What are the speakers discussing?

(A) Going to a conference
(B) Spending holidays overseas
(C) Hiring new staff members
(D) Meeting colleagues from another office

34. Where will the speakers most likely go on Wednesday?

(A) To a sales presentation
(B) To a social event
(C) To an airport
(D) To a job interview

---

35. What problem are the speakers discussing?

(A) A photocopier has not been delivered.
(B) A fax machine is not working.
(C) The downtown office is closed.
(D) An appointment has been canceled.

36. When is the deadline for submission?

(A) Today
(B) Tomorrow morning
(C) Tomorrow afternoon
(D) Next week

37. What does the man offer to do?

(A) Reschedule a meeting
(B) Contact a technician
(C) Send documents by e-mail
(D) Make some copies

---

38. Where most likely are the speakers?

(A) At a printing shop
(B) In a museum gift shop
(C) On a street corner
(D) At a ticket office

39. What are the speakers talking about?

(A) A print of a painting
(B) A home renovation
(C) A sculpture exhibit
(D) A gallery tour

40. What will the woman most likely do next?

(A) Admire a painting
(B) Purchase a ticket
(C) Follow the clerk
(D) Meet a popular artist

---

41. What is the problem?

(A) An item is damaged.
(B) A customer was overcharged.
(C) Some equipment is broken.
(D) An item was delivered to the wrong address.

42. What does the man agree to do?

(A) Give a discount
(B) Send another copy
(C) Call a delivery man
(D) Give some data

43. What does the woman request?

(A) Giving an opening address
(B) Renovating a porch
(C) Completing some forms
(D) Changing some delivery instructions

GO ON TO THE NEXT PAGE

44. Why did Carla request to change the meeting time?

(A) She is waiting for a customer.
(B) She has been on a business trip.
(C) Some information was delayed.
(D) A meeting room was not available.

45. When will the meeting most likely take place?

(A) On Wednesday morning
(B) On Wednesday evening
(C) On Thursday morning
(D) On Thursday afternoon

46. What will the man most likely do next?

(A) Make travel arrangements
(B) Prepare a marketing report
(C) Search for survey results
(D) Try to contact Carla

---

47. What is the man's problem?

(A) He does not have transportation now.
(B) He has lost his way in the airport.
(C) He forgot to take his bag with him.
(D) He is late for an appointment.

48. Where is the man?

(A) At an office
(B) On a plane
(C) At an airport
(D) In a taxi

49. What does the woman say she will tell Laura?

(A) The store is closing.
(B) The man is waiting.
(C) The flight was delayed.
(D) The clients have arrived.

---

50. Where does the conversation take place?

(A) At a café
(B) At a hardware store
(C) At a restaurant
(D) At a sign-making company

51. What does the man request?

(A) A price estimate
(B) A discount
(C) A catalog
(D) A contact number

52. What concern does the woman mention?

(A) She won't be here until next month.
(B) An item is out of stock.
(C) Some work cannot be started immediately.
(D) A catalog is missing.

---

53. What are the speakers discussing?

(A) Developing a new product
(B) Sales performance
(C) Negotiating a contract
(D) Work assignments

54. What does the man say the problem is?

(A) The wrong address was given.
(B) The price of products is not reasonable.
(C) The workload is increasing in the marketing team.
(D) The quality of products needs to be improved.

55. What does the woman imply when she says, "That's a good idea"?

(A) She wants to hold a meeting.
(B) She needs to buy a new computer.
(C) She plans to make a plane reservation.
(D) She hopes to hire a sales representative.

---

56. What does the woman indicate about the Legal Department?

(A) It is understaffed.
(B) It recently hired some employees.
(C) It is being relocated.
(D) It requested more funds.

57. What does the man intend to do this week?

(A) Revise his résumé
(B) Arrange some interviews
(C) Apply for a license
(D) Ask for legal advice

58. Why is the man concerned?

(A) He has lost some documents.
(B) The applicants do not seem to be qualified.
(C) He may not be able to meet a deadline.
(D) He will soon run short of cash.

---

59. What are the speakers mainly discussing?

(A) Meeting a client
(B) Sharing a ride
(C) Fixing a technical problem
(D) Leaving for a business trip

60. What does the woman mean when she says, "That'd be nice"?

(A) She wants to stop by a repair shop.
(B) She will contact a client.
(C) She agrees to take a taxi.
(D) She has to go to work early.

61. What will the man most likely do next?

(A) Book a taxi service
(B) Prepare for his presentation
(C) Contact a car repair shop
(D) Go to his office immediately

---

62. Who most likely are the speakers?

(A) Tour guides
(B) Newspaper reporters
(C) Event planners
(D) Interior designers

63. What does the woman imply when she says, "I can't believe it"?

(A) She thinks the restaurant is not that good.
(B) She feels sorry for the men.
(C) She is pleased that the restaurant is popular.
(D) She disagrees with the men's opinion.

64. What will the clients do tomorrow after lunch?

(A) Sign a contract
(B) Choose a design
(C) Visit a building
(D) Provide opinions

GO ON TO THE NEXT PAGE

Towns	General Details
Syracuse	Pets considered Cable TV
Bronx	Garage Smoking allowed
Bayside	Pets considered Garage
Medford	Cable TV Two bedrooms

65. Look at the graphic. Which is the ideal place for the man?

(A) Syracuse
(B) Bronx
(C) Bayside
(D) Medford

66. What is the man concerned about the apartment?

(A) The rent is expensive.
(B) The garage needs repairing.
(C) The bathroom doesn't have enough space.
(D) The furniture is too old-fashioned.

67. When does the man say he will call the woman?

(A) This Friday
(B) Next Friday
(C) Next weekend
(D) In a couple of weeks

Title / Director	Time
Great Banquet Lena Williams	20:40 22:10
Sisters James Watanabe	21:30
Heartbreak Tomas Burton	21:10 23:20
Forever Love Tim Leighton	23:30

68. Look at the graphic. Which movie will the man most likely see tonight?

(A) *Great Banquet*
(B) *Sisters*
(C) *Heartbreak*
(D) *Forever Love*

69. What does the man offer to do?

(A) Purchase a ticket
(B) Make dinner reservations
(C) Review a meeting agenda
(D) Create an advertisement

70. What does the woman say she will do tonight?

(A) Organize a company event
(B) Attend a formal banquet
(C) Watch a movie at home
(D) Meet with Tomas Burton

PART 4

Directions: You will hear some talks given by a single speaker. You will be asked to answer three questions about what the speaker says in each talk. Select the best response to each question and mark the letter (A), (B), (C), or (D) on your answer sheet. The talks will not be printed in your test book and will be spoken only one time.

71. Why is the announcement being made?
(A) To introduce a staff member
(B) To announce a new system
(C) To promote a special offer
(D) To evaluate a project

72. When can people first purchase annual memberships?
(A) In January
(B) In May
(C) In August
(D) In September

73. What type of benefits can members enjoy?
(A) Discounts
(B) Free gifts
(C) Advance reservation
(D) Admission to all exhibitions

---

74. What product is being advertised?
(A) A wristwatch
(B) A suitcase
(C) A map
(D) A compass

75. What is true about the product?
(A) It can be purchased in different sizes.
(B) It has been inspected by experts.
(C) It is available in many colors.
(D) It is rugged and waterproof.

76. What special offer is mentioned?
(A) A free coupon with every purchase
(B) A twenty-percent reduction in price
(C) A discount on a traveler's bag
(D) A two-year warranty

---

77. What is the purpose of the talk?
(A) To discuss Mr. Moore's promotion
(B) To advertise a new product
(C) To announce a job opening
(D) To review salary increases

78. What is James Moore's previous position?
(A) Economics professor
(B) Director of finance
(C) Director of Human Resources
(D) Senior manager

79. How long has Mr. Moore worked for Russel?
(A) For over 4 years
(B) For over 10 years
(C) For over 20 years
(D) For over 35 years

---

80. Who most likely is the listener?
(A) A job applicant
(B) An event planner
(C) A recruiting manager
(D) An entertainer

81. What is the purpose of the message?
(A) To give some feedback
(B) To provide a schedule
(C) To explain a process
(D) To describe an event

82. What does the speaker want the listener to do?
(A) Review her application
(B) Get more qualifications
(C) Contact the headquarters
(D) Apply again later

GO ON TO THE NEXT PAGE

83. Where is the announcement probably being made?

(A) In a post office
(B) In a library
(C) In a repair shop
(D) In a construction company

84. What will take place beginning on June 10?

(A) A main entrance will be closed.
(B) A parking lot will be renovated.
(C) A post office will reopen.
(D) The south entrance will be inaccessible.

85. What does the speaker mean when she says, "make sure to do that"?

(A) Patrons should understand why the library was built.
(B) Employees should find out the name of construction company.
(C) She has to check who built the post office.
(D) Patrons should know which alternate entrance to use.

---

86. What is the main topic of the conference?

(A) Community health
(B) Research methods
(C) Web site design
(D) Medical products

87. What does the speaker say about the small group sessions?

(A) They will be held in several locations.
(B) They are not listed in the program.
(C) They require preregistration.
(D) They feature product demonstrations.

88. According to the speaker, what can the listeners find on the Web site?

(A) Research reports
(B) An evaluation form
(C) Registration confirmation
(D) A program schedule

---

89. Where does the speaker probably work?

(A) At a delivery company
(B) At a factory
(C) At a photo studio
(D) At a publishing company

90. What does the speaker imply when he says, "Here's the thing"?

(A) He has to replace copies of some photographs quickly.
(B) He needs to have some pictures taken again.
(C) He wants some books reprinted.
(D) He will visit New Orleans tomorrow.

91. What does the speaker offer to do?

(A) Work overtime
(B) Pay a fee
(C) Send pictures by e-mail
(D) Extend a deadline

Item #	Quantity
1. Microscopes	5 pieces
2. Test tubes	15 pieces
3. Gloves	10 pairs
4. Protective goggles	15 pieces

92. What is the purpose of the message?

(A) To change an order
(B) To announce a special event
(C) To confirm an order of supplies
(D) To request a delivery address

93. Look at the graphic. What item should be removed from the list?

(A) Item 1
(B) Item 2
(C) Item 3
(D) Item 4

94. What does the speaker ask the listener to do?

(A) Mail a signed contract
(B) Provide a telephone number
(C) Return a phone call
(D) Gather information

Time	Title / Presenter
9:00 A.M. – 9:45 A.M.	Opening Address Billy Forbes
9:45 A.M. – 10:30 A.M.	"Dynamic Shifts" Dennis Lowe
10:30 A.M. – 11:15 A.M.	"Overseas Markets" Ken Shelton
11:15 A.M. – 12:00 P.M.	"The Global Economy" Frank Green

95. What is the purpose of the announcement?

(A) To notify employees of an upcoming event
(B) To report a schedule change
(C) To highlight a company's success
(D) To promote a conference that Mr. Shelton is hosting

96. By when should the listeners register for the seminar?

(A) Before January 8
(B) After January 8
(C) After January 10
(D) On January 10

97. Look at the graphic. Which presentation are the listeners especially encouraged to attend?

(A) Opening address
(B) Dynamic Shifts
(C) Overseas Markets
(D) The Global Economy

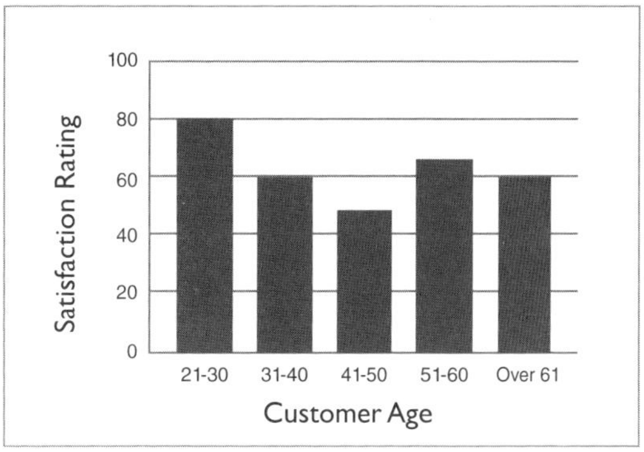

98. Where does the speaker most likely work?

(A) At an electronics company
(B) At an office supply store
(C) At a car manufacturer
(D) At an Internet-service provider

99. What is one advantage of the Bright Cleanette Sweeper?

(A) It is recommended by experts.
(B) It is economical to buy.
(C) It removes stains easily.
(D) It is lightweight.

100. Look at the graphic. What age group will Mr. Dalton talk about?

(A) 21-30
(B) 41-50
(C) 51-60
(D) Over 61

MP3와 해설 파일은 온라인에서 제공됩니다.

▸▸ **books.english.co.kr**

TEST 05

T5.mp3 | 정답 p.188

LISTENING TEST

In the Listening test, you will be asked to demonstrate how well you understand spoken English. The entire Listening test will last approximately 45 minutes. There are four parts, and directions are given for each part. You must mark your answers on the separate answer sheet.
Do not write your answers in your test book.

PART 1

Directions: For each question in this part, you will hear four statements about a picture in your test book. When you hear the statements, you must select the one statement that best describes what you see in the picture. Then find the number of the question on your answer sheet and mark your answer. The statements will not be printed in your test book and will be spoken only one time.

Statement (B), "They're shaking hands," is the best description of the picture, so you should select answer (B) and mark it on your answer sheet.

1.

TEST 05

2.

GO ON TO THE NEXT PAGE

3.

4.

5.

6.

GO ON TO THE NEXT PAGE

PART 2

Directions: You will hear a question or statement and three responses spoken in English. They will not be printed in your test book and will be spoken only one time. Select the best response to the question or statement and mark the letter (A), (B), or (C) on your answer sheet.

7. Mark your answer on your answer sheet.

8. Mark your answer on your answer sheet.

9. Mark your answer on your answer sheet.

10. Mark your answer on your answer sheet.

11. Mark your answer on your answer sheet.

12. Mark your answer on your answer sheet.

13. Mark your answer on your answer sheet.

14. Mark your answer on your answer sheet.

15. Mark your answer on your answer sheet.

16. Mark your answer on your answer sheet.

17. Mark your answer on your answer sheet.

18. Mark your answer on your answer sheet.

19. Mark your answer on your answer sheet.

20. Mark your answer on your answer sheet.

21. Mark your answer on your answer sheet.

22. Mark your answer on your answer sheet.

23. Mark your answer on your answer sheet.

24. Mark your answer on your answer sheet.

25. Mark your answer on your answer sheet.

26. Mark your answer on your answer sheet.

27. Mark your answer on your answer sheet.

28. Mark your answer on your answer sheet.

29. Mark your answer on your answer sheet.

30. Mark your answer on your answer sheet.

31. Mark your answer on your answer sheet.

PART 3

Directions: You will hear some conversations between two or more people. You will be asked to answer three questions about what the speakers say in each conversation. Select the best response to each question and mark the letter (A), (B), (C), or (D) on your answer sheet. The conversations will not be printed in your test book and will be spoken only one time.

32. What does the man ask the woman for?

(A) Help with a presentation
(B) Directions to another office
(C) Information about a meeting
(D) Traveling to Sydney together

33. What did the employees at the Sydney office do?

(A) They completed their training.
(B) They designed a new product.
(C) They increased their sales.
(D) They decreased their costs.

34. What will probably happen soon?

(A) A workshop will be held.
(B) A new sales manager will be hired.
(C) A trip to Sydney will be arranged.
(D) A new advertisement will be released.

---

35. What are the speakers discussing?

(A) Reviewing a movie
(B) Distributing catalogs
(C) Improving a catalog
(D) Planning a business trip

36. How did the woman find out about the change?

(A) From a newsletter
(B) From a meeting
(C) From an e-mail
(D) From a bulletin board

37. According to the woman, why will the change be made?

(A) To draw more clients
(B) To market a new product
(C) To lower printing costs
(D) To increase production

---

38. What event are the speakers discussing?

(A) A luncheon
(B) A workshop
(C) A concert
(D) A retirement party

39. What problem do the men mention about the Bourgeois?

(A) There are not enough seats.
(B) The price is too expensive.
(C) More staff members are needed.
(D) The menu needs to be revised.

40. What does the woman decide to do?

(A) Postpone an event
(B) Use a company facility
(C) Prepare an agenda
(D) Contact some other agencies

---

41. Where most likely are the speakers?

(A) In a medical clinic
(B) In an office building
(C) On a street
(D) At a construction site

42. Who is George Winston?

(A) A Web designer
(B) A lawyer
(C) A receptionist
(D) A security guard

43. Why did the man come to see Mr. Winston?

(A) To interview for a marketing position
(B) To explain his upcoming court case
(C) To discuss a design for his Web site
(D) To purchase a piece of real estate

GO ON TO THE NEXT PAGE

44. Where most likely does the conversation take place?

(A) At a furniture store
(B) At an art gallery
(C) At a hardware store
(D) At a museum

45. When does the man have to do the repair work?

(A) During the weekend
(B) During the hours of operation
(C) Early in the mornings
(D) Late in the evenings

46. What does the man mean when he says, "I'll let you know if there are any changes"?

(A) He thinks that the place might close early that day.
(B) He is happy that the facility is finally being renovated.
(C) He thinks there might be some unexpected problems.
(D) He is not sure who should be hired for the position.

---

47. What does the woman say she likes?

(A) A newspaper article
(B) The appearance of display
(C) The weekend get-away plan
(D) The sale signs on the window

48. What will happen next weekend?

(A) A new store will open.
(B) A sale will take place.
(C) New merchandise will arrive.
(D) A reporter will visit the store.

49. What does the man ask about the advertisement?

(A) Where it should be placed
(B) How much he should spend on it
(C) When it should be run
(D) How many days it should appear

---

50. What does the woman imply when she says, "I'm not surprised"?

(A) They have spent a lot of money on advertisements.
(B) There is a seasonal effect regarding ads.
(C) She has seen the advertisements before.
(D) She expected the ads would increase the business.

51. Where do the speakers probably work?

(A) At a department store
(B) At a caterer
(C) At a photo studio
(D) At an advertising agency

52. What might the speakers do on Friday?

(A) Shop for holiday gifts
(B) Make some wedding cakes
(C) Put in extra hours
(D) Do some painting

---

53. Which department does the woman work in?

(A) Accounting
(B) Marketing
(C) Technical Support
(D) Personnel

54. What are the speakers discussing?

(A) Scheduling a software installation
(B) Getting rid of computer viruses
(C) Purchasing a new computer
(D) Solving a technical problem

55. What does the woman say she will do?

(A) Fill out a request form
(B) Fix the problem herself
(C) Install a new program
(D) Cancel an installation

---

56. What special offer is available for new customers?

(A) Customized designs
(B) Overnight delivery
(C) An extended warranty
(D) Price discounts

57. Why does the woman want to put a sign?

(A) To indicate a location
(B) To promote a special sale
(C) To announce a relocation
(D) To show a parking area

58. What does the man recommend doing?

(A) Increasing the advertising expenses
(B) Visiting another store on Oak Street
(C) Using waterproof material
(D) Collecting client feedback

---

59. What is the man concerned about?

(A) Copying a document
(B) Finding a contract
(C) Being late for a meeting
(D) Contacting a person in charge

60. According to Mindy, what most likely is the problem?

(A) A cost has increased.
(B) An order was submitted late.
(C) An invoice was not paid.
(D) A file was deleted.

61. What does the man agree to do?

(A) Order a new photocopier
(B) Use another conference room
(C) Call a repair person
(D) Print the file at a nearby business

Model #	Size	Zoom Lens	Colors
Z2000	Compact	X	Black / White
Z2000 plus	Medium	X	Black
Z3000	Compact	√	Black / Silver
Z3000 plus	Compact	√	Black / White

62. What is the woman's job?

(A) Photographer
(B) Reporter
(C) Musician
(D) Sales person

63. What does the man say about the Z3000 series cameras?

(A) They are durable.
(B) Their prices are reasonable.
(C) They have a lot of memory.
(D) They have a powerful zoom lens.

64. Look at the graphic. What model does the woman probably purchase?

(A) Z2000
(B) Z2000 plus
(C) Z3000
(D) Z3000 plus

GO ON TO THE NEXT PAGE

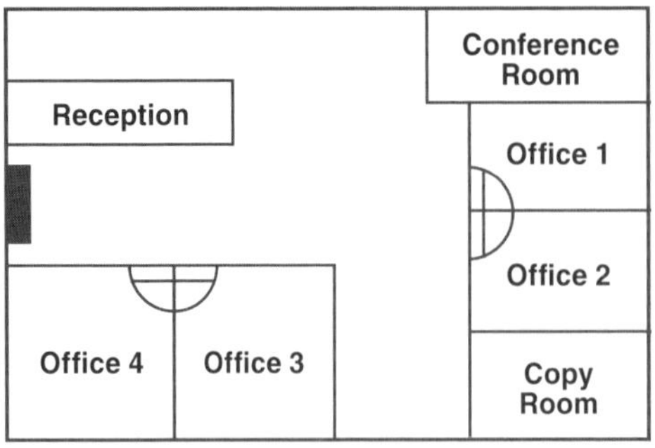

65. According to the woman, what is the man going to do?
(A) Contact the maintenance crew
(B) Apply for a loan for renovation
(C) Speak at a training workshop
(D) Meet with company executives

66. Look at the graphic. Which office has been assigned to the man?
(A) Office 1
(B) Office 2
(C) Office 3
(D) Office 4

67. What does the man say will take place this afternoon?
(A) A job interview
(B) A staff meeting
(C) A product demonstration
(D) Office renovations

Itinerary

Customer: Morgan Simpson

Departure Date	Destination
March 1 (Mon.)	London
March 4 (Thu.)	Madrid
March 5 (Fri.)	Paris
March 6 (Sat.)	Munich

68. What are the speakers mainly discussing?
(A) Taking a vacation
(B) Scheduling a relocation
(C) Visiting international clients
(D) Going on a business trip

69. What does the woman need to do?
(A) Make an appointment
(B) Give a presentation
(C) Leave a trade show early
(D) Reschedule a meeting

70. Look at the graphic. Where will the woman meet her relatives?
(A) In London
(B) In Madrid
(C) In Paris
(D) In Munich

PART 4

Directions: You will hear some talks given by a single speaker. You will be asked to answer three questions about what the speaker says in each talk. Select the best response to each question and mark the letter (A), (B), (C), or (D) on your answer sheet. The talks will not be printed in your test book and will be spoken only one time.

71. Where does the talk take place?
(A) At a real estate agency
(B) At a convention hall
(C) In a hotel lobby
(D) At a job fair

72. What does the speaker say was recently installed?
(A) Movable walls
(B) Soundproof equipment
(C) A security system
(D) An information counter

73. What is offered in January and February?
(A) Free hotel rooms
(B) Guided tours of the area
(C) Shuttle bus service
(D) Reduced rental prices

---

74. What kind of business does the speaker probably work for?
(A) A home inspection company
(B) A package delivery service
(C) An automobile repair shop
(D) A lighting store

75. What is the purpose of the message?
(A) To conduct a survey
(B) To provide inspection results
(C) To file an insurance claim
(D) To advertise a new service

76. What does the speaker ask the listener to do?
(A) Pay for the repairs in advance
(B) Give a credit card number
(C) Schedule a delivery date
(D) Authorize a repair service

---

77. According to the speaker, where can the listeners get bags?
(A) From the speaker
(B) From a store
(C) From a truck
(D) From a farmer

78. What should a person who needs help in a field do?
(A) Contact the farm supervisor
(B) Go back to the main building
(C) Go to the information desk
(D) Talk to a farm worker

79. What will the speaker most likely do next?
(A) Give a demonstration
(B) Explain a recent study
(C) Weigh the fruit the listeners picked
(D) Collect admission fees

---

80. What is the advertisement for?
(A) Summer vacation packages
(B) Cuisine classes
(C) French language classes
(D) A recently opened restaurant

81. Why does the speaker say, "someone who has been the head chef for fifteen years"?
(A) To advertise a vacant position
(B) To ask people to buy his books
(C) To encourage people to sign up
(D) To propose an alternate solution

82. What should listeners do to get more information?
(A) Visit an institute
(B) Call a toll-free number
(C) Attend an informational meeting
(D) Go to an online page

GO ON TO THE NEXT PAGE

83. Where is the announcement most likely taking place?

(A) At a movie theater
(B) At a comedy show
(C) At a sporting event
(D) At a music performance

84. What is the main purpose of the announcement?

(A) To advertise upcoming events
(B) To ask for volunteers for a show
(C) To request proper behavior
(D) To introduce the performers

85. What does the speaker mean when he says, "The entertainers will be available afterward"?

(A) He wants the audience to have a discussion with them in person.
(B) He predicts that the show will be a great success.
(C) He thinks that they would hold a signing event for audience.
(D) He acknowledges people want to spend some time with them.

---

86. What is the purpose of the talk?

(A) To report a job opening
(B) To recommend a former employee
(C) To honor an award winner
(D) To introduce a new employee

87. In which city did Ms. Diaz most recently work?

(A) San Francisco
(B) Atlanta
(C) Miami
(D) Seattle

88. What will the listeners probably do next?

(A) Travel to San Francisco
(B) Set up an interview
(C) Meet with the president
(D) Listen to Ms. Diaz's speech

---

89. What is the announcement mainly about?

(A) A change in a schedule
(B) The opening of a new theater
(C) The casting for a new play
(D) A show cancelation

90. How should listeners purchase tickets for the additional performance?

(A) By reserving them on a Web site
(B) By sending an e-mail to a dealer
(C) By visiting the theater in person
(D) By contacting a performance director

91. What does the speaker imply when she says, "this is a last-minute addition"?

(A) A discount will be given to the customers.
(B) Ticket prices won't be that expensive.
(C) The number of spectators will decrease.
(D) Tickets can be purchased only at a designated area.

---

92. Who most likely is the speaker?

(A) A sports presenter
(B) A radio journalist
(C) A football player
(D) A match referee

93. What prize will be awarded to a winner?

(A) Dinner with an athlete
(B) An autographed football shirt
(C) A two-week trip
(D) Tickets for the final

94. What information are listeners asked to provide?

(A) The title to a game
(B) The date of an event
(C) The name of the first scorer
(D) The total score of a team

BUSINESS HOURS

Monday – Friday 9:00 A.M. – 9:00 P.M.	
Saturday: 10:00 A.M. – 9:00 P.M.	
Sunday: 11:00 A.M. – 8:00 P.M.	

95. What will probably happen after the announcement?

(A) Customers will start shopping.
(B) Free gifts will be distributed to the customers.
(C) Some customers will pay for their purchases.
(D) Employees will take inventory.

96. Look at the graphic. Which day of the week is tomorrow?

(A) Monday
(B) Friday
(C) Saturday
(D) Sunday

97. What is stated about gift cards?

(A) They can be redeemed online.
(B) They are available at every register.
(C) They can be purchased with cash only.
(D) They are available at other stores in the mall.

EXPENSE REPORT

DATE	DESCRIPTION	AMOUNT
May 3	Hotel (4 days)	$280
May 5	Restaurant	$50
May 6	Car Rental	$100
May 7	Parking	$50

98. What is the purpose of the message?

(A) To change a reservation
(B) To cancel a trip to Las Vegas
(C) To request a missing document
(D) To correct a mistake the speaker made

99. Look at the graphic. Which expense needs to be confirmed?

(A) Hotel
(B) Restaurant
(C) Car Rental
(D) Parking

100. What does the speaker offer to do?

(A) Describe a process
(B) Handle a complaint
(C) Reschedule an appointment
(D) Contact a hotel for the listener

MP3와 해설 파일은 온라인에서 제공됩니다.

▸▸ **books.english.co.kr**

TEST 06

T6.mp3 | 정답 p.196

LISTENING TEST

In the Listening test, you will be asked to demonstrate how well you understand spoken English. The entire Listening test will last approximately 45 minutes. There are four parts, and directions are given for each part. You must mark your answers on the separate answer sheet.
Do not write your answers in your test book.

PART 1

Directions: For each question in this part, you will hear four statements about a picture in your test book. When you hear the statements, you must select the one statement that best describes what you see in the picture. Then find the number of the question on your answer sheet and mark your answer. The statements will not be printed in your test book and will be spoken only one time.

Statement (B), "They're shaking hands," is the best description of the picture, so you should select answer (B) and mark it on your answer sheet.

1.

2.

TEST 06

GO ON TO THE NEXT PAGE

3.

4.

5.

6.

GO ON TO THE NEXT PAGE

PART 2

Directions: You will hear a question or statement and three responses spoken in English. They will not be printed in your test book and will be spoken only one time. Select the best response to the question or statement and mark the letter (A), (B), or (C) on your answer sheet.

7. Mark your answer on your answer sheet.

8. Mark your answer on your answer sheet.

9. Mark your answer on your answer sheet.

10. Mark your answer on your answer sheet.

11. Mark your answer on your answer sheet.

12. Mark your answer on your answer sheet.

13. Mark your answer on your answer sheet.

14. Mark your answer on your answer sheet.

15. Mark your answer on your answer sheet.

16. Mark your answer on your answer sheet.

17. Mark your answer on your answer sheet.

18. Mark your answer on your answer sheet.

19. Mark your answer on your answer sheet.

20. Mark your answer on your answer sheet.

21. Mark your answer on your answer sheet.

22. Mark your answer on your answer sheet.

23. Mark your answer on your answer sheet.

24. Mark your answer on your answer sheet.

25. Mark your answer on your answer sheet.

26. Mark your answer on your answer sheet.

27. Mark your answer on your answer sheet.

28. Mark your answer on your answer sheet.

29. Mark your answer on your answer sheet.

30. Mark your answer on your answer sheet.

31. Mark your answer on your answer sheet.

PART 3

Directions: You will hear some conversations between two or more people. You will be asked to answer three questions about what the speakers say in each conversation. Select the best response to each question and mark the letter (A), (B), (C), or (D) on your answer sheet. The conversations will not be printed in your test book and will be spoken only one time.

32. Where does the man work?
(A) At an electronics store
(B) At a shipping center
(C) At an airport
(D) At a conference center

33. Why is the man contacting the woman?
(A) A shipment has arrived.
(B) A computer was found.
(C) An event has been postponed.
(D) A reservation is canceled.

34. What does the man offer to do?
(A) Send an item
(B) Revise a meeting agenda
(C) Fix a computer
(D) Make an appointment

---

35. Where most likely are the speakers?
(A) At a police station
(B) At a financial institute
(C) At a photo studio
(D) At an airline check-in counter

36. What does the woman request?
(A) An account number
(B) An identification
(C) A credit card
(D) A billing statement

37. What will the man most likely do next?
(A) Complete a form
(B) Take a picture
(C) Apply for a driver's license
(D) Close an account

---

38. What does the man want to do tomorrow?
(A) Leave work early
(B) Meet with a client
(C) Work from home
(D) Lead a presentation

39. What is the woman concerned about?
(A) Submitting the work on time
(B) Shopping for a present
(C) Organizing a committee
(D) Finding some documents

40. What does the woman say will happen next week?
(A) An office will be cleaned.
(B) Some equipment will be replaced.
(C) An employee will be unavailable.
(D) A proposal will be presented.

---

41. Who most likely is the woman?
(A) A cyclist
(B) A reporter
(C) A shop owner
(D) A researcher

42. What does the woman mention about the material?
(A) It is reasonably priced.
(B) It is easy to make.
(C) It is light and strong.
(D) It is environmentally friendly.

43. According to the woman, what will happen in 6 months?
(A) A new researcher will be hired.
(B) A product will be introduced to the market.
(C) A bike race will be held in town.
(D) An agreement will be signed.

GO ON TO THE NEXT PAGE

44. What is the man mainly considering to choose a car?

(A) A discounted price
(B) Comfortable seating
(C) Brand name
(D) The reliability of a car

45. According to the woman, what is offered to customers?

(A) A ten-percent discount
(B) A six-month warranty
(C) A coupon for free fuel
(D) An extra set of tires

46. Why does the man ask to see another model?

(A) He saw it in an advertisement.
(B) He would like a newer car.
(C) He prefers something smaller.
(D) He wants a car in a different color.

---

47. When is the conversation taking place?

(A) In the morning
(B) At noon
(C) In the afternoon
(D) At night

48. What does the man imply when he says, "You could try the fast-food restaurant around the corner"?

(A) His restaurant doesn't serve vegetarian dishes.
(B) The food usually takes longer to be served at his restaurant.
(C) His restaurant is about to close for the day.
(D) It is open 24 hours a day.

49. What does the man say about his restaurant?

(A) It closes at the same time every day.
(B) It is usually crowded on weeknights.
(C) It is especially popular on weekends.
(D) It has daily specials during the week.

---

50. Who is the woman most likely talking to?

(A) A colleague
(B) A store manager
(C) A salesperson
(D) A client

51. According to the man, what is the advantage of the lunch special?

(A) It comes with a beverage.
(B) It is served with side dishes.
(C) It is cheaper with a coupon.
(D) It uses organic products.

52. What will the speakers probably do next?

(A) Schedule a meeting
(B) Order some food
(C) Go back to the office
(D) Postpone a staff meeting

---

53. Where does this conversation take place?

(A) At a manufacturing plant
(B) At a repair shop
(C) In a research laboratory
(D) At an electric company

54. What is the man impressed with?

(A) The automation level of a factory
(B) The high price of some equipment
(C) The size of an assembly line
(D) The variety of goods on display

55. What does the woman ask the man to do?

(A) Repair some machines
(B) Provide a cost estimate
(C) Advertise a new product
(D) Join her company

---

56. What is the man looking for?

(A) A gift for a family member
(B) A restaurant with outdoor seating
(C) A location for a new store
(D) A piece of luggage

57. What does the man ask the woman for?

(A) The address of a shop
(B) An item in a different size
(C) An additional discount
(D) A warm drink

58. What does the woman mean when she says, "I got one for my friend"?

(A) She would like the man to meet her friend.
(B) Her friend is the same size as the man's wife.
(C) She is willing to pay for a purchase.
(D) She is emphasizing how good a product is.

---

59. Where do the speakers probably work?

(A) At an employment agency
(B) At a caterer
(C) At a theater
(D) At a restaurant

60. Why does the man ask the woman to help?

(A) Some employees are off duty today.
(B) The food has not been prepared.
(C) Some guests did not make reservations.
(D) An event has to be rescheduled.

61. What will the woman probably do next?

(A) Go to the patio
(B) Work with Philippe
(C) Put on different clothing
(D) Wait for the man's call

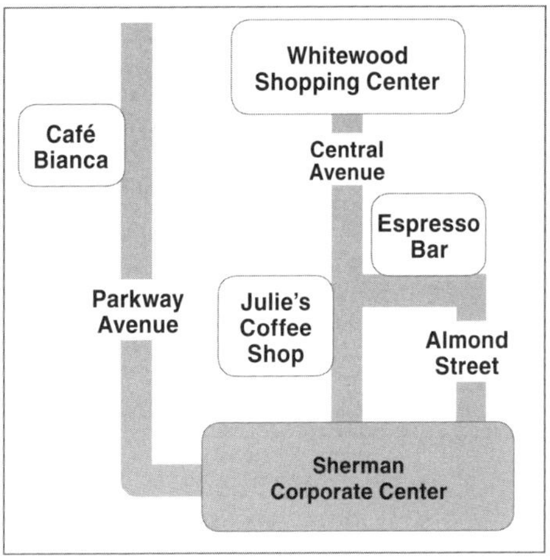

62. What does the man say about his new house?

(A) It is in a heavily populated area.
(B) It is closer to his office.
(C) It is in a business district.
(D) It is in a good neighborhood.

63. How does the man get to work now?

(A) By car
(B) By train
(C) By bicycle
(D) By bus

64. Look at the graphic. Where does the man go for coffee on his way to work?

(A) Café Bianca
(B) Espresso Bar
(C) Whitewood Shopping Center
(D) Julie's Coffee Shop

TEST 06

Conference Room A:
Wednesday

Time	*Event*
Noon	Luncheon Meeting
2:00 P.M.	Engineering Forum
3:00 P.M.	Networking Event
4:00 P.M.	Sales Strategy Workshop

65. Where do the speakers work?

(A) At a law firm
(B) At a newspaper
(C) At a manufacturing facility
(D) At a bookstore

66. Look at the graphic. According to the man, what event is Jason in charge of?

(A) The luncheon meeting
(B) The engineering forum
(C) The networking event
(D) The sales strategy workshop

67. What will the woman do next?

(A) Contact a client about a contract
(B) Conduct a job interview
(C) Ask a coworker to change rooms
(D) Revise a company policy

Elevator Closure

North Elevator	9:00 A.M. – 10:00 A.M.
East Elevator	10:30 A.M. – 11:30 A.M.
South Elevator	1:00 P.M. – 2:00 P.M.
West Elevator	2:30 P.M. – 3:30 P.M.

68. What did Ms. Yamada realize last week?

(A) A certificate will be no longer valid.
(B) New equipment was installed.
(C) New tenants will move in.
(D) Some machines should be fixed.

69. Look at the graphic. Which elevator is closest to the entrance?

(A) North Elevator
(B) East Elevator
(C) South Elevator
(D) West Elevator

70. What does the man suggest the woman do?

(A) Reschedule a meeting
(B) Call a technician
(C) Display a new sign
(D) Speak to a supervisor

PART 4

Directions: You will hear some talks given by a single speaker. You will be asked to answer three questions about what the speaker says in each talk. Select the best response to each question and mark the letter (A), (B), (C), or (D) on your answer sheet. The talks will not be printed in your test book and will be spoken only one time.

71. Where is the announcement being made?
(A) At a travel agency
(B) At a train station
(C) At an airport
(D) At a bus terminal

72. What is the cause of the problem?
(A) Overbooked flights
(B) Weather conditions
(C) Mechanical problems
(D) Traffic congestion

73. What will be provided for some passengers?
(A) Hotel accommodations
(B) Complimentary beverages
(C) Full refunds for their tickets
(D) Seating upgrades

---

74. What type of business is being advertised?
(A) An electronics store
(B) A food market
(C) A furniture store
(D) A car repair center

75. According to the advertisement, why do customers like the business?
(A) It provides good customer service.
(B) It offers online shopping.
(C) It is conveniently located.
(D) It has a variety of products.

76. What will the business do on September 12?
(A) Close for remodeling
(B) Host a celebration
(C) Count its inventory
(D) Hire a new staff member

---

77. Why did the speaker leave the message?
(A) To ask for a refund
(B) To request technical assistance
(C) To respond to an inquiry
(D) To arrange an appointment

78. Why does the speaker say, "I apologize for that"?
(A) To express her regret for a delay in delivery
(B) To explain why an accountant was late for a meeting
(C) To report an accident on the road
(D) To acknowledge that there has been an error

79. What might happen this afternoon?
(A) An official announcement will be made.
(B) Some money will be transferred.
(C) A delivery will be made.
(D) A part will be ordered.

---

80. Who most likely is the report intended for?
(A) Traffic police officers
(B) Commuters
(C) Shopping center managers
(D) Construction supervisors

81. What problem is the speaker discussing?
(A) A road closure
(B) An equipment breakdown
(C) Construction delays
(D) An increase in traffic

82. According to the report, what will happen in March?
(A) A construction project will begin.
(B) A department store will open.
(C) A highway will be closed.
(D) A new road will be built.

GO ON TO THE NEXT PAGE

83. What did Mr. Waters request?

(A) An airplane ticket
(B) A delivery schedule
(C) A price estimate
(D) A special warranty

84. What additional information does Mr. Waters have to provide?

(A) A telephone number
(B) A mailing address
(C) A payment option
(D) A delivery preference

85. What does the speaker mean when he says, "express air is probably a better choice"?

(A) Its price has been marked down.
(B) It is faster than the other option.
(C) He has used the service before.
(D) The other service is not available now.

---

86. What is being advertised?

(A) A nature course
(B) A travel book
(C) A TV show
(D) A holiday tour package

87. Who is Raquel Sylvia?

(A) A TV program host
(B) A university professor
(C) A tour guide
(D) An environmentalist

88. What can be found on the Web site?

(A) An application form
(B) The location of the station
(C) Some images
(D) A price list of packages

---

89. What type of business does Peter O'Malley own?

(A) An insurance company
(B) A building renovation company
(C) A furniture manufacturer
(D) A stationery store

90. What does the company plan to do by the end of the year?

(A) Renew a Web site
(B) Construct a building
(C) Hire some staff members
(D) Design a line of furniture

91. What does the speaker imply when she says, "most of his customers still place their orders by phone"?

(A) O'Malley's will increase its product prices soon.
(B) New employees will take customers' calls.
(C) Some new employees will get higher salaries.
(D) A store is moving to a new location.

---

92. What is the subject of Dr. Covey's recent book?

(A) Designing a Web site
(B) Teaching at a university
(C) Developing business strategies
(D) Publishing a novel

93. For how long has Dr. Covey worked as a consultant?

(A) 5 years
(B) 10 years
(C) 15 years
(D) 20 years

94. According to the speaker, what will probably happen next?

(A) Dr. Covey will discuss her experience.
(B) The interviewer will describe a book.
(C) The radio program will end.
(D) There will be a commercial break.

Flowchart for Yellowjeep

Create a design
▼
Build a model
▼
Conduct a field test
▼
Make design revisions
▼
Launch a marketing campaign

95. Who most likely is the speaker?
(A) A corporate executive
(B) A product developer
(C) A customer service representative
(D) A field test participant

96. Look at the graphic. According to the speaker, which step should be completed within the next month?
(A) Build a model
(B) Conduct a field test
(C) Make design revisions
(D) Launch a marketing campaign

97. What will the listeners probably do next?
(A) Develop a prototype
(B) Fill out a document
(C) Test a new product
(D) Look at a slide

Tour Schedule

Garden Tour	10:00 A.M.
Lunch	12:00 P.M.
Museum Visit	1:30 P.M.
Theater Performance	3:30 P.M.

98. What does the speaker say about the restaurant Baron?
(A) Its menu is updated daily.
(B) It has multiple locations nationwide.
(C) It recently won an award.
(D) It is the oldest restaurant in the city.

99. Look at the graphic. What time is the talk most likely being given?
(A) At 10:00 A.M.
(B) At 12:00 P.M.
(C) At 1:30 P.M.
(D) At 3:30 P.M.

100. What will the speaker distribute?
(A) Information booklets
(B) Admission tickets
(C) Bottles of water
(D) Local maps

MP3와 해설 파일은 온라인에서 제공됩니다.

▶▶ **books.english.co.kr**

TEST 07

T7.mp3 | 정답 p.204

LISTENING TEST

In the Listening test, you will be asked to demonstrate how well you understand spoken English. The entire Listening test will last approximately 45 minutes. There are four parts, and directions are given for each part. You must mark your answers on the separate answer sheet. Do not write your answers in your test book.

PART 1

Directions: For each question in this part, you will hear four statements about a picture in your test book. When you hear the statements, you must select the one statement that best describes what you see in the picture. Then find the number of the question on your answer sheet and mark your answer. The statements will not be printed in your test book and will be spoken only one time.

Statement (B), "They're shaking hands," is the best description of the picture, so you should select answer (B) and mark it on your answer sheet.

1.

2.

TEST 07

GO ON TO THE NEXT PAGE

3.

4.

5.

6.

TEST 07

GO ON TO THE NEXT PAGE

PART 2

Directions: You will hear a question or statement and three responses spoken in English. They will not be printed in your test book and will be spoken only one time. Select the best response to the question or statement and mark the letter (A), (B), or (C) on your answer sheet.

7. Mark your answer on your answer sheet.

8. Mark your answer on your answer sheet.

9. Mark your answer on your answer sheet.

10. Mark your answer on your answer sheet.

11. Mark your answer on your answer sheet.

12. Mark your answer on your answer sheet.

13. Mark your answer on your answer sheet.

14. Mark your answer on your answer sheet.

15. Mark your answer on your answer sheet.

16. Mark your answer on your answer sheet.

17. Mark your answer on your answer sheet.

18. Mark your answer on your answer sheet.

19. Mark your answer on your answer sheet.

20. Mark your answer on your answer sheet.

21. Mark your answer on your answer sheet.

22. Mark your answer on your answer sheet.

23. Mark your answer on your answer sheet.

24. Mark your answer on your answer sheet.

25. Mark your answer on your answer sheet.

26. Mark your answer on your answer sheet.

27. Mark your answer on your answer sheet.

28. Mark your answer on your answer sheet.

29. Mark your answer on your answer sheet.

30. Mark your answer on your answer sheet.

31. Mark your answer on your answer sheet.

PART 3

Directions: You will hear some conversations between two or more people. You will be asked to answer three questions about what the speakers say in each conversation. Select the best response to each question and mark the letter (A), (B), (C), or (D) on your answer sheet. The conversations will not be printed in your test book and will be spoken only one time.

32. What is the purpose of the man's visit?
(A) To schedule a meeting
(B) To review some contracts
(C) To pick up some documents
(D) To get a signature

33. According to the woman, where is Mr. Edwards?
(A) In a cafeteria
(B) In a meeting room
(C) In a staff lounge
(D) In his office

34. What does the woman say the man can do?
(A) Wait until Mr. Edwards is available
(B) Come back in 10 minutes
(C) Call Mr. Edwards later
(D) Leave the documents with her

---

35. When was the meeting supposed to take place?
(A) This afternoon
(B) This evening
(C) Tomorrow
(D) Next week

36. Why will the meeting be postponed?
(A) All meeting rooms are booked.
(B) Some information is not available yet.
(C) One participant cannot attend.
(D) The office is closing early.

37. What does the man suggest doing?
(A) Going to an airport
(B) Holding a teleconference
(C) Listening to a weather forecast
(D) Looking over a report

---

38. Where are the speakers?
(A) At a reception desk
(B) At a restaurant
(C) At a store
(D) At a party

39. What does the man say he did a few days ago?
(A) Ordered a cake
(B) Canceled an order
(C) Met with his sister
(D) Made dinner reservations

40. According to the man, what will probably happen today?
(A) He will send out some invitations.
(B) He will attend a birthday party.
(C) He will bake some special cakes.
(D) He will get an extra discount.

---

41. Where does this conversation probably take place?
(A) At a travel agency
(B) In a governmental office
(C) On a bus
(D) At an airport

42. Why is the man concerned about his trip?
(A) He might miss a flight.
(B) His luggage might be delayed.
(C) His passport has expired.
(D) His meeting might be canceled.

43. What does the woman offer to do?
(A) Talk to the flight attendant
(B) Arrange some transportation
(C) Postpone a meeting
(D) Confirm a reservation

GO ON TO THE NEXT PAGE

44. What are the speakers discussing?

(A) Booking an airline ticket
(B) Organizing a conference
(C) Reserving a hotel room
(D) Planning a vacation

45. What does the man imply when he says, "the prices were too expensive"?

(A) He wants to receive a membership discount.
(B) The hotel doesn't offer a special rate.
(C) He wants the company to cover a cost.
(D) He couldn't get the flight he wanted.

46. What information will the woman give the man?

(A) A colleague's e-mail address
(B) A travel guide for a trip
(C) A travel agent's contact number
(D) A brochure about a conference

---

47. What are the speakers mainly talking about?

(A) A television commercial
(B) A lack of space
(C) A need for more employees
(D) A surplus in the budget

48. Where do the speakers most likely work?

(A) At a real estate agency
(B) At a construction company
(C) At an advertising agency
(D) At an accounting firm

49. According to the woman, which department has the highest priority?

(A) Management
(B) Accounting
(C) Engineering
(D) Marketing

---

50. Where do the women most likely work?

(A) At an electronics store
(B) At an employment agency
(C) At a TV station
(D) At a movie theater

51. What job requirement do the speakers discuss?

(A) Being professionally certified
(B) Holding relevant degrees
(C) Having management experience
(D) Having a flexible schedule

52. What will the man do next?

(A) Show a video
(B) Provide references
(C) Tour a facility
(D) Submit some documents

---

53. What type of business is the man calling?

(A) A publisher
(B) A hotel
(C) A restaurant
(D) A bookstore

54. Why is the man calling?

(A) To reserve a venue for an event
(B) To book hotel rooms for his employees
(C) To cancel a reservation he made earlier
(D) To purchase airline tickets for participants

55. What does the woman say she will do?

(A) Prepare some equipment
(B) Clean up the conference rooms
(C) Write down some information
(D) Call a travel agency

---

56. What was the main topic of the seminar?

(A) Managing time more efficiently
(B) Running a responsible corporation
(C) Understanding consumer behavior
(D) Becoming a great instructor

57. What does the man mean when he says, "I was quite impressed with the instructor"?

(A) He thinks the instructor looks good.
(B) He has met the instructor before.
(C) He wants to be like the instructor.
(D) He thinks the instructor was efficient.

58. What will the man do next week?

(A) Work on a marketing strategy
(B) Buy a new car for his family
(C) Meet with corporate lawyers
(D) Train new employees

---

59. Where is the conversation taking place?

(A) At a paint store
(B) At a clothing store
(C) At a dry cleaner's
(D) At a dentist's office

60. What does the woman ask the man about?

(A) Contacting a different store
(B) Changing a meeting time
(C) Altering her blouse
(D) Removing a stain from clothing

61. What will the woman probably do next?

(A) Pay for her purchase
(B) Provide her contact information
(C) Return an item for a refund
(D) Wait for gift-wrapping

---

62. What is the main topic of the conversation?

(A) Giving a big presentation
(B) Responding to client complaints
(C) Launching a new product
(D) Holding a charity event

63. What does the woman imply when she says, "I volunteered last year"?

(A) She is able to train other volunteers.
(B) She is proud of doing volunteer work.
(C) She met someone at last year's event.
(D) She doesn't plan to attend an event today.

64. What does the man say he will do tomorrow?

(A) Raise some funds for an event
(B) Prepare a marketing questionnaire
(C) Discuss an issue at a meeting
(D) Conduct some product testing

GO ON TO THE NEXT PAGE

Invoice

Customer: TPC Corporation

Item	Quantity	Price
Invitations	200	$800
Catalogues	100	$900

Shipping: $30

Total: $1,730

65. What is the purpose of the conversation?

(A) To negotiate a price
(B) To explain a process
(C) To discuss a problem
(D) To review customer feedback

66. Look at the graphic. How much money will the speakers be refunded?

(A) $800
(B) $900
(C) $30
(D) $1,730

67. What does the woman want the store to do?

(A) Refund some money
(B) Expedite the rest of an order
(C) Change a delivery time
(D) Send an invoice via e-mail

From	Subject
Ilene Rosenthal	Attached: Travel Itinerary
David Choi	Sales Projection
Adrian Harris	Conference Agenda
Helen Edmond	Accounting Workshop

68. Why is the woman unable to access her e-mail?

(A) Her password has expired.
(B) She forgot to update some software.
(C) Her computer needs some repairs.
(D) Her Internet connection is not working.

69. Look at the graphic. Who sent the e-mail the speakers are referring to?

(A) Ilene Rosenthal
(B) David Choi
(C) Adrian Harris
(D) Helen Edmond

70. What does the woman ask the man to do?

(A) Call for technical assistance
(B) Prepare for a conference
(C) Print a document
(D) Review some sales figures

PART 4

Directions: You will hear some talks given by a single speaker. You will be asked to answer three questions about what the speaker says in each talk. Select the best response to each question and mark the letter (A), (B), (C), or (D) on your answer sheet. The talks will not be printed in your test book and will be spoken only one time.

71. What is the report about?

(A) Health
(B) Weather
(C) Sports
(D) Traffic

72. What does the speaker suggest the listeners do?

(A) Spend some time outside
(B) Drive carefully
(C) Dress warmly
(D) Stack up some groceries

73. What will the listeners hear next?

(A) An advertisement
(B) A music program
(C) An emergency report
(D) An interview with a guest speaker

---

74. What is the purpose of the message?

(A) To request some contact information
(B) To suggest some future repairs
(C) To report the completion of a job
(D) To advertise an auto product

75. What does the speaker mean when he says, "we are about to close for the day"?

(A) His place will be closed during the weekend.
(B) He thinks the work might be delayed.
(C) He wants the customer to hurry up.
(D) He doesn't want the customer to come today.

76. What did the speaker notice about the car?

(A) The wiper fluid needed to be refilled.
(B) The air conditioning was broken.
(C) The brake lights weren't working.
(D) The oil needed to be changed.

---

77. What is Elaine Perkins' profession?

(A) A board member
(B) An operator
(C) A tour guide
(D) A desk clerk

78. What are the listeners asked to do?

(A) Help a new employee
(B) Make a seating plan
(C) Put their names on a waiting list
(D) Greet some customers

79. What does the speaker say he will do this morning?

(A) Give a job interview
(B) Hire a trainer
(C) Give a tour
(D) Revise a manual

---

80. Why is Mr. Santos coming for a visit?

(A) A project has been completed.
(B) A new branch has opened.
(C) A sales record has been achieved.
(D) A new manager has been hired.

81. Why does the speaker say, "this isn't a formal inspection"?

(A) To remind the listeners of an event
(B) To reassure employees
(C) To dispute a claim
(D) To express disagreement

82. What event have the listeners been invited to?

(A) A retirement party
(B) A fashion show
(C) A welcome luncheon
(D) A product demonstration

---

83. Why did the speaker leave a message?

(A) To request a client list
(B) To report on a budgeting change
(C) To provide an update on travel plans
(D) To request missing documentation

84. What does the speaker ask the listener to do?

(A) Mail a package
(B) Send an e-mail
(C) Provide a forwarding address
(D) Fax a copy of a receipt

85. When does the speaker hope to receive a reply?

(A) By Tuesday
(B) By Wednesday
(C) By this week
(D) By this month

---

86. Where is the talk probably being given?

(A) At a company picnic
(B) At an awards ceremony
(C) At a company meeting
(D) At a job fair

87. What was completed this morning?

(A) An office renovation
(B) A meeting agenda
(C) A new Web site
(D) A sales report

88. What will happen later this month?

(A) Financial bonuses will be awarded.
(B) A revised agenda will be sent by e-mail.
(C) A celebration will be held.
(D) A new president will be named.

---

89. What kind of business is being advertised?

(A) A paint store
(B) A furniture store
(C) An office supply store
(D) A graphic design company

90. What does the upgraded Web site offer?

(A) Coupons for discounts on office furniture
(B) Faster speed to access information
(C) Clear directions to the store
(D) The convenience of online shopping

91. How can customers receive free delivery?

(A) By spending over a certain amount
(B) By making a purchase by credit card
(C) By applying for a membership card
(D) By completing a customer survey

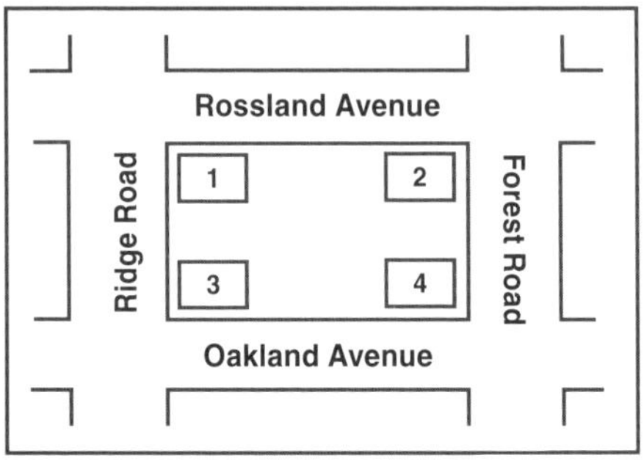

92. What is the purpose of the message?

(A) To cancel a meeting
(B) To schedule some repairs
(C) To confirm an appointment
(D) To ask for an address

93. What does the speaker recommend the listener do?

(A) Leave earlier than usual
(B) Use public transportation
(C) Come back later
(D) Bring some medical records

94. Look at the graphic. Which number shows where the annex building is?

(A) 1
(B) 2
(C) 3
(D) 4

Customer Feedback

	Jessie's Café	*All Flavors*
Low Prices	★★	★
Friendly Atmosphere	★	★★
A Variety of Menus	★★	★★
Good Customer Service	★★	★

95. What is the main topic of the talk?

(A) Relocation plans
(B) A potential acquisition
(C) Software upgrades
(D) A business performance

96. Who most likely is the speaker?

(A) A marketing researcher
(B) A business owner
(C) A news reporter
(D) A store clerk

97. Look at the graphic. What will the speaker most likely discuss next?

(A) Prices
(B) Atmosphere
(C) Menus
(D) Customer Service

SPEAKER	TIME
Chris Appleton	10 A.M.
Mark Elliot	2 P.M.
Lorena Kim	4 P.M.
Jennifer Lock	6 P.M.

98. What is offered to the listeners?

(A) A visitor's badge
(B) A bag of supplies
(C) A presentation ticket
(D) A complimentary drink

99. Look at the graphic. According to the speaker, who will make the first presentation?

(A) Chris Appleton
(B) Mark Elliot
(C) Lorena Kim
(D) Jennifer Lock

100. Why are the listeners invited to the Reedsburg Ballroom?

(A) To eat breakfast
(B) To attend a presentation
(C) To register for the event
(D) To meet people

MP3와 해설 파일은 온라인에서 제공됩니다.

▶▶ **books.english.co.kr**

TEST 08

T8.mp3 | 정답 p.212

LISTENING TEST

In the Listening test, you will be asked to demonstrate how well you understand spoken English. The entire Listening test will last approximately 45 minutes. There are four parts, and directions are given for each part. You must mark your answers on the separate answer sheet.
Do not write your answers in your test book.

PART 1

Directions: For each question in this part, you will hear four statements about a picture in your test book. When you hear the statements, you must select the one statement that best describes what you see in the picture. Then find the number of the question on your answer sheet and mark your answer. The statements will not be printed in your test book and will be spoken only one time.

Statement (B), "They're shaking hands," is the best description of the picture, so you should select answer (B) and mark it on your answer sheet.

1.

2.

GO ON TO THE NEXT PAGE

3.

4.

5.

6.

GO ON TO THE NEXT PAGE

PART 2

Directions: You will hear a question or statement and three responses spoken in English. They will not be printed in your test book and will be spoken only one time. Select the best response to the question or statement and mark the letter (A), (B), or (C) on your answer sheet.

7. Mark your answer on your answer sheet.

8. Mark your answer on your answer sheet.

9. Mark your answer on your answer sheet.

10. Mark your answer on your answer sheet.

11. Mark your answer on your answer sheet.

12. Mark your answer on your answer sheet.

13. Mark your answer on your answer sheet.

14. Mark your answer on your answer sheet.

15. Mark your answer on your answer sheet.

16. Mark your answer on your answer sheet.

17. Mark your answer on your answer sheet.

18. Mark your answer on your answer sheet.

19. Mark your answer on your answer sheet.

20. Mark your answer on your answer sheet.

21. Mark your answer on your answer sheet.

22. Mark your answer on your answer sheet.

23. Mark your answer on your answer sheet.

24. Mark your answer on your answer sheet.

25. Mark your answer on your answer sheet.

26. Mark your answer on your answer sheet.

27. Mark your answer on your answer sheet.

28. Mark your answer on your answer sheet.

29. Mark your answer on your answer sheet.

30. Mark your answer on your answer sheet.

31. Mark your answer on your answer sheet.

PART 3

Directions: You will hear some conversations between two or more people. You will be asked to answer three questions about what the speakers say in each conversation. Select the best response to each question and mark the letter (A), (B), (C), or (D) on your answer sheet. The conversations will not be printed in your test book and will be spoken only one time.

32. Where most likely is the conversation taking place?
(A) In an office meeting
(B) At a convention center
(C) At an airport
(D) In a university lecture room

33. What will the man receive?
(A) An entry pass
(B) An information booklet
(C) A registration form
(D) A free lecture

34. What does the man want to know?
(A) The attendees at an event
(B) The room where he will be staying
(C) The location of an event
(D) The fee for registration

---

35. Who is the woman?
(A) A researcher
(B) A press officer
(C) A decorator
(D) A market analyst

36. Why is the woman calling?
(A) To reorder some equipment
(B) To request product information
(C) To ask for advice on a project
(D) To report an invoice error

37. What does the man offer to do?
(A) Arrange for a house to be painted
(B) Change the amount of products ordered
(C) Organize a visit from a representative
(D) Mail some samples

---

38. What does the man want to know?
(A) The woman's schedule
(B) The reason for the woman's trip
(C) Directions to a downtown area
(D) The location of Chelsie's office

39. What will happen next Tuesday?
(A) A promotion of an employee
(B) A party for a coworker
(C) A business investment
(D) A staff meeting

40. What will the woman do before her trip?
(A) Stop by a gas station to fill up the tank
(B) Move to Korea to open a business
(C) Meet her colleague in person
(D) Visit the downtown office

---

41. What are the speakers discussing?
(A) The renovation of a building
(B) Promoting a new branch
(C) Reimbursement for expenses
(D) A sales performance

42. What is *Quest West*?
(A) A television program
(B) A computer game
(C) A guidebook
(D) A magazine

43. What will probably happen at the end of the month?
(A) A publicity campaign will begin.
(B) Overseas branches will be open.
(C) Some versions of a product will be available.
(D) A product will be popular with younger consumers.

GO ON TO THE NEXT PAGE

44. What problem does the woman mention?

(A) A receipt is missing.
(B) Some information can't be found.
(C) A popular item is out of stock.
(D) The price is higher than expected.

45. Why does the woman say, "This jacket looks great"?

(A) To explain the quality of an item
(B) To convince the man to buy a product
(C) To show interest in making a purchase
(D) To ask the man to check an inventory list

46. What does the man say he will do?

(A) Expand a product line
(B) Look for discount offers
(C) Print a receipt
(D) Check a Web site

---

47. What are the speakers mainly discussing?

(A) A computer upgrade
(B) A printing order
(C) A store refund
(D) An advance payment

48. What store policy is mentioned?

(A) Customers must use a shop design.
(B) Customers must place an order two weeks in advance.
(C) Services must be paid in full when ordering.
(D) Deliveries could cost extra depending on the location.

49. What does Ms. Yumi explain to the customer?

(A) A warranty cannot be extended.
(B) A replacement part should be ordered.
(C) An extra charge will be added.
(D) An account has been suspended.

---

50. What is the conversation mainly about?

(A) A payroll error
(B) A department reorganization
(C) Software development
(D) Decreased sales

51. According to the woman, what did the feedback show?

(A) The company should hire more employees.
(B) Some clients were dissatisfied with a program.
(C) Employees made some mistakes.
(D) Management communicated with employees well.

52. What will happen in March?

(A) Salaries will be increased.
(B) A workshop will be scheduled.
(C) Some customers will be interviewed.
(D) A product will be released.

---

53. What has the man been reading about?

(A) Personal relationships
(B) Art history
(C) Web design
(D) Architecture

54. What does the man ask the woman to do?

(A) Change a deadline
(B) Discuss a project
(C) Offer a lower price
(D) Provide a recommendation

55. Where does the man say he will go tonight?

(A) To a museum
(B) To a library
(C) To a bookstore
(D) To a gallery

---

56. What does Becky want to do?

(A) Change a work shift
(B) Refer a friend for employment
(C) Attend an employee training session
(D) Request a transfer to another department

57. What does the man mean when he says, "Junko has been here a long time"?

(A) Junko plans to retire soon.
(B) He was surprised about a mistake that Junko made.
(C) He thinks Junko should be promoted.
(D) Junko can answer a question instead.

58. What does Junko recommend doing?

(A) Consulting a professional counselor
(B) Picking up extra materials
(C) Visiting a Web site
(D) Talking to a manager in person

---

59. What type of business does the woman work for?

(A) A moving company
(B) A real estate agency
(C) A delivery company
(D) An advertising agency

60. What is the woman concerned about?

(A) Shipping delays
(B) New government regulations
(C) An increase in competition
(D) A staff shortage

61. What does the woman emphasize about the company?

(A) The affordable prices
(B) The design of Web site
(C) The speedy delivery service
(D) The customer service

Store Directory	
Aisle 1	Dairy
Aisle 2	Baked Goods
Aisle 3	Beverages
Aisle 4	Frozen Foods

62. What are the speakers planning to do?

(A) Organize a business dinner
(B) Attend a professional conference
(C) Participate in a sports competition
(D) Go hiking with employees

63. Look at the graphic. Which aisle should the speakers go to?

(A) Aisle 1
(B) Aisle 2
(C) Aisle 3
(D) Aisle 4

64. What does the woman remind the man to do?

(A) Fill out a form
(B) Ask for a discount
(C) Check a price online
(D) Present a membership card

GO ON TO THE NEXT PAGE

Spice World Restaurant Rating

Atmosphere
★★★★
Prices
★★
Customer Service
★★★
Food Quality
★★★★★

Weather Forecast

Wednesday	Thursday	Friday	Saturday
28°C Cloudy	25°C Sunny	27°C Sunny	30°C Storms

65. Who most likely is the woman?

(A) A waitress
(B) A chef
(C) A restaurant owner
(D) A food critic

66. Look at the graphic. What do the speakers want the restaurant to improve in?

(A) Atmosphere
(B) Prices
(C) Customer service
(D) Food quality

67. What does the man suggest doing?

(A) Lowering the prices of some dishes
(B) Offering cooking classes during the day
(C) Providing food samples for customers
(D) Asking employees for suggestions

68. What event are the speakers discussing?

(A) A company picnic
(B) An outdoor concert
(C) An awards ceremony
(D) A retirement party

69. Look at the graphic. Which day do the speakers choose?

(A) Wednesday
(B) Thursday
(C) Friday
(D) Saturday

70. What will the woman do next?

(A) Mail some invitations to participants
(B) Contact a food preparation company
(C) Book a venue for an event
(D) Call the weather bureau for more details

PART 4

Directions: You will hear some talks given by a single speaker. You will be asked to answer three questions about what the speaker says in each talk. Select the best response to each question and mark the letter (A), (B), (C), or (D) on your answer sheet. The talks will not be printed in your test book and will be spoken only one time.

71. What is the purpose of the talk?

(A) To announce an award winner
(B) To notify listeners of a company move
(C) To introduce a new employee
(D) To publicize a sports competition

72. What does the speaker indicate about Ms. Hanson?

(A) She used to work for a competing company.
(B) She has an advanced degree in accounting.
(C) She has been a good leader of her team.
(D) She can speak two languages.

73. What does the speaker invite Ms. Hanson to do?

(A) Join a sports team
(B) Review an employment contract
(C) Demonstrate her language skills
(D) Participate in a training session

---

74. Why is the speaker calling?

(A) To make inquiries about a gathering
(B) To book a dinner reservation
(C) To confirm an appointment
(D) To inform of a change in plans

75. What information did the speaker find on a Web site?

(A) Room sizes
(B) Options for meals
(C) Opening hours
(D) Large group discounts

76. What does the speaker want to do?

(A) Negotiate with a manager
(B) Visit the venue
(C) Receive an estimate
(D) Put down a deposit

---

77. Where does the talk most likely take place?

(A) At a science museum
(B) At a manufacturing plant
(C) At a trade convention
(D) At an electronics store

78. Why does the speaker say, "it's almost a three-hour tour"?

(A) To caution the listeners
(B) To announce a delay
(C) To correct some mistakes
(D) To express satisfaction with a situation

79. What does the speaker recommend the listeners do?

(A) Buy the safety equipment
(B) Create order forms
(C) Review the brochures
(D) Keep their tickets

---

80. What is the main topic of the announcement?

(A) A security system
(B) A new club membership
(C) A maintenance job
(D) A personal credit card

81. When will the new change go into effect?

(A) On Monday
(B) On Tuesday
(C) On Friday
(D) On Sunday

82. What should the listeners do if they don't receive their pass?

(A) Contact the security office
(B) Talk to a supervisor
(C) Register for one online
(D) Complete a request form

GO ON TO THE NEXT PAGE

83. What is the speaker mainly discussing?

(A) Conference arrangements
(B) A vacation itinerary
(C) Some visiting clients
(D) A restaurant opening

84. What change does the speaker mention?

(A) The menu at a restaurant
(B) The number of guests
(C) A price of admission
(D) The time of an appointment

85. What does the speaker imply when she says, "That exhibition received negative reviews"?

(A) She disagrees with the reviews.
(B) She wants some additional information.
(C) She assumes a place will not be crowded.
(D) She thinks a plan should be changed.

---

86. What is being advertised?

(A) A cleaning tool for offices
(B) A fabric stain remover
(C) A system for cleaning bathrooms
(D) A washing machine

87. What is mentioned about the product?

(A) It is simple to use.
(B) It takes a long time to make.
(C) It is cheaper than other brands.
(D) It is not sold at other stores.

88. What is the benefit of ordering now?

(A) Receiving an additional product for free
(B) Getting a product at half price
(C) Getting a discount voucher for future use
(D) Receiving complimentary shipping

---

89. According to the speaker, what has happened in recent months?

(A) A product release has been delayed.
(B) Customer complaints have increased.
(C) Employees have reported low satisfaction.
(D) Competition from other companies has increased.

90. What does the speaker imply when he says, "this is very important to our company's success"?

(A) He wants to change the terms of a contract.
(B) He expects employees to attend a seminar.
(C) He hopes to find an alternative solution.
(D) He acknowledges the listeners' effort.

91. What should the listeners send to the speaker?

(A) Training materials
(B) An expense report
(C) A feedback form
(D) A list of client contacts

---

92. Who is the speaker?

(A) A bank manager
(B) A radio producer
(C) A financial adviser
(D) A professional salesman

93. What is the speaker mainly discussing?

(A) How to purchase discounted goods
(B) How to be prepared for retirement
(C) How to become a financial counselor
(D) How to control spending

94. What does the speaker recommend?

(A) Making a budget for spending
(B) Going shopping less often
(C) Getting rid of unnecessary credit cards
(D) Visiting a Web site for further information

Late Payment Policy	
Days Late	**Fee**
5	$4.00
10	$10.00
15	$20.00
20	$30.00

95. Where does the speaker most likely work?

(A) At a financial institution
(B) At a utility company
(C) At a library
(D) At a customer service center

96. Look at the graphic. How much is the listener's late fee?

(A) $4.00
(B) $10.00
(C) $20.00
(D) $30.00

97. What should the listener provide to sign up for the service?

(A) Some contact information
(B) An invoice number
(C) A valid identification card
(D) Some payment details

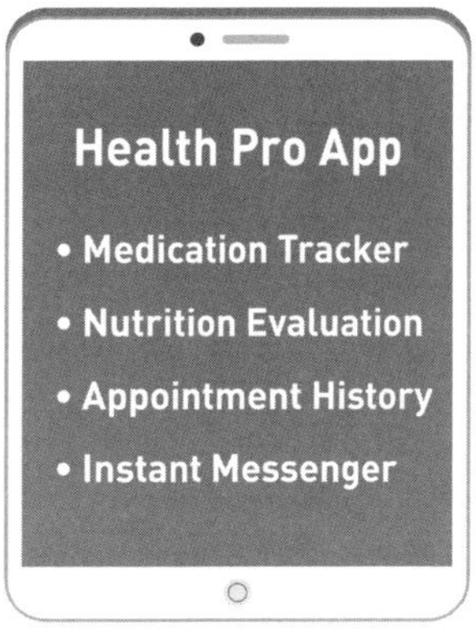

98. Where is the talk most likely taking place?

(A) At a community center
(B) At a medical clinic
(C) At a pharmacy
(D) At a fitness center

99. What are the listeners asked to do?

(A) Purchase some new software
(B) Give a product demonstration
(C) Try some new technology
(D) Read an instruction manual

100. Look at the graphic. What feature does the speaker think will be most useful?

(A) Medication Tracker
(B) Nutrition Evaluation
(C) Appointment History
(D) Instant Messenger

MP3와 해설 파일은 온라인에서 제공됩니다.

▸▸ **books.english.co.kr**

TEST 09

T9.mp3 | 정답 p.220

LISTENING TEST

In the Listening test, you will be asked to demonstrate how well you understand spoken English. The entire Listening test will last approximately 45 minutes. There are four parts, and directions are given for each part. You must mark your answers on the separate answer sheet. Do not write your answers in your test book.

PART 1

Directions: For each question in this part, you will hear four statements about a picture in your test book. When you hear the statements, you must select the one statement that best describes what you see in the picture. Then find the number of the question on your answer sheet and mark your answer. The statements will not be printed in your test book and will be spoken only one time.

Statement (B), "They're shaking hands," is the best description of the picture, so you should select answer (B) and mark it on your answer sheet.

1.

2.

GO ON TO THE NEXT PAGE

3.

4.

5.

6.

TEST 09

GO ON TO THE NEXT PAGE

PART 2

Directions: You will hear a question or statement and three responses spoken in English. They will not be printed in your test book and will be spoken only one time. Select the best response to the question or statement and mark the letter (A), (B), or (C) on your answer sheet.

7. Mark your answer on your answer sheet.

8. Mark your answer on your answer sheet.

9. Mark your answer on your answer sheet.

10. Mark your answer on your answer sheet.

11. Mark your answer on your answer sheet.

12. Mark your answer on your answer sheet.

13. Mark your answer on your answer sheet.

14. Mark your answer on your answer sheet.

15. Mark your answer on your answer sheet.

16. Mark your answer on your answer sheet.

17. Mark your answer on your answer sheet.

18. Mark your answer on your answer sheet.

19. Mark your answer on your answer sheet.

20. Mark your answer on your answer sheet.

21. Mark your answer on your answer sheet.

22. Mark your answer on your answer sheet.

23. Mark your answer on your answer sheet.

24. Mark your answer on your answer sheet.

25. Mark your answer on your answer sheet.

26. Mark your answer on your answer sheet.

27. Mark your answer on your answer sheet.

28. Mark your answer on your answer sheet.

29. Mark your answer on your answer sheet.

30. Mark your answer on your answer sheet.

31. Mark your answer on your answer sheet.

PART 3

Directions: You will hear some conversations between two or more people. You will be asked to answer three questions about what the speakers say in each conversation. Select the best response to each question and mark the letter (A), (B), (C), or (D) on your answer sheet. The conversations will not be printed in your test book and will be spoken only one time.

32. Where most likely are the speakers?
(A) At a doctor's office
(B) At a department store
(C) In a security office
(D) At a computer shop

33. What does the man ask for?
(A) A product manual
(B) A copy of some results
(C) A prescription
(D) A receipt of payment

34. Why is the woman unable to deal with the man's request immediately?
(A) Some systems are being examined.
(B) The office will close soon.
(C) The information has not come out yet.
(D) She is not good at using computers.

---

35. What is the man calling to confirm?
(A) An address
(B) A list of staff members
(C) A closing time
(D) An inventory

36. What does the woman ask about?
(A) Which items will be on sale
(B) How long a task will take
(C) How many workers will be coming
(D) What options can be selected

37. What does the woman say a security guard will do?
(A) Give a receipt
(B) Lock up a store
(C) Provide materials
(D) Issue a parking permit

---

38. What is the conversation mainly about?
(A) A flight cancelation
(B) Missing luggage
(C) Airfare
(D) Seat changes

39. What does the woman say she will do tomorrow?
(A) Move to a different city
(B) Check out a hotel
(C) Make a presentation
(D) Sign a contract

40. What does the man recommend the woman do?
(A) Check her passport
(B) Book a flight
(C) Use another form of transportation
(D) Read about a policy

---

41. What are the speakers discussing?
(A) Expanding a client base
(B) Hiring a new staff member
(C) Purchasing office supplies
(D) Preparing for a meeting

42. What has caused a problem?
(A) Some equipment is malfunctioning.
(B) Some data did not arrive.
(C) Their company is understaffed.
(D) A particular item is out of stock.

43. What does the man say he will do?
(A) Make copies at a store
(B) Reserve a meeting room
(C) Meet the maintenance staff
(D) Notify colleagues of a new deadline

GO ON TO THE NEXT PAGE

44. What does the man want to do?

(A) Stay an extra night
(B) Upgrade a room
(C) Take a city tour
(D) Receive a brochure

45. What does the man mean when he says, "That's fine, it's within my budget"?

(A) He doesn't need to cancel his reservation.
(B) He wants to try another place.
(C) He does not care about cost.
(D) He thinks the room rate is inexpensive.

46. What most likely will the man do next?

(A) Attend a workshop
(B) Review information
(C) Investigate a location
(D) Print out a document

---

47. What was printed?

(A) Sales promotions
(B) Training schedules
(C) Conference materials
(D) Invitation cards

48. What was the problem with the sample item?

(A) Some information was incorrect.
(B) Some pages were torn out.
(C) It was the wrong size.
(D) It was only printed in black.

49. What does the woman ask the man to do?

(A) Rearrange a meeting
(B) Revise a report
(C) Use a different printer
(D) Change a delivery date

---

50. What suggestion does the man make?

(A) Complying with regulations
(B) Prioritizing work assignments
(C) Making a list of goals
(D) Writing something to remember

51. What is the man planning to do?

(A) Write a book
(B) Arrange an interview
(C) Design a book
(D) Organize a meeting

52. What does the man mean when he says, "that's hard to say"?

(A) He is eager to talk about his future schedule.
(B) He doesn't understand what the woman said.
(C) He is reluctant to provide an answer.
(D) He wants to hear the question again.

---

53. What is the woman unable to do?

(A) Sign in to a computer
(B) Revise a document
(C) Print a report
(D) Find a place for a meeting

54. According to the man, what happened yesterday?

(A) A building had a power failure.
(B) A system was checked.
(C) An office was moved.
(D) A computer virus was detected.

55. What does the man offer to do?

(A) Call one of his colleagues
(B) Install some programs
(C) Restart a computer
(D) Submit a help request

---

56. What did the man do in Australia?

(A) Bought some souvenirs
(B) Attended some forums
(C) Visited some businesses
(D) Met some coworkers

57. What problem does the man mention?

(A) Some items are high-priced.
(B) A product is defective.
(C) Some clients complained about a contract.
(D) A schedule is too tight.

58. What does the woman suggest?

(A) Requesting some samples
(B) Refunding some money
(C) Placing an advertisement
(D) Renting a new office

---

59. Why is the man calling?

(A) To accept a proposal
(B) To inquire about a venue
(C) To negotiate a contract
(D) To change a schedule

60. What information does the woman request?

(A) The number of attendees
(B) The amount of money due
(C) The type of event
(D) The location of a hotel

61. What does the woman offer to do?

(A) Decorate a banquet hall
(B) Set up an alternative schedule
(C) Call the man back later
(D) Send the man a document

Item	Price
LAN Card	$50
Keyboard and Mouse	$80
Hard Drive	$100
Graphics Card	$250

62. Where does the conversation take place?

(A) At an electronics store
(B) At a computer class
(C) At a manufacturing facility
(D) At an Internet service company

63. According to the woman, what seems to be the problem?

(A) Some parts are out of stock.
(B) A system needs to be installed.
(C) An item is too old to use.
(D) A product is not working properly.

64. Look at the graphic. How much will the woman pay?

(A) $50
(B) $80
(C) $100
(D) $250

TEST 09

GO ON TO THE NEXT PAGE

Place	Time to Destination
National Museum	15 minutes
Art Gallery	30 minutes
Flea Market	45 minutes
Theme Park	60 minutes

65. Why does the man want to adjust the itinerary?

(A) A tour didn't receive favorable reviews.
(B) A place is far from the travel agency.
(C) Customers didn't like to visit a place.
(D) Some places need to be renovated.

66. Look at the graphic. Which place will be removed from the itinerary?

(A) National Museum
(B) Art Gallery
(C) Flea Market
(D) Theme Park

67. What does the woman suggest?

(A) Hiring more staff
(B) Buying additional bicycles
(C) Searching for a new manager
(D) Posting some information on the Internet

Company	Location
Forza	London
Sunrise	New York
Polypony	San Francisco
Cardine	Tokyo

68. What type of event is the company sponsoring?

(A) A race
(B) A music concert
(C) A fundraiser
(D) A fashion show

69. What is the man concerned about?

(A) Inclement weather conditions
(B) A customer complaint
(C) A limited budget
(D) A defective product

70. Look at the graphic. Which company will the speakers most likely choose?

(A) Forza
(B) Sunrise
(C) Polypony
(D) Cardine

PART 4

Directions: You will hear some talks given by a single speaker. You will be asked to answer three questions about what the speaker says in each talk. Select the best response to each question and mark the letter (A), (B), (C), or (D) on your answer sheet. The talks will not be printed in your test book and will be spoken only one time.

71. Where most likely are the listeners?

(A) On an airplane
(B) On a subway
(C) On an airport shuttle
(D) At a bus stop

72. What is the cause of the delay?

(A) A reservation has been canceled.
(B) A vehicle has broken down.
(C) There is an unexpected weather change.
(D) Some passengers have not yet arrived.

73. What does the speaker say will happen?

(A) The weather will be getting worse.
(B) The listeners will arrive as scheduled.
(C) Some refreshments will be provided.
(D) Some seats will not be available.

---

74. Why did the speaker meet with Mr. Oscar?

(A) To introduce a product
(B) To make a contract
(C) To review a sales report
(D) To discuss a design

75. What does the speaker offer Mr. Oscar?

(A) A company tour
(B) A job opportunity
(C) A free coupon
(D) A special discount

76. According to the speaker, what should Mr. Oscar do before Friday?

(A) Complete some paperwork
(B) Submit an application
(C) Make a decision
(D) Take a photograph

---

77. What event is being introduced?

(A) A restaurant reopening
(B) A cooking competition
(C) A cooking class
(D) An international food fair

78. What did Mr. Jarre recently do?

(A) Designed a menu
(B) Renovated a restaurant
(C) Published a cookbook
(D) Opened a new restaurant

79. According to the speaker, why should some listeners see Mr. Jarre after the event?

(A) To taste new dishes
(B) To obtain cooking information
(C) To register for another cooking class
(D) To buy his cookbook

---

80. What is the talk mainly about?

(A) Holding a charity event
(B) Being environmentally friendly
(C) Revising the company policies
(D) Reducing electricity use

81. Why does the speaker say, "let's start with the simplest one"?

(A) To express concerns about an event
(B) To ask for more effort to succeed
(C) To relieve the listeners from the burden of a change
(D) To invite the listeners to make a decision

82. What are the listeners asked to do?

(A) Order paper in different size
(B) Print in black and white
(C) Replace a part of the copy machine
(D) Make full use of paper

GO ON TO THE NEXT PAGE

83. What does the factory produce?

(A) Furniture
(B) Stationery
(C) Computer parts
(D) Automobiles

84. What does the speaker imply when he says, "one thousand units is a lot for us"?

(A) He needs to hire additional employees.
(B) The order is too expensive.
(C) He is delighted to receive such a big order.
(D) The order may have to be changed.

85. What does the speaker say about the factory?

(A) It will discontinue production.
(B) It is moving to a new location.
(C) It has a limited production capacity.
(D) It can manufacture different types of products.

---

86. Where does the speaker most likely work?

(A) At a university
(B) At an employment agency
(C) At an advertising agency
(D) At a newspaper

87. What change to a program does the speaker mention?

(A) Staff members will provide more feedback.
(B) The internships will be postponed.
(C) Students will receive other assignments.
(D) The company will hire more staffers to train the interns.

88. What is the purpose of the change?

(A) To provide more benefits for journalists
(B) To simplify the hiring process
(C) To decrease the program cost
(D) To store records efficiently

---

89. According to the speaker, what service will the company be offering?

(A) International shipping
(B) Customized designs
(C) Free installation
(D) Online orders

90. Why has the company decided to offer the service?

(A) Competition has been fierce.
(B) Demand has increased.
(C) Cost-cutting programs have been introduced.
(D) Customers are not satisfied with the ongoing service.

91. What does the speaker say he will do over the next few months?

(A) Develop new products
(B) Deal with customer complaints
(C) Conduct a survey
(D) Monitor company profits

---

92. What is being advertised?

(A) Sporting goods
(B) Laundry detergent
(C) Apparel
(D) Home appliances

93. What does the speaker mean when she says, "then look no further"?

(A) A product is on sale.
(B) Customers will like the product.
(C) Some merchandise has poor quality.
(D) There is no option to consider.

94. Why does the speaker suggest that listeners visit a Web site?

(A) To check some information
(B) To post a product review
(C) To request a free sample
(D) To make an online purchase

Sessions	Time
How to Be a Leader	1:00 – 2:00 P.M.
Creative Thinking	2:00 – 3:00 P.M.
Communication Skills	4:00 – 5:00 P.M.
Efficient Work Environments	5:00 – 6:00 P.M.

95. What is the purpose of the announcement?

(A) To introduce a new staff member
(B) To select the most popular lecturer
(C) To inform listeners of a change in a schedule
(D) To review the agenda for a meeting

96. What are some listeners asked to do?

(A) Pick up some materials
(B) Remain seated
(C) Turn off their phones
(D) Submit their reports

97. Look at the graphic. What time will Dr. Diane be speaking?

(A) 1:00 P.M.
(B) 2:00 P.M.
(C) 4:00 P.M.
(D) 5:00 P.M.

HS Grocery Promotional Sales	
Fruits	15% off
Meat & Fish	20% off
Dairy Products	30% off
Bread	40% off

98. Why is the store having a sale?

(A) To help revive the local economy
(B) To introduce some new items
(C) To celebrate an anniversary
(D) To raise additional funds

99. Where is a full list of discounts available?

(A) By the doorway
(B) On the Web site
(C) Near the bakery
(D) On a flyer

100. Look at the graphic. What is the discount rate on today's special item?

(A) 15%
(B) 20%
(C) 30%
(D) 40%

MP3와 해설 파일은 온라인에서 제공됩니다.

▸▸ **books.english.co.kr**

TEST
10

T10.mp3 | 정답 p.227

LISTENING TEST

In the Listening test, you will be asked to demonstrate how well you understand spoken English. The entire Listening test will last approximately 45 minutes. There are four parts, and directions are given for each part. You must mark your answers on the separate answer sheet.
Do not write your answers in your test book.

PART 1

Directions: For each question in this part, you will hear four statements about a picture in your test book. When you hear the statements, you must select the one statement that best describes what you see in the picture. Then find the number of the question on your answer sheet and mark your answer. The statements will not be printed in your test book and will be spoken only one time.

Statement (B), "They're shaking hands," is the best description of the picture, so you should select answer (B) and mark it on your answer sheet.

1.

2.

TEST 10

3.

4.

5.

6.

TEST 10

PART 2

Directions: You will hear a question or statement and three responses spoken in English. They will not be printed in your test book and will be spoken only one time. Select the best response to the question or statement and mark the letter (A), (B), or (C) on your answer sheet.

7. Mark your answer on your answer sheet.

8. Mark your answer on your answer sheet.

9. Mark your answer on your answer sheet.

10. Mark your answer on your answer sheet.

11. Mark your answer on your answer sheet.

12. Mark your answer on your answer sheet.

13. Mark your answer on your answer sheet.

14. Mark your answer on your answer sheet.

15. Mark your answer on your answer sheet.

16. Mark your answer on your answer sheet.

17. Mark your answer on your answer sheet.

18. Mark your answer on your answer sheet.

19. Mark your answer on your answer sheet.

20. Mark your answer on your answer sheet.

21. Mark your answer on your answer sheet.

22. Mark your answer on your answer sheet.

23. Mark your answer on your answer sheet.

24. Mark your answer on your answer sheet.

25. Mark your answer on your answer sheet.

26. Mark your answer on your answer sheet.

27. Mark your answer on your answer sheet.

28. Mark your answer on your answer sheet.

29. Mark your answer on your answer sheet.

30. Mark your answer on your answer sheet.

31. Mark your answer on your answer sheet.

PART 3

Directions: You will hear some conversations between two or more people. You will be asked to answer three questions about what the speakers say in each conversation. Select the best response to each question and mark the letter (A), (B), (C), or (D) on your answer sheet. The conversations will not be printed in your test book and will be spoken only one time.

32. What does the woman invite the man to do?

(A) Go on a tour
(B) Give a talk
(C) Conduct some research
(D) Register for a class

33. What information does the woman provide?

(A) The length of a document
(B) Directions to a location
(C) The number of participants
(D) The date of an event

34. What does the woman ask for permission to do?

(A) Invite city officials
(B) Select a conference site
(C) Change a travel itinerary
(D) Put some materials online

---

35. What is the man asking about?

(A) The rules of a game
(B) The length of a wait
(C) The cost of a ticket
(D) The time of a show

36. What does the woman tell the man?

(A) The game costs ten dollars to play.
(B) The line will be shorter later in the day.
(C) The park closes at five in the evening.
(D) The show is sold out for the day.

37. What will the man probably do next?

(A) Play some games
(B) Wait in line
(C) Eat some lunch
(D) Attend a show

---

38. According to the man, why is the accounting firm moving to a new office?

(A) The rent is high.
(B) The current location is far from downtown.
(C) The space is small.
(D) The transportation is inconvenient.

39. What does the man want to add to his office?

(A) A breakroom
(B) A fitness center
(C) A storage area
(D) Extra parking spaces

40. What will most likely happen at the end of August?

(A) A lease will expire.
(B) An inspection will take place.
(C) A conference will be held.
(D) Some executives will visit the premises.

---

41. What is the purpose of the woman's call?

(A) To ask about a bill
(B) To order some groceries
(C) To make a reservation
(D) To invite the man to an event

42. According to the man, what is the problem?

(A) No seats are available.
(B) A restaurant went out of business.
(C) There are no vegetarian options.
(D) A place does not take reservations.

43. What does the man suggest?

(A) Trying another option
(B) Going to a waiting area
(C) Visiting another location
(D) Coming back another day

---

44. According to the woman, what is Gina most likely doing?
(A) Recruiting internship candidates
(B) Meeting with potential clients
(C) Enjoying her vacation
(D) Attending a press conference

45. What does the man want Gina to do?
(A) Interview some people
(B) Lead a training session
(C) Make travel arrangements
(D) Postpone a business trip

46. What does the woman mean when she says, "Phillip has some experience with that kind of work"?
(A) The speakers should hire Phillip for a position.
(B) Gina and Phillip used to work in the same department.
(C) Phillip organized an internship program last year.
(D) Phillip should be able to assist the man.

---

47. What does the man need help with?
(A) Installing a new computer program
(B) Downloading anti-virus software
(C) Transferring photos to a computer
(D) Dialing into a conference call

48. Why is the woman unable to help the man right now?
(A) She has to participate in a meeting.
(B) She has to show a client a property.
(C) She has to visit a print shop.
(D) She has too many e-mails to send.

49. What will the man probably do next?
(A) Contact another colleague
(B) Look for help online
(C) Wait until tomorrow
(D) Visit a store

---

50. What does the man ask Jennifer to do?
(A) Sign up for a university class
(B) Visit a client out of town
(C) Work at a business function
(D) Interview a job candidate

51. What is the man supposed to do on Friday?
(A) Go on a business trip
(B) Visit a university
(C) Finish a report
(D) Meet with some clients

52. What does the man offer to do for Diana?
(A) Rearrange some schedules
(B) Organize an event
(C) Work overtime
(D) Volunteer for a project

---

53. Why is the woman calling?
(A) To ask for driving directions
(B) To get relocation assistance
(C) To request help planning a trip
(D) To change an itinerary

54. What does the man suggest the woman do?
(A) Book a trip online
(B) Cancel a trip
(C) Speak to another agent
(D) Call back another time

55. What does the woman say is important to her?
(A) Not going over her budget
(B) Arriving on time for an appointment
(C) Finding a comfortable hotel
(D) Minimizing travel time

---

56. What kind of service does the woman's company provide?

(A) Construction and remodeling
(B) Financial counseling
(C) Residential property management
(D) International shipping

57. Why does the man say, "Europe is pretty far away"?

(A) To express concern
(B) To show excitement
(C) To turn down an offer
(D) To get a price estimate

58. What will the speakers most likely discuss next?

(A) A delivery location
(B) A rental price
(C) Detailed measurements
(D) Personnel requirements

---

59. Why did Mr. Wiley call?

(A) To order some materials
(B) To schedule a meeting
(C) To cancel an appointment
(D) To check on the status of a work

60. What does the man say he is doing right now?

(A) Reconfirming some information
(B) Making a telephone call
(C) Leaving for the day
(D) Revising some plans

61. What does the woman suggest the man do?

(A) Finish a project
(B) Deliver some drawings
(C) E-mail Mr. Wiley
(D) Call a supplier

TOUR (1 HOUR LONG)	TICKET AVAILABILITY
10:00 A.M.	2 tickets
11:30 A.M.	SOLD OUT
1:00 P.M.	6 tickets
2:30 P.M.	5 tickets

62. What do the speakers plan to tour?

(A) A historic site
(B) A government building
(C) A cooking school
(D) An ancient palace

63. What does the man remind the woman about?

(A) Attending a presentation
(B) Eating lunch with colleagues
(C) Coming back for a reception
(D) Bringing photo identification

64. Look at the graphic. When will the speakers go on a tour?

(A) 10:00 A.M.
(B) 11:30 A.M.
(C) 1:00 P.M.
(D) 2:30 P.M.

TEST 10

www.getimage.com
Categories

1	Food & Dining	▼
2	Sports & Hobbies	▼
3	Travel & Destinations	▼
4	Companies & Workplaces	▼

65. What project is the man working on?
(A) Designing a brochure
(B) Organizing a sports competition
(C) Revising a portfolio
(D) Planning an itinerary

66. Look at the graphic. Which category will the man most likely search?
(A) Category 1
(B) Category 2
(C) Category 3
(D) Category 4

67. Why does the woman recommend using getimage.com?
(A) Photographs are available for free.
(B) Photographs come in various sizes.
(C) It was recommended by professionals.
(D) It offers a large selection of photographs.

Hollywood Bedframe Parts List

Item	Quantity
Corner plates	4
Mending plates	12
T plates	8
Universal plates	5

68. What does the woman say she is trying to do?
(A) Repair an appliance
(B) Return a defective item
(C) Get a discount from a store
(D) Assemble some furniture

69. Look at the graphic. What is the woman missing?
(A) Corner plates
(B) Mending plates
(C) T plates
(D) Universal plates

70. What is the woman asked to bring with her?
(A) The original package
(B) An instruction manual
(C) A store receipt
(D) A product warranty

PART 4

Directions: You will hear some talks given by a single speaker. You will be asked to answer three questions about what the speaker says in each talk. Select the best response to each question and mark the letter (A), (B), (C), or (D) on your answer sheet. The talks will not be printed in your test book and will be spoken only one time.

71. According to the report, what is unusual about the weather this week?

(A) The high temperatures
(B) The low temperatures
(C) The heavy rain
(D) The strong winds

72. What has the government issued due to the weather conditions?

(A) A cold wave watch
(B) Water restrictions
(C) A state of emergency
(D) Food rations

73. When will the weather be better for outdoor activities?

(A) On Wednesday
(B) On Thursday
(C) On Friday
(D) On Saturday

---

74. What is the speaker doing?

(A) Explaining a registration process
(B) Apologizing for a delay
(C) Giving an overview of a tour
(D) Complimenting the product quality

75. Who is Paul Lehman?

(A) An actor
(B) A tour guide
(C) An art collector
(D) An architect

76. What will the listeners most likely do next?

(A) Meet Ms. Bickerstaff
(B) Proceed to a living room
(C) Stop by a gift shop
(D) Gather around an entrance

---

77. What does the store sell?

(A) Clothing
(B) Electronics
(C) Food
(D) Books

78. Why does the speaker say, "The store will be closing in approximately 30 minutes"?

(A) The store should start checking inventory.
(B) The special discount will last for half an hour.
(C) Customers need to pay for their purchases soon.
(D) Customers should return products they do not want.

79. Where has a clearance display been placed?

(A) Next to the manager's office
(B) In a rear corner
(C) On the second floor
(D) Near the main entrance

---

80. What does the speaker say will happen tomorrow?

(A) An office will be closed.
(B) A corporate executive will visit.
(C) A sales meeting will be held.
(D) A company will file for bankruptcy.

81. What does the report say?

(A) Sales have increased.
(B) Costs have decreased.
(C) Profits are less than expected.
(D) A company has met its goals.

82. What does the speaker request?

(A) Details about convention participants
(B) A completed report for the board
(C) Suggestions for reducing costs
(D) A revised marketing strategy

GO ON TO THE NEXT PAGE

83. What type of business is the speaker calling from?

(A) An insurance firm
(B) A fitness club
(C) A telecom company
(D) A financial institution

84. Why is the speaker calling?

(A) To verify some information
(B) To discuss the benefits offered
(C) To quote the mortgage interest rates
(D) To schedule an appointment

85. According to the speaker, why should Ms. Stotesbury call back right away?

(A) An offer will expire soon.
(B) A position is still available.
(C) An application deadline has passed.
(D) An account has been closed.

---

86. Why has the speaker arranged the meeting?

(A) To introduce a new sales manager
(B) To discuss an interview format
(C) To provide feedback on a project
(D) To prepare for a sales meeting

87. What are the listeners asked to do?

(A) Ask assigned questions
(B) Complete a sales report
(C) Create portfolios for an interview
(D) Apply for a position

88. What does the speaker mean when he says, "We'll meet at 4 o'clock today"?

(A) He has to take care of some urgent businesses now.
(B) The majority of the people are available then.
(C) They need to conduct additional interviews.
(D) A final decision will be delayed until later.

---

89. What is the purpose of the talk?

(A) To go over sales performance
(B) To describe a factory layout
(C) To explain a workshop schedule
(D) To announce the winner of a competition

90. Who most likely is the speaker?

(A) A plant supervisor
(B) A repair technician
(C) A financial consultant
(D) A professional instructor

91. What does the speaker imply when she says, "there are some vending machines at the end of the hallway"?

(A) The listeners should fix them before lunch.
(B) The listeners should meet there.
(C) The listeners should buy food from them.
(D) The listeners need to move them to another location.

---

92. What is the main purpose of the talk?

(A) To announce the opening of a factory
(B) To introduce a new employee
(C) To explain a new procedure
(D) To discuss details of a production process

93. What does the speaker mention about Ms. Choi?

(A) She studied manufacturing processes in college.
(B) She has worked for the company for three years.
(C) She can speak several foreign languages.
(D) She has experience doing a similar job.

94. What is the company trying to do now?

(A) Launch a new product line
(B) Relocate their headquarters to China
(C) Translate a manual into other languages
(D) Redesign some facilities overseas

ELEVATOR DIRECTORY ▶

Floors 2–4	E
Floors 5–10	F
Floors 11–17	G
Floors 18–25	H

95. What will most likely be discussed at the meeting tomorrow?

(A) An open position
(B) A home renovation
(C) A business acquisition
(D) A landscaping project

96. What should the listener do at the security desk?

(A) Pick up a visitor pass
(B) Get a parking permit
(C) Contact the person in charge
(D) Ask for a floor map

97. Look at the graphic. On which floor is the speaker's office located?

(A) 2nd floor
(B) 5th floor
(C) 11th floor
(D) 18th floor

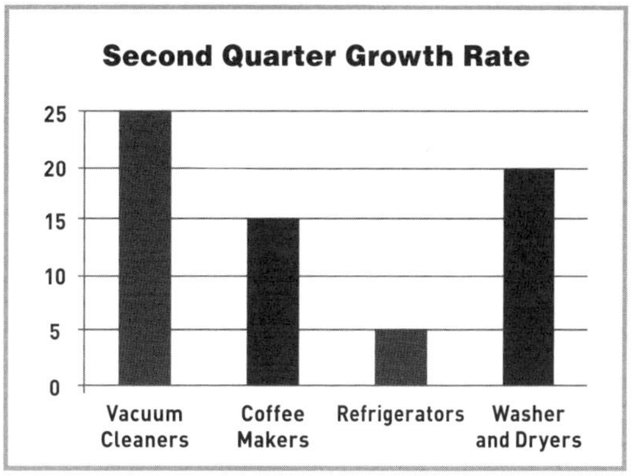

98. Who most likely are the listeners?

(A) Stockholders
(B) Product designers
(C) Sales associates
(D) Accounting clerks

99. Look at the graphic. Which category is the speaker concerned about?

(A) Vacuum Cleaners
(B) Coffee Makers
(C) Refrigerators
(D) Washers and Dryers

100. What has the company decided to do?

(A) Research competitors
(B) Reduce prices
(C) Hire a consultant
(D) Launch a new advertising campaign

▸ 상세 해설 파일은 온라인에서 제공됩니다. ▸▸ books.english.co.kr

정답 및 스크립트

TEST 01

| p.14

1	(C)	2	(C)	3	(A)	4	(C)	5	(A)
6	(B)	7	(C)	8	(B)	9	(B)	10	(A)
11	(B)	12	(C)	13	(B)	14	(C)	15	(B)
16	(C)	17	(C)	18	(C)	19	(C)	20	(B)
21	(C)	22	(A)	23	(A)	24	(B)	25	(B)
26	(C)	27	(C)	28	(C)	29	(B)	30	(A)
31	(B)	32	(C)	33	(A)	34	(A)	35	(D)
36	(C)	37	(A)	38	(C)	39	(A)	40	(D)
41	(D)	42	(A)	43	(C)	44	(D)	45	(B)
46	(B)	47	(C)	48	(A)	49	(D)	50	(C)
51	(B)	52	(D)	53	(D)	54	(B)	55	(D)
56	(C)	57	(C)	58	(D)	59	(D)	60	(A)
61	(C)	62	(B)	63	(B)	64	(D)	65	(B)
66	(C)	67	(D)	68	(C)	69	(D)	70	(B)
71	(B)	72	(C)	73	(D)	74	(A)	75	(C)
76	(C)	77	(A)	78	(D)	79	(D)	80	(D)
81	(B)	82	(A)	83	(B)	84	(B)	85	(D)
86	(D)	87	(C)	88	(A)	89	(A)	90	(C)
91	(D)	92	(B)	93	(C)	94	(B)	95	(B)
96	(B)	97	(D)	98	(D)	99	(B)	100	(C)

Part 1

1 (A) The woman is watering the plant.
(B) The woman is putting on a suit.
(C) The woman is talking into a microphone.
(D) The woman is rehearsing on the stage.

2 (A) They are boarding the plane.
(B) They are getting off the bus.
(C) They are standing near a bus.
(D) They are packing their bags.

3 (A) A vehicle is at the intersection.
(B) They are building houses along the road.
(C) A car is waiting to enter the garage.
(D) Pedestrians are crossing the street.

4 (A) A stone archway is being restored.
(B) They are strolling through the doorway.
(C) Shadows are being cast across the walkway.
(D) They are building the brick wall.

5 (A) Most of the seats are occupied.
(B) A sign is being hung on the wall.
(C) All of the people are facing the front.
(D) Most of the people are standing near the table.

6 (A) The worker is fixing the roof of the house.
(B) Some lines are painted on the ground.
(C) The man is pushing the door open.
(D) The man is polishing the glasses.

Part 2

7 How do you get to work every day?
(A) By express mail.
(B) No, I didn't send it.
(C) I walk there.

8 What's the name of the recently released product?
(A) It will be launched next month.
(B) You should check our Web site for it.
(C) I don't think that's new.

9 When will the car repairs be finished?
(A) She will be driving your car.
(B) As soon as the necessary parts arrive.
(C) It needs some new tires.

10 Have you sent out the shipment yet?
(A) No, I have to pack everything first.
(B) No, I'm not traveling by boat.
(C) Sure, I can give you one if you want.

11 Who should I contact if I have any problems?
(A) The contract was signed yesterday.
(B) That would be me.
(C) No, she doesn't have any problems.

12 Why are you packing those documents?
(A) To the conference center.
(B) Everything is all set for the meeting.
(C) So I can look over them on the plane.

13 Don't you need more office supplies?
(A) Everything in the store is on sale.
(B) Yes, I put in a request already.
(C) Yes, we have to know what customers want.

14 Could you please call room service?
(A) The room is not tidy enough.
(B) The receptionist will answer the phone.
(C) Sure, what do you want?

15 We'll accept a passport or a valid driver's license for identification.
(A) Yes, I am.
(B) I don't have either.
(C) Can you order one for me?

16 When is your birthday?
(A) What would you like as a present?
(B) I'll order some cake for you, too.
(C) Actually, it was a couple of months ago.

17 Would you like a soup or a salad with your meal?
(A) Yes, I tried everything, but it didn't work.
(B) We need to buy some more vegetables.
(C) What kind of soup do you have?

18 Couldn't we change our meeting to tomorrow?
(A) They have already met.
(B) No, the policies need to be changed.
(C) I'm afraid I'll be out of town then.

19 Would you like to ride with us or take the subway?
(A) After the training is over.
(B) He will try to find us at the station.
(C) The subway should be better at this time of the day.

20 Why don't we invite Sally, too?
(A) The invitation was delayed.
(B) She would like that very much.
(C) Yes, the lecture was canceled.

21 Will the final interview be conducted next month?
(A) I'm looking for a new employee.
(B) The conductor will lead the orchestra.
(C) That's what they say.

22 Why are those signs painted yellow?
(A) To make them more visible.
(B) The sign says to turn right.
(C) The painter was hired to do the job.

23 Where are Baxtor automobiles manufactured?
(A) Primarily in Sweden.
(B) Around 45,000 euros.
(C) A very reliable car.

24 How much are the painting classes at the community center?
(A) About five kilometers away.
(B) Ninety dollars for ten classes.
(C) From 9 A.M. to 7 P.M.

25 That art museum is open late tonight, isn't it?
(A) Several new exhibitions.
(B) No, only on Saturdays and Sundays.
(C) I don't think the admission is free.

26 Did you ask Sarah if you could borrow the projector?
(A) This month's projection seems low.
(B) No, you cannot take that much.
(C) Yes, I asked her last Monday.

27 Which application should I fill out to apply for a job as a member of the sales staff?
(A) The employment contract is for six months.
(B) In the first-floor display area.
(C) The one that's in the green box.

28 Should we lock these files up?
(A) He's from far away.
(B) I'd like an aisle seat, please.
(C) Yes, please. They are confidential.

29 The computer works fine, doesn't it?
(A) I'm fine, too.
(B) It should be now.
(C) About two hundred people commute.

30 We'll be able to open a new store next month.
(A) We need some extra help to do that.
(B) Please close it when you leave.
(C) I'll see you in two weeks.

31 Is this e-mail message okay, or should I revise it?
(A) Fifty unread messages.
(B) I think it should be shorter.
(C) In a recently published magazine.

Part 3

Questions 32-34 refer to the following conversation.

W Hi. This is Melinda Hines from TSN Studios. I'm calling to check on our order for two office chairs.

M Oh, hi, Ms. Hines. Thank you for calling. Yes, we processed your order and shipped them out last Friday.

W Oh, great. So when can I expect to receive them? I need those chairs as soon as possible.

M It usually takes three to four business days to arrive, but I can find out the exact date for you. I'll check the computer system right away.

32 What does the woman ask about?
(A) Payment options
(B) The price of a product
(C) The status of an order
(D) A shipping address

33 What products are the speakers discussing?
(A) Office furniture
(B) Telephones
(C) Cameras
(D) Computers

34 What does the man offer to do?
(A) Check a delivery date
(B) Reduce a price
(C) Expedite a shipment
(D) Cancel an order

Questions 35-37 refer to the following conversation.

M Hello. I would like to apply for a business loan. Who do I need to speak with?

W You need to meet with Mike Jenkins, the commercial loan officer, but he is with another client right now. He should be finished in the next thirty minutes. You can have a seat in the lobby, and I'll let him know you are here.

M Actually, I've got some other errands to run right now. Will he be available this afternoon?

W Yes, this is his last scheduled appointment today. I will let him know that you came by and expect you later this afternoon.

35 What does the man want to do?
(A) Transfer some money
(B) Open a bank account
(C) Deposit some money
(D) Apply for a loan

36 What problem does the man have?
(A) Mr. Jenkins is at lunch.
(B) The bank is closing in 30 minutes.
(C) Mr. Jenkins is busy at the moment.
(D) There is a long line of people.

37 What does the woman suggest the man do?
(A) Sit in a waiting area
(B) Make an appointment
(C) Try another location
(D) Fill out a form

Questions 38-40 refer to the following conversation.

W I need to update the sales figure on our monthly progress report. But my Internet is running unusually slow today. Are you experiencing the same problem?

M Yes, it's been rather slow all morning. I already called the Technical Support Department, and they are sending a technician over this afternoon.

W Oh, well, but I need to do some research online right now.

M Hmm... then I'm going to go upstairs to the Accounting Department to see if they have the same issue with the Internet first.

38 What does the woman want to do?
(A) Arrange a meeting
(B) Set a sales goal
(C) Revise a report
(D) Upgrade a software

39 What does the woman imply when she says, "I need to do some research online right now"?
(A) She does not want to wait until the technician arrives.
(B) She thinks the man can solve the problem.
(C) She is concerned she will not meet the deadline.
(D) She wants to hire someone with lots of experience.

40 What does the man say he will do?
(A) Call the IT Department
(B) Shop for a new computer
(C) Send an e-mail
(D) Go to another floor

Questions 41-43 refer to the following conversation.

W Hello. I'm calling from the Customer Service Department at Helvesco Shoes. You recently purchased a pair of boots from us, and I want to know if you're satisfied with your purchase.

M Oh, yes. I'm very pleased with your service. I was especially impressed that I could order a pair of shoes and receive them the very next day.

W That's great. We appreciate the positive feedback. Would you mind if we share your comments on our Web site?

M I would not mind as long as it doesn't take much of my time.

W It's very simple, and you won't have to do anything. And we'll give you bonus points that can be used for your next purchase once your comment is uploaded on our site.

41 Why is the woman calling?
(A) To offer a refund
(B) To verify an address
(C) To promote a new product
(D) To collect feedback

42 What does the man say about the service?
(A) The delivery was fast.
(B) Returning merchandise was easy.
(C) The service agents were helpful.
(D) The fees are reasonable.

43 What does the woman want to do?
(A) Postpone a shipping date
(B) Substitute an item
(C) Post some comments
(D) Confirm an order quantity

Questions 44-46 refer to the following conversation.

M Michelle, can I catch a ride with you to the product show in Atlanta on Tuesday?

W Actually, I'm not going to drive this time. I'm planning to take the bus. Why don't you go with me? In that way, we'll have a chance to practice our product demonstration before the show.

M Oh, okay. That's not a bad idea. But I just assumed you were driving since you usually do. Why aren't you driving this time?

W My car is in the shop. I'm having problems with the transmission.

M Do you think your car will be fixed by next week? Maybe we could wait for a while before making a bus reservation.

44 What does the man request?
(A) A ticket to Atlanta
(B) A sample of a product
(C) A bus schedule
(D) A ride to an event

45 What will the speakers probably do on Tuesday?
(A) Leave work early
(B) Give a demonstration
(C) Participate in a conference call
(D) Pick up a car from a shop

46 Why does the woman say she will take the bus?
(A) It is less expensive.
(B) Her car is being repaired.
(C) It will save her time.
(D) She cannot find anyone to ride a car with.

Questions 47-49 refer to the following conversation with three speakers.

M Heather, I'm trying to locate the file with the new client questionnaires, but it's not in the file cabinet. I'm scheduled to meet with my new client, Hampton Industries, this afternoon, and I would like to review it before the meeting.

W1 Tonya met a new client this morning, and I bet she has it. Tonya, have you seen the file for new clients?

W2 Well, I'm updating some of the contents. All of the questionnaires are submitted electronically, so we should have all copies on the company server.

M Could one of you print a copy of the questionnaire and bring it to my office?

W1 I'll take care of it as soon as I'm done with this report.

M I really appreciate that.

47 What is the man looking for?
(A) A customer list
(B) A timetable
(C) A questionnaire
(D) A menu

48 Who will the man meet this afternoon?
(A) A client
(B) An employee
(C) A job candidate
(D) A manager

49 What does the man ask the women to do?
(A) Review a file
(B) E-mail a document
(C) Conduct a survey
(D) Print a document

Questions 50-52 refer to the following conversation.

W Hi, Mark. Are you going to the baseball game sponsored by our company this Sunday?

M I rearranged my schedule so that I could go, but it's supposed to be rather cool this weekend. I'm just getting over a cold, so I might not go.

W Don't worry about the weather. The company purchased tickets in a suite, so we'll be very comfortable. They even arranged for us to have free food and drinks during the game. It should be a great time, so you shouldn't miss it.

50 What are the speakers discussing?
(A) A baseball team
(B) A nearby restaurant
(C) A company-sponsored event
(D) An awards ceremony

51 Why is the man considering not attending the event?
(A) He has somewhere else to be.
(B) He is concerned about the weather.
(C) He doesn't like baseball.
(D) He thinks the tickets are too expensive.

52 According to the woman, what will the company provide?
(A) Transportation to an event
(B) Paid vacation time
(C) A hotel room
(D) Complimentary refreshments

Questions 53-55 refer to the following conversation.

M Hi. I would like to get a credit card from Colonial Bank. How can I apply for one?

W Actually, all credit card applications at the bank must be completed online. You can visit our Web site at www.colonialbank.com to submit an application.

M Great. How long does it usually take to get approval?

W You can expect to receive a decision about ten to fifteen business days after you make your submission. If you have any other questions, you can either call again or check the FAQ section on our Web site.

53 What are the speakers talking about?
(A) Registering for an online course
(B) Paying with a credit card
(C) Arranging for an appointment
(D) Getting a new card

54 What does the woman give the man?
(A) An application form
(B) A Web site address
(C) A credit card number
(D) A deposit slip

55 Why does the man say, "How long does it usually take to get approval"?
(A) He is eager to get a loan as soon as possible.
(B) He wants to talk to a service agent in person.
(C) He is ready to apply for another position.
(D) He wants to get details about a process.

Questions 56-58 refer to the following conversation.

M Hi, Iris. What are you still doing here? I thought you were working only a half day today so that you could leave for your vacation.

W That was my plan, but the weather report is calling for rain this weekend. It's supposed to be nicer next weekend.

M So will you go next week instead?

W Yeah, I think I'll stay in town this week and head for the beach next Friday. I'd rather go when the weather is better.

M Well, if that schedule works for you, I'm happy for you. But you know the deadline for the marketing proposal has been moved to next week.

W I know, so I might have to work overtime during the week to meet the deadline. Actually, I'm going to call the overseas offices now to get some data for my report.

56 What is the conversation mainly about?
(A) Working over the weekend
(B) An overdue report
(C) A change in plans
(D) A marketing plan

57 What is the woman concerned about?
(A) The ticket price
(B) The missing data
(C) The inclement weather
(D) The lack of budget

58 What will the woman do next?
(A) Visit a marketing office
(B) Ask for a deadline extension
(C) Call a travel agency
(D) Contact other departments

Questions 59-61 refer to the following conversation.

M How many people have registered for the international finance class this semester?

W So far, twenty-six students have registered. That's a bit more than I expected. The classroom can only hold thirty students, and enrollment is open for another week. The class is only offered in the spring, and I don't want some students to be turned away.

M You should check with the department head to see if he'd be willing to let you use another room and increase the class size. He's fairly flexible on matters like that.

W I think you're right. Do you happen to know what his office hours are? I'd like to stop by and speak with him in person. We can put up a new sign to attract more students once the class size is adjusted.

59 Where most likely are the speakers?
(A) At a community center
(B) At a public library
(C) At a real estate agency
(D) At a university

60 What does the man suggest the woman do?
(A) Meet with a superior
(B) Cancel a class
(C) Teach an additional class
(D) Close enrollment

61 What does the woman ask for?
(A) A phone number
(B) Textbooks
(C) Business hours
(D) A list of students

Questions 62-64 refer to the following conversation and schedule.

M How is the construction on our new distribution center in Spring Hills going?

W I'm afraid the project is a bit behind schedule. We were able to get approval on the design on March first as scheduled. But the next phase of construction took longer than we had planned.

M Do you think we can meet the deadline on April first? If we don't, that might create another problem. Without the distribution center ready in time, we might not have space for the merchandise we're currently carrying.

W When does the lease on the old warehouse expire? We may need to extend it for another month just in case.

M I believe it expires at the end of the month. Could you call the property manager to ask if we can get an extension?

W Good idea. It's better to be safe than sorry.

62 What are the speakers talking about?
(A) Budget approval
(B) A construction project
(C) The purchase of property
(D) The distribution of merchandise

63 Look at the graphic. Which job took longer than expected?
(A) Design (B) Wiring
(C) Flooring (D) Roofing

64 What does the man ask the woman to do?
(A) Postpone a project deadline
(B) Cancel a product shipment
(C) Revise a construction design
(D) Request a lease extension

Questions 65-67 refer to the following conversation and map.

W Excuse me. Could you help me with this map? This station is a little confusing.

M Sure, we're at Grand Central Station right here. Where do you want to go?

W I'm trying to get to the airport, but I'm not sure which line I should take. I'd normally take Line A, but it's closed for repairs right now.

M I'd take this route. It's not an express route though. You'll have to stop at Downtown Crossing, but it's relatively fast.

W Thank you for your help. I really appreciate it.

M In fact, I'm on my way to that platform myself. So I can walk you there if you want.

W Actually, I need to grab a quick bite to eat at a nearby restaurant, but thanks for the offer.

65 Where does the conversation take place?
(A) At an airport
(B) At a subway station
(C) At a sales seminar
(D) At a restaurant

66 Look at the graphic. Which line does the man suggest the woman take?
(A) Line A (B) Line B
(C) Line C (D) Line D

67 What does the man offer to do?
(A) Draw a subway map
(B) Find out a train schedule
(C) Buy the woman some food
(D) Accompany the woman to a platform

Questions 68-70 refer to the following conversation and table.

W Hello. I'm opening an online shop to sell cosmetics I make by using organic ingredients, and I'm interested in your shipping service. Can you tell me about your rates?

M Sure. Our regular shipment rate is based on weight. Once you find out the weight of your product, you can use the calculator on our Web site to determine the cost. We also offer extra services at additional rates. Here is a list of the special services we offer and their prices.

W Hmm... I only sell my cosmetics to domestic customers, so regular delivery is fine. But some of the bottles holding cosmetics are made of glass, and I'm worried they might break during delivery.

M Then we can ship them as fragile items. We put extra filling in the packages and handle them with special care.

68 What does the woman want to sell?
(A) Bottled water
(B) Organic food
(C) Cosmetics
(D) Domestic produce

69 According to the man, what can be done on a Web site?
(A) Ordering products at discounted prices
(B) Purchasing shipping materials
(C) Tracking the locations of delivery trucks
(D) Determining the cost of mailing a package

70 Look at the graphic. Which special fee will the woman most likely pay?
(A) $10 (B) $15
(C) $17 (D) $20

Part 4

Questions 71-73 refer to the following talk.

Welcome, everyone, and congratulations on joining the great team here at Tri-Star Corporation. My name is Josh Malcom, and I'll be training you on how to use the company's IT network and server. I heard that some of you have been issued user IDs and passwords and already logged into the company server. If you haven't yet done so, let's do it together. Please enter your user ID on the start page on your computer, and the system will prompt you to create a password. If you have any problems, let me know, and I will assist you. Please also remember to review the company's network and Internet policies and regulations. It is included in the Human Resources packet you received this morning. In about twenty minutes, Laurie Mason will be here to explain the employee benefits of our company. She'll review the health insurance options and the 401k plan.

71 What department does the speaker probably work for?
(A) Human Resources
(B) Information Technology
(C) Accounting
(D) Security

72 What are the listeners instructed to do?
(A) Submit a résumé
(B) Present identification
(C) Log into a network
(D) Fill out some forms

73 What will mostly likely happen in 20 minutes?
(A) User IDs will be issued.
(B) A tour of the office will be provided.
(C) Managers will be introduced.
(D) Company benefits will be explained.

Questions 74-76 refer to the following announcement.

May I have your attention, please? We've now arrived at our port destination of the day, Cayman Island, which is one of the most beautiful islands in the Caribbean. The island is a popular tourist destination, where you may enjoy great shopping, play water sports, or simply lounge on the stunning beaches. Be sure to take all personal belongings that you need today as the boat will be inaccessible until 5 P.M. You have about six hours starting now to enjoy this gorgeous island. Be sure to return to the dock by 5 P.M. as we'll be leaving promptly at 5:30 P.M.

74 Who most likely is the speaker?
(A) A travel guide
(B) A store manager
(C) A hotel employee
(D) A bus driver

75 What does the speaker imply when she says, "Be sure to take all personal belongings"?
(A) She will discuss a new topic now.
(B) She thinks more items will be needed.
(C) She wants to prevent possible mishaps.
(D) She wants to encourage the listeners to shop more.

76 Where are the listeners asked to return?
(A) To an office
(B) To a hotel
(C) To a dock
(D) To a tour bus

Questions 77-79 refer to the following telephone message.

Hello, Ms. Wade. This is Jeff Coates from Ferguson Custom Cabinets. We've run into a delay with the cabinets you ordered for your kitchen. We were scheduled to receive the products on Tuesday, but the factory hasn't finished making them yet. I spoke with the factory manager, and he assured me that production will be complete by the end of the week. This means the soonest we can install them is next Monday. Could you please call me back and let me know if Monday will work for you? If not, we'll be happy to reschedule a time that is convenient for you. Thank you.

77 Where does the speaker most likely work?
(A) At a furniture company
(B) At a delivery service
(C) At a restaurant
(D) At a clothing factory

78 What is the problem?
(A) A delivery truck is not working.
(B) An installer is busy on the scheduled day.
(C) The wrong item was delivered.
(D) An order is not ready.

79 What does the speaker ask the listener to do?
(A) Change her order
(B) Schedule a meeting
(C) Give directions to her home
(D) Confirm a date

Questions 80-82 refer to the following excerpt from a meeting.

Good afternoon. I'm Charles Strasburg. As the company president, I'd like to welcome all of you to our company's annual meeting. I'll begin today's meeting by introducing our new chief financial officer, Rebecca Nuckols. Ms. Nuckols has worked here at the McNeal Corporation for almost eight years. She most recently held the position of head manager in the Accounting Department. Her immediate focus will be the upcoming stockholders' meeting that is set for October. This is an exciting time for our company, and we are fortunate to have someone as knowledgeable as her on our staff. At this time, I'd like to welcome Ms. Nuckols to the podium.

80 What is the purpose of the talk?
(A) To report some financial figures
(B) To raise funds for charity
(C) To introduce an award winner
(D) To announce an employee's promotion

81 According to the speaker, what was Ms. Nuckols' latest position?
(A) Company president
(B) Head manager
(C) Corporate accountant
(D) Chief financial officer

82 What will Ms. Nuckols do in the future?
(A) Prepare for an upcoming event
(B) Retire from the McNeal Corporation
(C) Be promoted to company president
(D) Join the Accounting Department

Questions 83-85 refer to the following announcement.

Welcome, everyone. I hope you enjoyed the introductory dinner. I'm Diane Choi, the coordinator for this year's leadership conference. To get started, let's take a look at the conference schedule you received during registration. At the top of the schedule, you'll see that today's featured speaker will be well-known inspirational speaker Dr. Morgan Collier. His presentation will begin in about ten minutes right here in this ballroom. Upon the conclusion of Dr. Collier's session, coffee and dessert will be served. And please remember throughout the conference that there will be books and videos for sale in the main hall at twenty percent off. So be sure to take a look at them.

83 What are the listeners asked to do?
(A) Attend a dinner
(B) Look at a schedule
(C) Give a presentation
(D) Register in the main hall

84 What does the speaker say will happen in 10 minutes?
(A) Coffee and dessert will be served.
(B) Dr. Collier will speak.
(C) Conference registration will begin.
(D) Books and videos will be distributed.

85 What does the speaker imply when she says, "be sure to take a look at them"?
(A) It is important to meet the speaker in person.
(B) The discount rate is the biggest of the year.
(C) Books will be autographed by the author.
(D) It is a good opportunity to purchase some products.

Questions 86-88 refer to the following excerpt from a meeting.

Now that we've reviewed our productivity numbers for this past quarter, I'd like to talk a little about the new manufacturing procedures that we are implementing this month. As you know, in three weeks, we will begin using new manufacturing equipment in the plant. As production managers, you are required to attend a briefing on the new equipment to learn how it will affect our manufacturing processes. It will be held at the Westfield plant next Tuesday. Sometime before then, I'd like all of you to get together with your production teams to review the new procedures. Everyone should have received the training manuals last month, but it would be good to meet so that you can clear up any questions they might have.

86 What is the main purpose of the talk?
(A) To create a training schedule
(B) To discuss quarterly production figures
(C) To announce the launch of a new product
(D) To prepare for a new procedure

87 In which division do the listeners most likely work?
(A) Accounting
(B) Personnel
(C) Manufacturing
(D) Maintenance

88 What are the listeners asked to do?
(A) Meet with their teams
(B) Purchase some equipment
(C) Distribute the training manuals
(D) Submit ideas to improve efficiency

Questions 89-91 refer to the following telephone message.

Good afternoon, Ms. Lavin. This is Warren Hatfield calling from Hatfield Washing Service. I'm calling to confirm that I'll be sending over a crew to your office on Wednesday morning to wash the windows. As usual, I'll leave the invoice with your receptionist in the main lobby. Please note that we recently changed our mailing address, so you can mail the payment to our new one, which will be on the invoice. I'll highlight the new address on it to make the words stand out. Thanks and have a nice day.

89 Why is the speaker leaving the message?
(A) To confirm an appointment
(B) To advertise a new business
(C) To request a service
(D) To make a reservation

90 What does the speaker imply when he says, "I'll highlight the new address"?
(A) He needs to provide a reason for the company's relocation.
(B) He is suggesting that the listener visit his office.
(C) He wants to save the listener the trouble of finding information.
(D) He is pointing out that the office will be closed soon.

91 What does the speaker say about the payment?
(A) He has not received money for previous services.
(B) It should be left with the receptionist.
(C) His company accepts only cash.
(D) The address to mail it has recently changed.

Questions 92-94 refer to the following excerpt from a meeting.

Welcome to the April meeting of the Fredericksburg Home Project Organization. It's been nearly three years since we started this organization with the objective of building homes for needy families in Fredericksburg. I am extremely proud of the progress we've made during that time. Tonight, we're going to discuss some of the projects that have been underway. The project coordinators will give us updates on what their groups have accomplished as well as upcoming activities. There are also signup sheets for each project on the table in the back of the room. If there's a specific activity you would like to volunteer for, such as painting, carpentry, or roofing, please make sure to add your name to the appropriate sheet before you leave. Now let's start with an update on the Thompson's home.

92 What is the talk mainly about?
(A) An organization's finances
(B) Some project updates
(C) A new board member
(D) Future projects

93 What is the main goal of the organization?
(A) To organize social events
(B) To help contractors network
(C) To construct homes for the poor
(D) To provide food for the homeless

94 What are the listeners invited to do?
(A) Speak to a project coordinator
(B) Sign up on a list
(C) Attend a separate meeting
(D) Send an e-mail to the group

Questions 95-97 refer to the following announcement and map.

Attention, passengers. Flight 25 with service to Singapore is now boarding at Gate 16. The attendant must scan your boarding pass before you may board, so please have it ready. As a reminder, each passenger may bring one small piece of luggage to be stored in the overhead compartment. For passengers who need to check in their extra baggage, the airline's temporary check-in counter is operating directly opposite the Gate 17, so please make use of the service. We will start by boarding passengers with tickets in rows 60 to 80 at Gate 16. Passengers with children can board at this time, too. The remaining passengers will board shortly. Thank you for your cooperation.

95 What is the purpose of the announcement?
(A) To inform passengers of a departure time change
(B) To get passengers ready for the boarding process
(C) To warn about the mishandling of baggage
(D) To give information about a travel destination

96 What are the passengers asked to get ready?
(A) Their ID cards
(B) Their boarding passes
(C) Their customs forms
(D) Their passports

97 Look at the graphic. Where should the passengers who want to check in their bags go to?
(A) Gate 16
(B) Gate 17
(C) Counter A
(D) Counter B

Questions 98-100 refer to the following announcement and schedule.

I would like to give you a quick overview of the schedule for today. The tour groups for ancient palaces will be arriving at 10 A.M., so those of you that are tour guides for the palace need to be ready at that time. The groups will return from the palace at 12 P.M. for the buffet lunch. Those of you conducting the outdoor tours should be ready for the situation when the weather gets bad. The weather forecast is predicting showers in the afternoon, but we won't cancel any tours unless we have to. And please note that there will be a private tour for VIP guests that is not on the schedule. That was a last-minute decision. We have some free time after the garden tours, so I've arranged a private tour in that time slot. Now, let's begin our day.

98 Who most likely are the listeners?
(A) Palace guards
(B) Tourists
(C) Gardeners
(D) Tour guides

99 What does the speaker say about the weather?
(A) Some tours must be canceled because of it.
(B) Rain has been predicted for the afternoon.
(C) It is going to be sunny all day.
(D) The weather bureau needs to be contacted to check it.

100 Look at the graphic. What time will the private tour be conducted?
(A) At 9:00 A.M.
(B) At 11:00 A.M.
(C) At 2:00 P.M.
(D) At 4:00 P.M.

TEST 02

p.28

1	(D)	2	(C)	3	(C)	4	(B)	5	(A)
6	(D)	7	(B)	8	(A)	9	(C)	10	(B)
11	(A)	12	(B)	13	(C)	14	(A)	15	(C)
16	(C)	17	(A)	18	(B)	19	(A)	20	(C)
21	(C)	22	(A)	23	(A)	24	(B)	25	(B)
26	(C)	27	(B)	28	(C)	29	(B)	30	(A)
31	(A)	32	(A)	33	(C)	34	(D)	35	(B)
36	(C)	37	(C)	38	(A)	39	(B)	40	(D)
41	(B)	42	(C)	43	(A)	44	(A)	45	(B)
46	(D)	47	(A)	48	(D)	49	(C)	50	(A)
51	(A)	52	(C)	53	(B)	54	(A)	55	(D)
56	(A)	57	(C)	58	(B)	59	(D)	60	(A)
61	(B)	62	(B)	63	(C)	64	(C)	65	(C)
66	(D)	67	(D)	68	(D)	69	(A)	70	(B)
71	(B)	72	(A)	73	(C)	74	(A)	75	(C)
76	(C)	77	(A)	78	(D)	79	(C)	80	(C)
81	(D)	82	(C)	83	(C)	84	(C)	85	(B)
86	(B)	87	(B)	88	(D)	89	(C)	90	(B)
91	(A)	92	(D)	93	(B)	94	(C)	95	(D)
96	(D)	97	(A)	98	(B)	99	(B)	100	(C)

Part 1

1 (A) The woman is removing her apron.
(B) The woman is eating at a restaurant.
(C) The woman is handing over a plate.
(D) The woman is pouring a mixture.

2 (A) Workers are installing some wires.
(B) The bridge is being expanded.
(C) Pedestrians are walking on a bridge.
(D) They are building a skyscraper near the bridge.

3 (A) Some cakes are being cut into slices.
(B) Desserts are being served to a customer.
(C) A selection of baked goods is on display.
(D) The dishes on the table are empty.

4 (A) The man is unloading boxes from the back of the truck.
(B) The man is wheeling a cart on the street.
(C) The man is waiting for the light to change.
(D) The man is moving cartons into the warehouse.

5 (A) They are standing near a sign.
(B) They are riding through the park.
(C) They are putting on their helmets.
(D) They are signaling to one another.

6 (A) Some refreshments have been set on a table.
(B) Picture frames are being hung on the wall.
(C) The room is decorated with lights on the ceiling.
(D) Power cord is plugged into an outlet.

Part 2

7 Who should I ask for when I call back?
(A) You can buy it on the second floor.
(B) Talk to Jenny at the reception desk.
(C) It was returned yesterday.

8 When is Dr. Wilson heading to Montreal?
(A) Very soon.
(B) A round-trip ticket, please.
(C) He will resign as head of department.

9 Where is the sales seminar being held?
(A) At 9:30 A.M.
(B) Forty-five hundred euros.
(C) In the auditorium.

10 What is your supervisor's name?
(A) Almost two years now.
(B) It's Melanie Taylor.
(C) Sure, I've met her.

11 You just started working here, didn't you?
(A) Yes, about a month ago.
(B) Yes, but it's already finished.
(C) Sorry. No one is working at the moment.

12 We should be able to meet the deadline after all.
(A) Let's meet around nine.
(B) That's good news.
(C) All of them should participate.

13 Why didn't you buy the latest model?
(A) All the models are on display.
(B) Let's put them in the corner.
(C) Because it was more expensive.

14 Which channel is the nine o'clock business report on?
(A) I believe it's Channel seven.
(B) No, I didn't buy tickets in business class.
(C) I'll finish the report as soon as possible.

15 Should we hire an accountant or an analyst for the new assignment?
(A) I didn't count them.
(B) I can't find her office.
(C) Either would be helpful.

16 Has the mail arrived yet?
(A) We haven't received any phone calls.
(B) Yes, we should apply extra postage.
(C) I'll check on that right away.

17 Why did the company change the application procedure?
(A) To increase efficiency.
(B) Yes, I think it did.
(C) We need at least five new employees.

18 What was on sale at the supermarket?
(A) No, she wasn't at dinner with us.
(B) Some fruits and vegetables.
(C) It's on Main Street.

19 Couldn't you find a place to sit down?
(A) No, the café was full.
(B) You can sit here.
(C) It's row 54, seat number B.

20 What is the problem with that clock?
(A) I'd like to reserve a table for eight o'clock.
(B) She knows how to fix the computer.
(C) It needs new batteries.

21 How much longer will this task take?
(A) Almost seven meters long.
(B) Eric will take it to the office.
(C) It should be completed by Wednesday.

22 Should we meet for lunch or dinner on Saturday?
(A) I'm free all day. Anytime is okay.
(B) Yes, the food was excellent there.
(C) Sure, I'd love to see you, too.

23 How about hiring an outside consultant to help with the project?
(A) That might be a better solution.
(B) He works at a consulting firm.
(C) Yes, the projection was off target.

24 Let's turn on the air conditioning now to cool down before our meeting.
(A) No, it's a right turn, not a left one.
(B) Yes, it's very hot in here.
(C) Maybe I'll bring my car instead.

25 Do you know who posted the memo on the company bulletin board?
(A) Peter just went to the post office.
(B) I believe the supervisor did.
(C) Okay, I'll make the announcement right away.

26 Lisa forgot to bring her security badge today.
(A) The lost and found desk.
(B) Why don't you ask the security guard first?
(C) I'm always forgetting mine, too.

27 How is the feature article for the magazine selected?
(A) At least 800 words on it.
(B) The editors vote on it.
(C) In a future issue.

28 You can hand in the survey results by tomorrow, can't you?
(A) To get more detailed data.
(B) Yes, the company needs more money.
(C) Actually, I'm still compiling them.

29 Did we just miss our subway stop?
(A) I stopped taking the bus.
(B) No, it's the next one.
(C) Yes, it'll start ten minutes early.

30 Could I pick up my car at 7:30?
(A) Sorry. We close at six.
(B) She'll travel by plane.
(C) It comes in many different colors.

31 The vice president of the bank retired last month.
(A) I wonder if they hired a replacement.
(B) Yes, I made this month's payment.
(C) You can try the Busan office.

Part 3

Questions 32-34 refer to the following conversation.

W Good morning. My husband and I want to check in. Here's our reservation number. We've been assigned to seats in row 30 in the economy section. But we wonder if it's too late to upgrade them to business class.

M Let me see your tickets, please. You're going to Los Angeles, right? Well, I do happen to have a couple of business class seats available, but each one will cost an extra 100 dollars. Is that okay with you?

W It's a little more than I expected. I think it should be okay, but let me check with my husband before I pay for them.

32 Where is the conversation probably taking place?
(A) In an airport
(B) In an airplane
(C) In a theater
(D) In a train station

33 What does the woman ask for?
(A) A refund
(B) A meal
(C) A seat change
(D) An updated schedule

34 What will the woman do next?
(A) Book a different flight
(B) Cancel a reservation
(C) Buy something to eat
(D) Talk to her husband

Questions 35-37 refer to the following conversation.

W Phil, I can't find the report that I'm supposed to hand in today. I thought I had it in my briefcase when I left work yesterday.

M Try looking in your briefcase again. It might be hidden in one of the compartments.

W It's not in here. I already double-checked. Could you go ahead and set up the projector in the conference room? I have to go back to my office to print another copy of the report.

M Okay, but try not to be late for the meeting. This is a very important presentation for our department.

35 Why is the woman concerned?
(A) She lost her briefcase.
(B) She cannot find a document.
(C) She missed a presentation.
(D) She is late for a meeting.

36 What is the man asked to do?
(A) Call her secretary
(B) Make another copy
(C) Set up equipment
(D) Postpone a meeting

37 Where will the woman probably go next?
(A) To a store
(B) To her house
(C) To her office
(D) To a conference room

Questions 38-40 refer to the following conversation.

M Is it okay if I come in a bit late tomorrow? I have a dentist's appointment at nine o'clock in the morning. One of my teeth has been bothering me for days.

W That should be fine. When you arrive tomorrow, let's get started on that assignment we discussed with the Sales Department. They want us to start preparing a promotional brochure that features all our new services. What time will you be here?

M I should be finished at the dentist's office by ten o'clock, so I'm going to be here no later than ten thirty.

W Perfect. I'll be in a meeting until ten anyway. I'll have all the materials ready for us to review before you arrive. We can meet in your office at ten thirty then.

38 What are the speakers discussing?
(A) A plan for a workday
(B) A reservation for dinner
(C) An upcoming business trip
(D) A dental procedure

39 What does the woman suggest?
(A) Canceling the dentist's appointment
(B) Undertaking a specific work
(C) Taking a vacation day
(D) Rescheduling a meeting

40 What time will the speakers meet?
(A) At 9:00 A.M. (B) At 9:30 A.M.
(C) At 10:00 A.M. (D) At 10:30 A.M.

Questions 41-43 refer to the following conversation with three speakers.

W Good morning, everyone. Next month, our magazine will have a special feature on local restaurants and cafés. Is anyone interested in this assignment?

M1 Yes, I'd love to write an article about Café a Roma. It recently won an award for the best coffee and desserts.

W Thanks, Hiroshi. Why don't you set up an interview with the owner?

M1 That sounds great. Hey, Kevin, can you go along to the interview with me and take some photographs of the place?

M2 Sure, I've been hoping to check out that café myself anyway.

W Great. You both can work out the details later on then.

41 Where does the conversation take place?
(A) At a local café
(B) At a magazine company
(C) At a photography gallery
(D) At an awards ceremony

42 What is mentioned about Café a Roma?
(A) It has expanded its menu.
(B) It is hiring new employees.
(C) It was recently awarded a prize.
(D) It is a good location for an event.

43 What is Kevin asked to do?
(A) Take pictures
(B) Edit some articles
(C) Contact the café owner
(D) Prepare some food

Questions 44-46 refer to the following conversation.

M Excuse me. This line doesn't seem to be moving. Have you been waiting long?

W Yes, much longer than I expected. I have to make a deposit, but I need to get back to my office soon. For some reason, my bank card isn't working, so I can't use the automated teller machine.

M That's too bad. I have to exchange some currency, but I have a meeting with a client in a few minutes. I guess I'll just come back around three.

W Sounds good. The bank should be less crowded then. I'm going to stay and wait a few more minutes. I wish there were more tellers working at this time of the day.

44 Where most likely are the speakers?
(A) In a bank
(B) In a meeting room
(C) In an office building
(D) In an electronics store

45 What problem are the speakers discussing?
(A) A client missed a meeting.
(B) There is a long wait.
(C) A machine is malfunctioning.
(D) A payment is late.

46 What does the man say he will do?
(A) Use an ATM
(B) Reschedule an appointment
(C) Send another check
(D) Return later

Questions 47-49 refer to the following conversation.

M Hello. I was wondering if you could help me. I bought a stereo from your store about ten months ago, but the CD player just stopped playing yesterday.

W Well, all of our merchandise has a one-year warranty. Since you've only had it for ten months, your stereo is still covered. You can bring it back to the store, and we'll fix it for you at no charge.

M Hmm... I'm afraid <u>that's not going to work for me.</u> I recently moved and now live quite far from your place.

W No problem. You can mail it directly to the manufacturer, and they'll either repair or replace it. Let me give you the address of where to send it. Make sure to include a copy of your sales receipt with the shipment.

47 What is the purpose of the call?
(A) To discuss a defective product
(B) To ask for a receipt
(C) To report a lost item
(D) To inquire about a new model

48 What does the man imply when he says, "that's not going to work for me"?
(A) He is not working tomorrow.
(B) He wants his money back.
(C) He cannot arrive at the place on time.
(D) He cannot visit a store in person.

49 What will the woman probably do next?
(A) Send a package
(B) Call a manufacturer
(C) Provide information
(D) Fix the stereo herself

Questions 50-52 refer to the following conversation.

M Hi, Claire. I just got a call from Mr. Humphrey. He's a little upset that he hasn't received his travel itinerary.

W That's really odd. I definitely e-mailed the itinerary to him on Monday.

M Really? Are you sure you sent it to the right address?

W Yes, I'm sure. I got it directly from his company's Web site.

M Well, Mr. Humphrey is one of our biggest clients. We should do something about it right away.

W Okay, I'll print a hard copy of the itinerary and take it to his office on my way out.

50 Why is Mr. Humphrey upset?
(A) He did not receive a schedule.
(B) He misplaced an important file.
(C) He found an error in a document.
(D) He doesn't like his schedule.

51 What did the woman do on Monday?
(A) She sent an e-mail.
(B) She updated contact information.
(C) She made some copies.
(D) She called Mr. Humphrey.

52 What does the woman say she will do?
(A) Check an e-mail address
(B) Fax a report
(C) Deliver a document
(D) Sign a contract

Questions 53-55 refer to the following conversation.

W Mr. Hoffman, can we discuss the schedule for the interviews that we need to conduct for the financial analyst position?

M Sure, I'll be in the office until the middle of next week. But I have to leave for the International Finance Convention in London on Thursday. How about doing the interviews on Tuesday or Wednesday before I go?

W Sorry. That would be difficult for me because I have to travel to Amsterdam on Tuesday. So I think it's best if we plan the interviews for Monday, when we will both be here. We really need to add another person to the finance team soon. That department is understaffed, and they have deadlines to meet.

M You're right. We need some help in that department as soon as possible.

53 What is the conversation mainly about?
(A) Making some investments
(B) Coordinating some schedules
(C) Laying off some employees
(D) Receiving some applications

54 When will the speakers probably conduct the interviews?
(A) On Monday
(B) On Tuesday
(C) On Wednesday
(D) On Thursday

55 Why is the company hiring a new financial analyst?
(A) Someone is retiring soon.
(B) It is opening a new international division.
(C) Customers are complaining about a slow process.
(D) The department has too much work.

Questions 56-58 refer to the following conversation.

W Harry, the chef just told me that we're almost out of the ingredients for the seafood soup, one of the specials. We'll have to let the servers know and have them stop taking orders for the soup.

M Good idea. Besides, we have a big party coming in soon at eight o'clock, and I think some of those customers pre-ordered the seafood soup. We have to have enough for them.

W Right, but it is still being advertised on the menu board. Shouldn't I remove it?

M Yes, you should. We'll have to come up with another dish as a substitute for the special soup, too.

56 What is the topic of the conversation?
(A) The availability of a special dish
(B) The skill of a new chef
(C) The location of a restaurant
(D) The addition of new ingredients

57 What does the man say will happen?
(A) Some groceries will be delivered.
(B) Some new staffers will be trained.
(C) A group of customers will arrive.
(D) A restaurant will be closed for renovations.

58 What does the woman ask about?
(A) What time she can leave work
(B) Whether she should update the menu
(C) Where they should store the supplies
(D) How many customers are in a party

Questions 59-61 refer to the following conversation.

M Hey, Rita. You know, I've been meaning to look at the comment cards that store customers filled out. I was just going through them right now, and some of the suggestions would be helpful to our store.

W Oh, sorry. I've been really busy checking inventory. Did you find anything interesting?

M Yeah, several people suggested that we extend our business hours during the holidays to make things more convenient for customers.

W That's actually a good idea. Many of our competitors do that, so maybe we should do that as well.

M Great. I'll make a note of that and present the idea at next week's meeting.

59 What did the man recently do?
(A) He registered for a seminar.
(B) He did some holiday shopping.
(C) He sent out some product brochures.
(D) He reviewed customers' feedback.

60 Why does the woman say, "I've been really busy checking inventory"?
(A) To provide an excuse
(B) To prepare for a change
(C) To ask for help
(D) To confirm a meeting time

61 What will the man suggest at next week's meeting?
(A) Updating some materials
(B) Extending hours of operation
(C) Holding a special sale
(D) Expanding a product line

Questions 62-64 refer to the following conversation and map.

W Hi there. I'm here to see Mr. Campbell in the IT Department for an important meeting.

M Okay, could you please fill in the sign-in sheet? I'll also give you a visitor's ID badge, which you should wear while on the premises.

W Sure. In addition, would you mind directing me to Mr. Campbell's office? I forgot to ask where his office is when I scheduled the meeting last week.

M He is on the fifth floor. Go straight down the hall after you get off the elevator, and you should see the sign for his office. It's right across from the main conference room. You should have no trouble finding it.

62 What does the man ask the woman to do?
(A) Use a different entrance
(B) Wear an ID badge
(C) Turn off her cell phone
(D) Come back at a later time

63 What did the woman do last week?
(A) She got Mr. Campbell's signature.
(B) She discussed a project plan.
(C) She set up a meeting.
(D) She asked for some advice.

64 Look at the graphic. Which office does the woman need to visit?
(A) Suite 501 (B) Suite 502
(C) Suite 503 (D) Suite 504

Questions 65-67 refer to the following conversation and list.

M Good afternoon, Wendy. I'm calling to discuss your food order for your business networking seminar next week. Are you still expecting ten people?

W Actually, there were a couple of late additions. We will have twelve participants on next Friday. Like I said before, I would like coffee, juice, bagels, and fruit in the morning and sandwiches and soft drinks for lunch.

M No problem. I'll have that order ready for you on Friday morning. The total comes to 285 dollars for both breakfast and lunch. We applied a special corporate discount as we discussed.

W Thank you. Oh, there is one more thing. Could you add some cookies to the lunch order?

65 Why is the man calling the woman?
(A) To organize an event
(B) To make a reservation
(C) To confirm an order
(D) To apologize for a delay

66 What information does the woman provide?
(A) The reason for a gathering
(B) The topic of a meeting
(C) The name of a venue
(D) The number of attendees

67 Look at the graphic. How much is the item the woman wants to add?
(A) $12 (B) $10
(C) $8 (D) $6

Questions 68-70 refer to the following conversation and sign.

M Don't you have baggage to check in, Debra? You're traveling lightly for someone heading to a four-day conference.

W Actually, I can't stay for the whole conference. I have to get back for a very important meeting with a client. Rescheduling would be inconvenient for the client. So I'm returning right after my presentation tomorrow.

M That's too bad. Hey, we should probably go down to the departure gate. My boarding pass says it's Gate B12.

W Let's check the departure board. Hmm... B12. There it is. It says our flight's on time, but I think we still have some time for a cup of coffee.

68 What type of event are the speakers traveling to?
(A) An awards banquet
(B) A sports competition
(C) A cultural festival
(D) A business function

69 Why is the woman staying at her destination for a short time?
(A) She must return for a meeting.
(B) She has to meet some colleagues.
(C) She has a limited budget.
(D) Her flight schedule has changed.

70 Look at the graphic. What city are the speakers flying to?
(A) New York
(B) Boston
(C) Chicago
(D) Minneapolis

Part 4

Questions 71-73 refer to the following announcement.

Good evening, shoppers. Welcome to Fresh Foods Grocery Store, where we provide you with delicious food at low prices every day. This week, we have some great deals in the Produce Department. Check out aisle four for a special twenty percent discount on all organic vegetables. As you know, we offer the widest selection of organic vegetables in town, so don't miss out on this sale. And don't forget that if there aren't food items you want on the shelves, please ask one of our employees to help you find what you are looking for. As always, thank you for shopping at Fresh Foods.

71 Where does the announcement take place?
(A) At a food manufacturer
(B) In a grocery store
(C) In a restaurant
(D) At a farmers' market

72 What does the speaker say she will provide this week?
(A) Lower prices
(B) Expedited delivery
(C) Product samples
(D) Gift certificates

73 What should the listeners do to buy products which are not on display?
(A) Ask the supervisor for a special order
(B) Place an order online
(C) Ask for help from a store employee
(D) Visit a manufacturer's Web site

Questions 74-76 refer to the following talk.

Good morning. My name is Juno Lee, and I will be leading this class on interviewing skills for students entering the job market. The goal of this program is to provide tips and suggestions on how to interview and secure a job after graduation. The class will be broken into morning and afternoon sessions with an hour break for lunch. This morning, we'll watch a video and then have a group discussion. The video will show effective interviewing techniques and examples of interview questions. During the afternoon session, we will be using the course book. If you haven't already purchased it, you should stop by the bookstore during the lunch break and buy it. I think the book is twelve dollars.

74 For whom is the talk intended for?
(A) University students
(B) Company employees
(C) Business managers
(D) Professors

75 What will most likely happen in the morning session?
(A) Some skills will be tested.
(B) Textbooks will be provided.
(C) A video will be shown.
(D) Experts will give a lecture.

76 According to the speaker, what can the listeners do during lunch?
(A) Register for another seminar
(B) Have a group talk
(C) Buy a book
(D) Discuss the course materials

Questions 77-79 refer to the following advertisement.

Whether you're traveling to New York, London, Hong Kong, or any other major city around the world, you don't need to look any further than Skyline International Hotels. We offer luxurious rooms at the most affordable prices. Right now, if you book a room online for two nights, we'll give you the third night for absolutely free. Promotions like this made *Urban Traveler* magazine rank us as the number one hotel for online reservations for two years in a row. So make your life easier by booking your next stay online with us. Visit www.skylinehotel.com today.

77 According to the speaker, what is an advantage of the hotel?
(A) Reasonable rates
(B) Friendly staff
(C) A pleasant environment
(D) A convenient location

78 Why does the speaker say, "make your life easier by booking your next stay online with us"?
(A) To introduce a new online system
(B) To announce further discounts
(C) To promote its renovated facilities
(D) To encourage people to try some services

79 What does the speaker say about *Urban Traveler* magazine?
(A) It offers some useful travel tips.
(B) It introduces a variety of hotel chains.
(C) It highly evaluated the company.
(D) Its subscribers can get special treatment.

Questions 80-82 refer to the following announcement.

We're extremely pleased with the wonderful turnout for this month's meet-the-author event at Valleyfield Bookstore. As most of you know, the meet-the-author series gives the general public a chance to hear renowned writers read from their own works and speak in an open forum. Tonight's guest is none other than Tom Welker. Mr. Welker has published many famous works, including several bestselling novels. His most recent novel, *The Long Road Home*, has once again achieved bestseller status. This evening, he will describe the process he undertakes to turn an idea into an actual living, breathing story. Afterward, he will be willing to answer your questions and sign copies of his books, which will be available for sale.

80 Where most likely are the listeners?
(A) At a retail store
(B) At an employment agency
(C) At a bookstore
(D) At a publisher

81 Who is Tom Welker?
(A) An editor
(B) A job counselor
(C) A bookstore owner
(D) A novelist

82 What will happen at the end of the event?
(A) A new book will be released.
(B) Samples will be distributed.
(C) Books will be signed.
(D) Interviews will be held.

Questions 83-85 refer to the following announcement.

Good morning, ladies and gentlemen, and welcome to White Falls Mountain. My name is Jason, and I'll be your guide today. Our tour will last about three hours, and we will hike about four kilometers as we stop to see the three waterfalls on the mountain. You're welcome to pause to take photographs during the tour. Just make sure not to fall too far behind the group. In addition, please don't venture off the trail as it's easy to get lost because of the dense forest. I will be sure to take extra time at the most scenic points on the tour. One last thing: I suggest that you use the restroom before we leave because there aren't any public restrooms on the mountain. Let's meet back here in ten minutes to start the hike.

83 What is the purpose of the announcement?
(A) To begin a lecture
(B) To introduce an employee
(C) To describe a tour
(D) To cancel an event

84 What are the listeners allowed to do?
(A) Eat lunch early
(B) Buy souvenirs
(C) Take photographs
(D) Carry personal belongings

85 What does the speaker suggest?
(A) Changing into warm clothes
(B) Using the restroom in advance
(C) Buying some food or drinks
(D) Turning off cell phones

Questions 86-88 refer to the following excerpt from a meeting.

Good morning, members of the urban planning commission. It's my honor and privilege to present the design proposal for the renovation of the downtown museum. As city planning members, you all recognize that the museum is almost fifty years old, so it is in dire need of renovations. However, as you'll see from our design, there are certain features that we would like to keep, such as the large exterior pillars. We propose preserving the best of the existing structures and adding new features such as an atrium in the main lobby. This approach should minimize costs and rejuvenate a landmark that has been an integral part of our community. Now, let me present you with the details of the proposal.

86 What is the main topic of the talk?
(A) Applications for a construction permit
(B) Design plans for a renovation
(C) Reviewing a proposal
(D) Tips for operating a museum

87 What does the speaker imply when he says, "the museum is almost 50 years old"?
(A) It has a large number of collections.
(B) It needs to be fixed in many places.
(C) He wants to sell the property for a high price.
(D) It is the oldest museum in the area.

88 What will the speaker probably do next?
(A) Turn off the lights for better viewing
(B) Listen to the guest lecturer
(C) Visit the museum himself
(D) Show the listeners some plans

Questions 89-91 refer to the following excerpt from a meeting.

Good afternoon, everyone. I've called this managers' meeting to discuss the results of our most recent customer satisfaction survey. As all of you know, the intention of the survey was to determine how we can improve our customer service. Overall, customers are quite pleased with our competitive pricing and the quality of our products. They also appreciate how quickly we respond to their individual requests. But there is still room for improvement. One obvious complaint was that our automated voicemail system was inefficient and difficult to use. I've provided everyone with the complete results of the survey, and I'd like to review each item in detail with all of you right now.

89 Who is the speaker talking to?
(A) Customers
(B) Accountants
(C) Managers
(D) Designers

90 What did customers complain about?
(A) Billing services
(B) The voicemail system
(C) Delivery delays
(D) The quality of the products

91 According to the speaker, what will happen next?
(A) Survey results will be discussed.
(B) A group project will be presented.
(C) All customers will be contacted.
(D) Response cards will be distributed.

Questions 92-94 refer to the following telephone message.

Hi, Teddy. It's Angela. It was great to see you again when I visited my old office at Research Panorama last week. I still prefer my new home-based job though. I'm calling because I misplaced the phone number and e-mail address for the company you always hire to clean the office carpets. I remember that its staff did excellent work. Remember how the cleaning crew got all the stains out of the old rugs in the client lounge? The carpets looked brand new when they finished being cleaned. Anyway, I need a crew to come over soon. Could you text or call me back with that information? Thanks, Teddy.

92 What is the purpose of the message?
(A) To inquire about a job
(B) To ask about business hours
(C) To report on the status of a project
(D) To ask for some information

93 What does the speaker mention about the cleaning service?
(A) It is out of business.
(B) It offered high quality work.
(C) It launched a new product.
(D) It changed its location.

94 What does the speaker mean when she says, "I need a crew to come over soon"?
(A) She wants to complain in person.
(B) An emergency has occurred at her home.
(C) She has carpets that need to be cleaned.
(D) She needs help meeting a client.

Questions 95-97 refer to the following announcement and schedule.

Good morning and welcome to the seventh annual Professional Realtors Conference for residential and commercial real estate agents. For those who planned to participate in the Communications workshop at 11 A.M., I'm afraid this session has been postponed. Due to bad weather, our guest speaker's flight was delayed, so he won't be arriving until after lunch. As a result, we switched his workshop with the last one on the schedule. We apologize for any inconvenience this may cause. For everyone who has already registered for this session, please go to the conference registration desk to inform the person there if you still wish to attend. Thank you for your cooperation, and we hope you enjoy the conference.

95 Who most likely are the listeners?
(A) Receptionists
(B) Local students
(C) Travel agents
(D) Realtors

96 Look at the graphic. According to the speaker, when will the workshop on Communications start?
(A) At 10:00 A.M.
(B) At 11:00 A.M.
(C) At 1:00 P.M.
(D) At 2:00 P.M.

97 What are some listeners asked to do?
(A) Go to the registration desk
(B) Listen to further instructions
(C) Attend another workshop
(D) Request a different schedule

Questions 98-100 refer to the following excerpt from a meeting and chart.

I'd like to start the staff meeting by sharing the results of the member survey our staff recently conducted. As you know, our biggest concern is to make sure our current members are satisfied with our services. Here are the top four answers to the following question: what changes would you like to see in our fitness club? Although most members said that they would like to have new showers in the locker room, we simply don't have enough money to renovate the facilities. However, we could afford to hire a couple more staff members so we can accommodate the second most popular choice. If you know some qualified people that you think would be interested in this job, please let me know.

98 According to the speaker, what is the center's main concern?
(A) Observing industry regulations
(B) Satisfying current members
(C) Reducing operating costs
(D) Expanding to a new market

99 Look at the graphic. What item does the speaker want to address?
(A) Renovations
(B) Diverse classes
(C) Better equipment
(D) Longer hours

100 What does the speaker ask the listeners to do?
(A) Tour a facility
(B) Take a certification class
(C) Refer potential employees
(D) Request a transfer

TEST 03

| p.42

1	(B)	2	(B)	3	(C)	4	(D)	5	(C)
6	(C)	7	(A)	8	(A)	9	(B)	10	(A)
11	(B)	12	(C)	13	(A)	14	(C)	15	(A)
16	(A)	17	(C)	18	(C)	19	(B)	20	(C)
21	(C)	22	(B)	23	(A)	24	(B)	25	(C)
26	(A)	27	(A)	28	(C)	29	(A)	30	(B)
31	(C)	32	(B)	33	(B)	34	(D)	35	(D)
36	(D)	37	(C)	38	(B)	39	(A)	40	(D)
41	(D)	42	(B)	43	(D)	44	(D)	45	(C)
46	(B)	47	(C)	48	(D)	49	(A)	50	(C)
51	(D)	52	(A)	53	(B)	54	(D)	55	(C)
56	(D)	57	(B)	58	(C)	59	(B)	60	(D)
61	(C)	62	(A)	63	(D)	64	(D)	65	(B)
66	(B)	67	(D)	68	(B)	69	(D)	70	(D)
71	(C)	72	(B)	73	(B)	74	(B)	75	(D)
76	(C)	77	(B)	78	(A)	79	(D)	80	(D)
81	(C)	82	(A)	83	(D)	84	(B)	85	(D)
86	(D)	87	(B)	88	(A)	89	(D)	90	(A)
91	(A)	92	(C)	93	(C)	94	(D)	95	(C)
96	(A)	97	(D)	98	(D)	99	(A)	100	(D)

Part 1

1 (A) The man is fixing his guitar.
(B) The man is playing an instrument.
(C) The audience is waiting to be seated.
(D) The man is standing on the stage.

2 (A) The doctor is prescribing some medicine to the patient.
(B) The woman is being examined by the doctor.
(C) The patient is being discharged from the hospital.
(D) Both of them are facing the same direction.

3 (A) Books are being arranged on the shelf.
(B) There are many notices on the board.
(C) Reading material has been placed on racks.
(D) Shoppers are browsing in the store.

4 (A) The people are getting off the train.
(B) There are some chairs on a platform.
(C) Passengers are walking toward the ticket counter.
(D) Some people are carrying things on their backs.

5 (A) Both men are wearing glasses.
(B) One man is handing something to the other.
(C) The men are greeting each other.
(D) One of the men is putting on a jacket.

6 (A) Some people are walking up the staircase.
(B) The railings are being removed.
(C) The steps lead to the next level.
(D) The floor is being polished to shine.

Part 2

7 How long is the trip to Beijing?
(A) Three hours by plane.
(B) Really? I'd like to go there, too.
(C) I've been there twice already.

8 What color should we paint the interior?
(A) How about light blue?
(B) That was really useful.
(C) The exterior walls need some repairs.

9 Are you working tomorrow?
(A) Yes, it's been working fine.
(B) Actually, it's my day off.
(C) I usually take the bus to work.

10 When did you get back from your vacation?
(A) Early this morning.
(B) For about two weeks.
(C) It was better than I had expected.

11 This is your work number, isn't it?
(A) Actually, he didn't call me.
(B) No, it's for my mobile phone.
(C) Let's walk over there.

12 I had a job interview last week.
(A) Yes, I could get that job.
(B) Let's meet another time.
(C) How did it go?

13 Did you make the plane reservation for Mr. Sanders?
(A) I took care of it yesterday.
(B) At international terminal B.
(C) Sure, I'd love to go with you if that's okay.

14 Who will lead the next seminar in the lecture series?
(A) The guests will be here soon.
(B) They are talking about the future of the publishing industry.
(C) They haven't announced it yet.

15 Can you call the warehouse to confirm our delivery?
(A) I already talked with someone there this morning.
(B) Only a few more boxes are needed.
(C) I'm afraid they are fully booked.

16 Do you know where the mailroom is?
(A) It's on the third floor.
(B) I'll use regular mail.
(C) Yes, to the New York office, please.

17 Didn't Mr. Dawson say he completed the research?
(A) Sure, I can work on the research and development team.
(B) No, I couldn't find the address.
(C) Yes, he finished everything last week.

18 We'll replace any damaged parts at no charge.
(A) No, it's not yours.
(B) I saw only a part of it.
(C) That's good to know.

19 What does Mr. Lewis say he does?
(A) Sure, I'll talk to him right away.
(B) He works at St. Martin's General Hospital.
(C) He updated the personnel file last night.

20 Do you want to take the item yourself or have it delivered?
(A) There will be a delivery charge.
(B) I'm full. Thank you.
(C) I'll pick it up later.

21 Ms. Jenkins, should I mail this package now?
(A) No, I didn't mean it.
(B) The meeting was delayed.
(C) Thanks. Will you do that for me?

22 Why do we have to leave so early?
(A) They don't live around here.
(B) The traffic might be bad downtown.
(C) He will be here any moment.

23 Haven't you ordered some more paper for the photocopier?
(A) Yes, it should be here tomorrow.
(B) No, the printer is not broken.
(C) Let's put them in the right order.

24 When will we be hearing about the results from the selection committee?
(A) From the store nearest your house.
(B) They'll contact you within a week.
(C) The construction will take about a month.

25 Mr. Yamamoto retired recently, didn't he?
(A) Yes, I'm so tired.
(B) No, I'll be ready by tomorrow.
(C) Yes, he left last month.

26 Have you tried the new restaurant that opened up on Main Street?
(A) Yes, the food was great.
(B) No, it's not that new.
(C) No, it's on Second Avenue.

27 Would you like me to make a reservation?
(A) That won't be necessary.
(B) You can look at the menu if you want.
(C) My flight doesn't leave until tomorrow.

28 Where did you find this document?
(A) In the middle of December.
(B) I'm fine. Thank you.
(C) Carlos gave it to me.

29 The earnings report should be ready soon.
(A) Can it be finished by tomorrow?
(B) The reporter works for the company.
(C) Yes, they'll send them by express mail.

30 Why don't we get our sales employees new mobile phones?
(A) Sure, let's move to a new location.
(B) We don't have enough money in our budget.
(C) New employees must go through some training.

31 This property is more affordable than I thought it would be.
(A) Okay, let me show you another one then.
(B) Just pull over right next to that house.
(C) Yes, the price is quite reasonable.

Part 3

Questions 32-34 refer to the following conversation.

M Hi. I own a small restaurant, and I need to rent some storage units while my business is being renovated.

W What size are you looking for? Most of our larger units are taken. We only have several smaller units. Would a two-meter-by-three-meter unit work for you?

M I'm not sure. I need to store all my kitchen utensils and furniture while construction is going on in the store.

W Why don't I visit your restaurant next week to take some measurements, and then I can give you an estimate? When would be good for you?

32 Who most likely is the man?
(A) A warehouse worker
(B) A restaurant owner
(C) A real estate agent
(D) A building architect

33 What does the man say about his business?
(A) It offers special discounts.
(B) It will be renovated.
(C) It opens every weekend.
(D) It changed its hours.

34 What does the woman offer to do?
(A) Have dinner together
(B) Return his call as soon as possible
(C) Give him some funding
(D) Come to his restaurant

Questions 35-37 refer to the following conversation.

W Hi, Scott. I'm calling to let you know I took a careful look at your manuscript, and the sample chapter looks very intriguing and promising. I am interested in publishing it.

M That is great! Do you have any feedback for me?

W Well, you might want to spend more time outlining the book before you actually write the whole thing. I have written down some comments for you, and I can give them to you next time we meet. Are you available to discuss this project next week?

35 What does the woman want to do?
(A) Write a children's story
(B) Conduct more research
(C) Find a writer
(D) Publish a book

36 What does the man ask for?
(A) A deposit for a property
(B) A deadline for a report
(C) Product samples
(D) Advice on a project

37 What will the speakers most likely do next?
(A) Sign a contract
(B) Visit a bookstore
(C) Arrange a meeting
(D) Write a new chapter

Questions 38-40 refer to the following conversation.

W Thank you for showing me around, Mr. Norman. This is the most interesting apartment your agency has shown me so far.

M I'm glad you like it. These units are extremely popular.

W I've never seen an apartment in an old factory, but it seems quite unique and spacious, too.

M Yes, it's rather unusual. You know, the building was repaired and divided into apartments just last year. This is the only one left to rent.

W I can see why it's so popular. I'd like to rent it.

M Good decision. You won't regret it.

W Has anyone else shown any interest in the apartment? I can give you the money for the security deposit today.

38 Who most likely is the man?
(A) A factory supervisor
(B) A rental agent
(C) An interior designer
(D) A loan officer

39 According to the man, what happened last year?
(A) A building was remodeled.
(B) An employee was hired.
(C) A plant was shut down.
(D) A contract was canceled.

40 What does the woman offer to do?
(A) Purchase some supplies
(B) Apply for a position
(C) Provide a list of references
(D) Make a payment immediately

Questions 41-43 refer to the following conversation.

M Did you hear the morning news report?

W No, I had an early morning meeting with a client. What did I miss?

M There was a story about how the city council finally approved the plan to build a new highway between Grover City and Marshall Road downtown.

W That's good news. I guess my commute will be shortened after the highway is completed since I live in the Grover City area.

41 Why was the woman unable to hear the news report?
(A) She was visiting another branch.
(B) She was meeting her family.
(C) She got stuck in traffic.
(D) She was with a client.

42 What is the subject of the news report?
(A) A company policy
(B) A council's decision
(C) A marketing plan
(D) A traffic jam

43 Why is the woman pleased?
(A) She can move to Grover City.
(B) Her deadline has been extended.
(C) Her office will be relocated.
(D) Her trip home from work will be faster.

Questions 44-46 refer to the following conversation.

M Hi. I just got a new eyeglasses prescription from my eye doctor. She suggested coming to your store to get it filled.

W Certainly. We have a great selection of frames. Actually, we just got a shipment yesterday.

M Great. I did want to get some new frames. I've had these for a while. And this is my first time buying glasses here. How long does it usually take to make them?

W Well, we can usually make them in about an hour. However, we have a problem today because one of our technicians called in sick. But if you select your frames and leave your prescription, we should have them ready by five.

44 Where most likely is the conversation taking place?
(A) In a camera store
(B) In a pharmacy
(C) In a laboratory
(D) In an eyeglasses store

45 What does the man want to do?
(A) Change an order
(B) Make an appointment
(C) Fill a prescription
(D) Return a purchase

46 What problem does the woman report?
(A) A product has been discontinued.
(B) An employee is out sick today.
(C) Some test results are not ready.
(D) Some equipment is broken.

Questions 47-49 refer to the following conversation.

M Hi, Pham. I have a meeting tomorrow with Mr. and Ms. Robinson about their small business loan. Would you mind taking my place? I have an appointment with my son's teacher.

W Sure, I can meet with the Robinsons. I have their application form with me. What else should I bring to the meeting?

M All you need is the list of additional documents they have to send us in two weeks. I can e-mail it today. Tell them how important it is to submit all the necessary information before the actual evaluation.

47 What is the woman asked to do?
(A) Go to a hospital
(B) Arrange a schedule
(C) Meet with some clients
(D) Send out an application

48 Why does the man make the request?
(A) He has to get a diploma.
(B) He is not feeling well.
(C) He is vacationing with his family.
(D) He has a scheduling conflict.

49 What does the man say he will send the woman?
(A) A list of some documents
(B) A cost estimate
(C) A timetable for a process
(D) An application form

Questions 50-52 refer to the following conversation.

W Tim, have you been to the old office supply store in the shopping center? It's going through some renovations and being completely reorganized.

M Well, it's about time. That place is outdated and needs some serious work done.

W I noticed that some things were being rearranged the last time I went there. An office furniture section was also being made.

M Does the store have any selections that we could use in our office?

W Yes, there are all kinds of desks, chairs, and cabinets on display, and the prices are quite reasonable.

M Well, I've been thinking about getting a new chair myself. Maybe I should check out the place during my lunch break.

W Good idea. I'll go with you.

50 Who most likely are the speakers?
(A) Furniture salespeople
(B) Professional movers
(C) Office workers
(D) Store clerks

51 What does the man mean when he says, "it's about time"?
(A) He is late for the meeting.
(B) A store needs more workers to meet demand.
(C) They need to get off work soon.
(D) Some work has been needed for a long time.

52 What will most likely happen at lunch time?
(A) The speakers will visit a store.
(B) The speakers will purchase some paper.
(C) The speakers will rearrange the office.
(D) The speakers will repair some furniture.

Questions 53-55 refer to the following conversation.

M Excuse me. I got an e-mail telling me that the book I have reserved is available, but when I checked with the librarian at the main reception desk, she told me that it's been checked out by someone else. She said I should talk to you about it.

W When did you get the e-mail? Our policy is to hold the book for ten days, and then we put it back on the shelves so that others can use the book, too.

M Actually, I got the e-mail two weeks ago. I didn't know there was a policy in terms of how long you would keep it for me.

W You could put it on reserve again if you want. Would you like to do that?

53 What is the man's problem?
(A) A library policy has changed.
(B) The book he wants is not available.
(C) He has been overcharged.
(D) He returned a book too late.

54 When did the man receive an e-mail?
(A) Today (B) Yesterday
(C) Ten days ago (D) Fourteen days ago

55 What does the woman offer to do?
(A) Send another e-mail
(B) Bring a book from a shelf
(C) Make a new reservation
(D) Provide a copy of the policy

Questions 56-58 refer to the following conversation.

W Hi, Sam. Can you update me on getting a new senior editor for *Arts Weekly* magazine?

M Well, we have received quite a few applications, but only a couple of individuals seemed qualified enough to do the job.

W Well, more doesn't necessarily mean better. We only need one good candidate for the job.

M You're right. So I'm trying to set up interviews with them. Will next Monday work for you?

W Actually, I'm leaving for a business trip on Friday and won't be back until Monday afternoon. I have some free time on Wednesday morning.

M Okay, great. I'll contact them right away and have them come over on Wednesday.

56 What position are the candidates applying for?
(A) Board member
(B) Clerical assistant
(C) Personnel manager
(D) Senior editor

57 What does the woman imply when she says, "more doesn't necessarily mean better"?
(A) She wants to hire more people.
(B) She focuses on quality than quantity.
(C) She thinks the company benefits could be improved.
(D) She needs to move to another branch.

58 Why do the speakers mention Wednesday?
(A) The woman is leaving for a business trip on that day.
(B) They need to make a reservation by then.
(C) The woman is available to meet people then.
(D) They need to launch a new magazine on that day.

Questions 59-61 refer to the following conversation.

M Ms. Lorain, after reviewing your résumé and interviewing you, we've decided to offer you a job as a sales manager at our company.

W Thank you, Mr. Sanderson. I'd like to accept that offer. When I first heard about this position, I knew this would be the perfect opportunity to utilize my background in marketing.

M Great. We expect a lot from you. Now, you'll have to see Ms. Evans in Human Resources to complete some forms and to sign the contract. By the way, when can you start? Would two weeks be long enough to wrap things up at your current company?

W Actually, I need at least a month if that's okay with you.

59 What kind of job is being offered?
(A) Marketing assistant
(B) Sales manager
(C) Human Resources director
(D) Delivery person

60 Why should the woman visit the Personnel Department?
(A) To pick up an application
(B) To hand in her résumé
(C) To meet the personnel director
(D) To fill out some paperwork

61 When does the woman say she could start working?
(A) In one week
(B) In two weeks
(C) In four weeks
(D) In two months

Questions 62-64 refer to the following conversation with three speakers.

M1 Have you guys realized we only have one month before the next stockholders' meeting? How are the preparations coming along?

W Yes, the venue was confirmed, and I'm searching for a proper caterer for the after-meeting reception.

M2 And we're also working on sending the annual report to all of our major stockholders.

W That reminds me. Would you like it printed in black and white or in color?

M2 I think our customers love them in color.

W I agree. Printing in color is more expensive, but it will be worth every penny.

M1 Good point. Our sales have increased substantially after introducing a new printer, so I think we can afford to go with color this year.

W That's good news. I'll contact the printer right away.

62 What are the speakers mainly discussing?
(A) Getting ready for an event
(B) Ordering some office supplies
(C) Sending out product catalogues
(D) Having the office painted

63 What does the woman ask the men to decide?
(A) The type of equipment
(B) The size of an order
(C) The method of delivery
(D) The appearance of a document

64 What does the woman mean when she says, "it will be worth every penny"?
(A) They don't have enough money.
(B) They need to postpone the meeting.
(C) The price of the stock has gone up.
(D) They should choose the color option.

Questions 65-67 refer to the following conversation and form.

W Excuse me, sir. I was on the one twenty Northwest Airlines flight from Michigan, and my luggage didn't arrive at baggage claim with everyone else's. I've been waiting for almost an hour.

M It might have been misdirected. You have to file a lost luggage report at your airline's service counter. Most of the time, lost luggage is returned to its owner within a few hours.

W Thank you. Can you tell me where I can find the service desk for Northwest Airlines?

M Its customer service desk is on the first floor next to the security office in Terminal G.

W Thank you so much.

M Be sure to indicate a personal phone number so that you can be reached right away once your luggage is found.

65 What is the woman's concern?
(A) Her arrival time has been changed.
(B) She is unable to locate her bags.
(C) She might miss her connecting flight.
(D) She is late for her appointment.

66 Where does the man suggest the woman go?
(A) To the international terminal
(B) To the customer service desk
(C) To the baggage claim area
(D) To the security office

67 Look at the graphic. Which information should be changed?
(A) Flight number
(B) Flight time
(C) Date of travel
(D) Contact information

Questions 68-70 refer to the following conversation and list.

W Warrick, how have the new vehicles been doing internationally?

M All of the foreign branches made some progress last year, but some regions had more difficult times than other places.

W We just closed down the branch which made the lowest increase in sales, so let's leave it out of the discussion. Then what seems to be the problem in the United States and Europe?

M I think our prices don't match those of other brands. In the small-to-medium-sized car market, customers prefer cars with basic features and reasonable prices both in America and Europe.

W Other companies have models with similar features and prices, but they are selling better than ours.

M Hmm... Good point. Well, if that's not the problem, then I think we should try a new marketing strategy, such as using a different advertising media.

68 What are the speakers discussing?
(A) The shipment of parts
(B) Overseas sales
(C) Travel destinations
(D) International trade

69 Look at the graphic. Which region will the speakers NOT address?
(A) The United States (B) Europe
(C) Middle East (D) Africa

70 What does the man suggest?
(A) Reducing the price by half
(B) Adding some new features
(C) Modifying current designs
(D) Changing marketing plans

Part 4

Questions 71-73 refer to the following news report.

Thank you for listening to FM 95.7, your local station for news, traffic, and weather. I'm Bill Henderson with your hourly traffic update. There is a thirty-minute delay on Burton Avenue near Huntington Park due to repair work on the southbound lanes. You might want to take an alternate route to avoid the delay. Traffic is moving smoothly on all of the other major roads. In addition, this is just a reminder that this Saturday night, there will be a fireworks festival near the Huntington River, so mark your calendars for that event. We'll be right back with the top local news after some short commercials from our sponsors.

71 What is the report about?
(A) Some recent elections
(B) The local weather
(C) The area traffic
(D) A traffic accident

72 Why is there a delay on Burton Avenue?
(A) There is a local festival.
(B) There is some construction work.
(C) There is a stalled car.
(D) There are bad weather conditions.

73 What will the listeners most likely hear next?
(A) Local news
(B) Advertisements
(C) The weather forecast
(D) An event schedule

Questions 74-76 refer to the following introduction.

Ladies and gentlemen, I'm pleased to announce this year's sales employee of the year award goes to Ms. Jennifer Wong. Ms. Wong started her career at Fantasy World two years ago, and in that short time, she has helped to double the sales of children's toys and publications at the Kerrytown branch, and profits there went up almost thirty-five percent. She is responsible for developing new promotional events such as book-reading sessions and demonstrations targeting children. Now, let's invite Ms. Wong to the stage and listen to the secrets to her success.

74 What is the purpose of the introduction?
(A) To launch an advertising campaign
(B) To recognize an employee's work
(C) To welcome a new vice president
(D) To announce the retirement of an employee

75 In what department does Ms. Wong work?
(A) The product development team
(B) The overseas marketing team
(C) The accounting team
(D) The sales team

76 What will probably happen next?
(A) A new product will be demonstrated.
(B) A video will be shown.
(C) A speech will be given.
(D) The audience will listen to a book reading.

Questions 77-79 refer to the following telephone message.

Hello, Mr. Booth. My name is Sandy, and I'm calling from Dr. Choi's office. You called yesterday to ask about refilling your medication, and I asked the doctor. Well, Dr. Choi said you have to visit the office and see him in order to have your prescription filled. You haven't had a physical examination in over a year. So Dr. Choi wants to check your progress before he gives you any more medication. Please give me a call to set up an appointment. We're open from Monday through Friday between nine and five.

77 Where does the speaker most likely work?
(A) At a pharmaceutical company
(B) At a medical facility
(C) At an employment agency
(D) At a laboratory research center

78 Why did the listener contact the speaker?
(A) To refill a prescription
(B) To change an appointment
(C) To ask about the business hours
(D) To find out the results of a test

79 Why does the Dr. Choi want to see the listener?
(A) To prescribe new medicine
(B) To request payment
(C) To ask him to fill out a form
(D) To examine him

Questions 80-82 refer to the following telephone message.

Hi, Mr. Sherman. I guess you're out of the office now. This is Ashley Benson from the public relations division. I have an important presentation for my clients scheduled in the main conference hall tomorrow morning at eleven. The problem is that when I rehearsed it with my staff today, the projector did not work properly. Even though the machine was on, nothing was projected on the screen. We need to show many visuals and charts to our clients. We cannot do that without proper projection equipment. Could you send someone to the conference room right away? Maybe we need a new projector. I'm not sure. Please give me a call on my mobile phone. I'll be waiting to hear from you.

80 Why is the speaker making the call?
(A) To order a new projector
(B) To return a product
(C) To reserve a conference room
(D) To report a problem

81 What problem does the speaker mention?
(A) A piece of equipment is out of stock.
(B) An important meeting was canceled.
(C) Some equipment malfunctioned.
(D) There were not enough participants.

82 What does the speaker ask the listener to do?
(A) Send a technician
(B) Book a venue
(C) Review a manual
(D) Prepare a presentation

Questions 83-85 refer to the following announcement.

Good morning, Huntsville Supermarket patrons. We proudly present our supermarket's own line of ice cream and frozen yogurt available on aisle ten. The ice cream comes in five different flavors, including vanilla, chocolate, and strawberry. It is good alone or with fresh baked pies from the bakery section. They come in easy-to-carry plastic cups, and we're offering a special one-day sale on all flavors. If you buy two cups of any flavor, we will give you the third one for free. But remember that these great deals are for today only. So make sure you check them out today and save money for you and your family!

83 What product is being promoted?
(A) Frozen beverages (B) Fresh fruits
(C) Baked goods (D) Ice cream

84 What is said about the product packaging?
(A) It is strong and durable.
(B) It is convenient to carry.
(C) It is made from recycled materials.
(D) It keeps the product fresh.

85 What does the speaker mean when she says, "make sure you check them out today"?
(A) Customers should find out about the closing time.
(B) Customers should become members.
(C) Customers should present special coupons.
(D) Customers should purchase the sale items.

Questions 86-88 refer to the following news report.

Now, in local news, the Newberry Scientific Society announced its plans to begin construction of a new regional museum. The president of the society, Richard Olson, is responsible for raising the necessary funds for the project. He hopes that many local business owners will participate to improve the quality of scientific education in the area. The museum plans to have hands-on experiment rooms and exhibition halls where children and adults can see, touch, and learn all the basic concepts of science. They will also have a small library with books on science from other countries. Mr. Olson said the society is eager to take the next step and to finalize the design of the building as early as next month.

86 What is the report mainly about?
(A) A famous scientific researcher
(B) The history of a local community
(C) A world-famous exhibit
(D) The construction of a museum

87 Who is Richard Olson?
(A) An architect (B) A president
(C) A librarian (D) A reporter

88 What is the next step in the project?
(A) Completing the architectural design
(B) Hiring a consultant for the construction
(C) Selecting a suitable site for the building
(D) Creating a budget to support the project

Questions 89-91 refer to the following announcement.

Good morning, employees. Today is Friday, September fifteenth. This announcement is to remind you about our new policy, which will be effective starting next Monday. For security reasons, all employees must wear their new identification badges before entering the facility and while on the factory floor. It's a must for all employees. The new photo ID card contains information about you and your department and will be used to enter and exit the building. This will allow us to maintain a safe environment on the plant floor. If you haven't received your new ID yet, you must contact the Human Resources office immediately to get one. There is a notice on the bulletin board in the employee lounge that explains the details of the new system. Please refer to it. Now, let's start the day at Bluemont Motors.

89 What is the purpose of the talk?
(A) To introduce a new plant manager
(B) To promote a new product
(C) To identify problems on the factory floor
(D) To explain a new security policy

90 What does the speaker mean when he says, "It's a must"?
(A) It's mandatory for all employees to wear badges.
(B) The work must be done by the end of the day.
(C) Access to the building is restricted to staff only.
(D) Some employees have to find new jobs.

91 What should the listeners do if they have not received their cards yet?
(A) Contact the personnel office
(B) Go to the employee lounge
(C) Visit the company Web site
(D) Report to their supervisors

Questions 92-94 refer to the following telephone message and form.

Hi, Kathy. This is Lana. I'm calling about the plans for next week's dealers meeting. I'm taking care of the presentations and the conference materials. I'd like you to take charge of the meal after the meeting. Could you call the caterer and let them know that we are expecting forty-five people? We also need some vegetarian options for the main course. Let's get together tomorrow to finalize all the details of the meeting and the reception. This year, we have some great speakers and programs. I hope everything goes well.

92 What is the message mainly about?
(A) Organizing the committee
(B) Hiring additional staffers
(C) Preparing for a meeting
(D) Making a hotel reservation

93 Look at the graphic. According to the speaker, what information needs to be changed?
(A) Client
(B) Date
(C) Number of People
(D) Special Request

94 Why does the speaker want to meet with the listener?
(A) To change the date of the event
(B) To evaluate some company records
(C) To set up some equipment together
(D) To make some final decisions on details

Questions 95-97 refer to the following announcement and program.

Thank you for coming to the opening day of the public speaking seminar. As you can see in your program, we have an exciting day for you today. But before we start, I have a brief announcement about the schedule. Today's keynote speech on image training at nine thirty will be delayed by thirty minutes and will start at ten o'clock due to some technical difficulties in meeting room B. We're sorry for the inconvenience, but I'm sure the speech will be worth the wait. There will be a break for lunch at noon as scheduled. For your convenience, we've provided a list of local restaurants on the back page of the program, and you can also visit the downstairs cafeteria. In the afternoon, we will break into groups, and you can either take an intensive workshop at two o'clock or visit the exhibition halls. I hope you enjoy everything we have prepared for you.

95 What is the purpose of the announcement?
(A) To promote local restaurants
(B) To present an award
(C) To provide an overview of a schedule
(D) To introduce a new presenter

96 Look at the graphic. What program do the participants have to wait 30 minutes for?
(A) Dr. Randolph's
(B) Ms. Nelson's
(C) Workshop
(D) Ms. Connelly's

97 Where can the listeners find a list of restaurants?
(A) On the bulletin board
(B) At the information desk
(C) On a local map
(D) In the conference program

Questions 98-100 refer to the following excerpt from a meeting and schedule.

Everyone, listen carefully. The company's board of directors will be visiting our factory on July tenth, which is three weeks from today. As a result, special departmental meetings have been scheduled throughout next week in the main meeting room. At these meetings, as department managers, you'll have to come up with a list of things that can be improved before the board's visit. The schedule is posted on the bulletin board in the employee lounge. There will be one change though. The meeting for quality control has been pushed back to the following day, Friday, because Mr. Brown, the factory supervisor, will be out of town on Thursday. Be sure to check to see what time your department's meeting will be held. This is a very important matter. We need to make the best impression possible on our board members. I expect your full support in the coming weeks.

98 When is the board of directors scheduled to visit?
(A) Before the end of the day
(B) Tomorrow
(C) Next week
(D) In three weeks

99 What will each department discuss at the meetings?
(A) Preparations for a visit
(B) Transfers to a different location
(C) Staff evaluations by the personnel division
(D) The revision of the meeting schedule

100 Look at the graphic. According to the speaker, when will the meeting for Quality Control be held?
(A) On June 21
(B) On June 22
(C) On June 23
(D) On June 24

TEST 04

| p.56

1	(D)	2	(B)	3	(A)	4	(A)	5	(B)
6	(D)	7	(A)	8	(C)	9	(A)	10	(A)
11	(A)	12	(C)	13	(A)	14	(B)	15	(A)
16	(C)	17	(A)	18	(C)	19	(A)	20	(B)
21	(B)	22	(B)	23	(C)	24	(C)	25	(A)
26	(A)	27	(A)	28	(B)	29	(C)	30	(C)
31	(B)	32	(A)	33	(D)	34	(B)	35	(B)
36	(A)	37	(C)	38	(B)	39	(A)	40	(C)
41	(A)	42	(B)	43	(D)	44	(C)	45	(C)
46	(D)	47	(A)	48	(C)	49	(B)	50	(D)
51	(A)	52	(C)	53	(B)	54	(B)	55	(A)
56	(A)	57	(B)	58	(C)	59	(B)	60	(C)
61	(B)	62	(D)	63	(C)	64	(C)	65	(C)
66	(A)	67	(A)	68	(C)	69	(A)	70	(A)
71	(C)	72	(C)	73	(A)	74	(A)	75	(D)
76	(B)	77	(C)	78	(B)	79	(D)	80	(A)
81	(A)	82	(D)	83	(B)	84	(A)	85	(D)
86	(A)	87	(C)	88	(C)	89	(D)	90	(A)
91	(B)	92	(C)	93	(D)	94	(C)	95	(A)
96	(A)	97	(C)	98	(A)	99	(C)	100	(A)

Part 1

1 (A) A man is examining a patient.
(B) A man is taking off his safety goggles.
(C) A man is working on a laptop computer.
(D) A man is wearing a lab coat.

2 (A) Some cars are parked along the road.
(B) Several bicycles have been secured to the post.
(C) A cyclist is riding past the bus station.
(D) Some people are waiting in line for a bus.

3 (A) The hills are covered with trees and grass.
(B) A path leads to a village.
(C) Some trees are being planted.
(D) People are enjoying the view from the top of the mountain.

4 (A) Chairs have been set up around the tables.
(B) Some plates have been piled on the counter.
(C) Dishes of food have been set on the tables.
(D) The restaurant is closed.

5 (A) A car is being serviced at a repair shop.
(B) The trunk of the car has been left open.
(C) A man is packing his suitcase.
(D) A man is giving a woman a ride.

6 (A) There is a child sitting on the bench.
(B) There are children playing a game indoors.
(C) The ride is currently unavailable.
(D) Some children are enjoying their time on the playground.

Part 2

7 Where is the trade fair taking place?
(A) At the convention center.
(B) This Friday.
(C) The weather turned fair.

8 Which project should I work on next?
(A) It's due on the second.
(B) This afternoon, I think.
(C) The one with the Stars Company.

9 Who's looking into the problems with the computer?
(A) No one has had a chance yet.
(B) David is looking for a job.
(C) I surf the Internet every morning.

10 Isn't the CCTV system supposed to be installed today?
(A) No, they changed the schedule.
(B) Yes, I think it's the camera.
(C) They are everywhere.

11 Are you still waiting for Ms. Williams to call?
(A) No, I talked to her this morning.
(B) No, I can't wait.
(C) No way. She is highly qualified for it.

12 Is the shopping mall closed on Sundays?
(A) Yes, I bought it last weekend.
(B) No, close to the street.
(C) No, it's open every day.

13 Why is the factory increasing its hours of operation?
(A) To fill a special order.
(B) Because he is too busy.
(C) I think more employees can come then.

14 Could you tell me when parking rates will go up?
(A) The price will rise by five percent.
(B) During the first week of April.
(C) I live right next to the parking lot.

15 Lisa, you used to live in Tokyo, didn't you?
(A) When I was a child.
(B) I'm used to doing this.
(C) The day after tomorrow.

16 How did you manage to land a good job?
(A) I'm a marketing manager.
(B) I've been working for two years now.
(C) My interview went well.

17 Don't you want to bring a laptop to the meeting?
(A) Yes, it's in my bag.
(B) Why don't you try it again?
(C) No, I'll meet some clients.

18 Let's go for a walk in the park during our lunch break.
(A) No, it's not broken.
(B) I'll have some sandwiches for lunch.
(C) Sure, we need some fresh air.

19 Excuse me. When will Dr. Tyler be available?
(A) I'm afraid she's busy all day.
(B) It's available now.
(C) Yes, the gate is open 24 hours a day.

20 Why is Central Park so crowded today?
(A) Yes, I agree with you.
(B) There's a free concert.
(C) Let's go there.

21 Don't forget to order more office supplies.
(A) I need to get all these documents in order by today.
(B) Don't worry. I won't.
(C) Yes, it was surprising news.

22 Melissa's flight is scheduled to arrive at six, isn't it?
(A) No, there will be eight people.
(B) I'll call the airline to find out.
(C) It's a live broadcast.

23 How can I get the light fixture replaced?
(A) The place is worth a visit.
(B) The one on the right.
(C) Check with the maintenance staff.

24 I worked until three in the morning due to the project.
(A) I have been to three countries so far.
(B) Why did you get up so early?
(C) You must be exhausted.

25 Is the laboratory going to be remodeled soon?
(A) Actually, the work has already begun.
(B) The lab sent it yesterday.
(C) When are you planning to remodel your house?

26 What does the seminar registration fee include?
(A) All conference sessions and meals.
(B) You can register in the lobby.
(C) Yes, the fee is $500 for each person.

27 Do you need a ride when you go to the airport?
(A) Thanks. That would be a big help.
(B) Yes, I'll pick him up later.
(C) Whenever he needs it.

28 I'd like to cancel my reservation for this Saturday, please.
(A) After this weekend.
(B) I can help you with that.
(C) No, it's been postponed.

29 Is Dr. Bella coming to the seminar in person, or will she attend it online?
(A) As soon as you arrive at the clinic.
(B) I'd rather take this one.
(C) She will be here soon.

30 Have you sent out promotional e-mails to our customers?
(A) Because sales were high.
(B) You will be promoted soon.
(C) I haven't received the list yet.

31 Can you tell all the managers about the schedule changes, or would you like me to do it?
(A) I don't think they'll be able to though.
(B) I'm sorry, but I'm too busy today.
(C) I'll let her know.

Part 3

Questions 32-34 refer to the following conversation.

M Do you know when the sales representatives from the Beijing office will be arriving? I've been looking forward to meeting them, but I'm leaving for Helsinki on Friday.

W Oh, you won't miss them. All the international representatives are coming on Tuesday.

M That's good. We talked so often on the telephone, and all of them were very nice.

W I know. The welcome reception on Wednesday evening will give everyone else in the Sales Department a chance to get to know one another.

32 Who most likely are the speakers?
(A) Sales representatives
(B) Travel agents
(C) Hotel receptionists
(D) Telephone operators

33 What are the speakers discussing?
(A) Going to a conference
(B) Spending holidays overseas
(C) Hiring new staff members
(D) Meeting colleagues from another office

34 Where will the speakers most likely go on Wednesday?
(A) To a sales presentation
(B) To a social event
(C) To an airport
(D) To a job interview

Questions 35-37 refer to the following conversation.

W Have you called the Technical Department yet? These documents have to be sent to the downtown office today by fax. However, the fax machine is still down.

M I called them this morning, but they said they wouldn't be able to send a technician until next week.

W The deadline for these documents is today. I guess I'll have to deliver them myself, but I have an important meeting with my client.

M Why don't I send the documents by e-mail? I can type all of them within an hour. It's the fastest way, isn't it?

35 What problem are the speakers discussing?
(A) A photocopier has not been delivered.
(B) A fax machine is not working.
(C) The downtown office is closed.
(D) An appointment has been canceled.

36 When is the deadline for submission?
(A) Today
(B) Tomorrow morning
(C) Tomorrow afternoon
(D) Next week

37 What does the man offer to do?
(A) Reschedule a meeting
(B) Contact a technician
(C) Send documents by e-mail
(D) Make some copies

Questions 38-40 refer to the following conversation.

M Hello. How may I help you?
W I'm looking for a print. Do you have the prints of the paintings in the exhibition?
M Sure, we have a lot of prints on sale. Which ones are you interested in?
W *Spring Thaw on Goose Pond* by Richard Lytle. I saw it displayed in the Modern Art Wing.
M Could you please tell me what it looks like? We have quite a few reproductions of Lytle's paintings, so I'm a little confused.
W Well, the painting was mostly blue and had some flowers in it.
M Okay, I see. That one is very popular. We have reproductions available in several different sizes. Come this way, and I'll show you some.

38 Where most likely are the speakers?
(A) At a printing shop
(B) In a museum gift shop
(C) On a street corner
(D) At a ticket office

39 What are the speakers talking about?
(A) A print of a painting
(B) A home renovation
(C) A sculpture exhibit
(D) A gallery tour

40 What will the woman most likely do next?
(A) Admire a painting
(B) Purchase a ticket
(C) Follow the clerk
(D) Meet a popular artist

Questions 41-43 refer to the following conversation.

M Good afternoon. *Daily News Chronicle* circulation desk. How may I help you?
W My copy of the *Daily News Chronicle* is all wet from the rain, and I can't read it. Could I have another one delivered, please?
M Oh, I'm sorry about that. You most certainly can. If you give me your name and address, I will have another copy sent to you as soon as the driver returns from his route.
W Oh thanks, I will, but you know, this isn't the first time that my paper's gotten wet. I wonder if you can ask the delivery person to put it on my porch from now on.

41 What is the problem?
(A) An item is damaged.
(B) A customer was overcharged.
(C) Some equipment is broken.
(D) An item was delivered to the wrong address.

42 What does the man agree to do?
(A) Give a discount
(B) Send another copy
(C) Call a delivery man
(D) Give some data

43 What does the woman request?
(A) Giving an opening address
(B) Renovating a porch
(C) Completing some forms
(D) Changing some delivery instructions

Questions 44-46 refer to the following conversation.

W Good morning. Have you heard from Carla about scheduling the marketing meeting for Wednesday?
M She just called me. The customer survey results she was expecting only came in this morning. She still has to analyze all the data, so she asked if we could move the meeting to Thursday.
W I am leaving on a business trip on Thursday afternoon. However, a morning meeting would be all right. Will you please call Carla and schedule the meeting for then?
M Certainly. I'll send you a text message as soon as I reach her.

44 Why did Carla request to change the meeting time?
(A) She is waiting for a customer.
(B) She has been on a business trip.
(C) Some information was delayed.
(D) A meeting room was not available.

45 When will the meeting most likely take place?
(A) On Wednesday morning
(B) On Wednesday evening
(C) On Thursday morning
(D) On Thursday afternoon

46 What will the man most likely do next?
(A) Make travel arrangements
(B) Prepare a marketing report
(C) Search for survey results
(D) Try to contact Carla

Questions 47-49 refer to the following conversation.

M Hi, Kate. It's Larry. I'm at the Baltimore Washington International Airport. Laura was supposed to give me a ride, but she isn't here. I tried calling her several times, but I can't reach her by phone. Do you know where she might be?
W Laura said your flight would be arriving at five. She must still be having lunch with her colleagues.
M Do you know when she'll be back in the office? If she'll be out for a while, I can just take a taxi or limousine.
W Hold on. She just walked in the office. I'll tell her you're waiting for her. She'll be there as soon as she can.

47 What is the man's problem?
(A) He does not have transportation now.
(B) He has lost his way in the airport.
(C) He forgot to take his bag with him.
(D) He is late for an appointment.

48 Where is the man?
(A) At an office (B) On a plane
(C) At an airport (D) In a taxi

49 What does the woman say she will tell Laura?
(A) The store is closing.
(B) The man is waiting.
(C) The flight was delayed.
(D) The clients have arrived.

Questions 50-52 refer to the following conversation.

W Good morning. How can I help you?

M I'd like to have a new sign made for my café. I really like the sign you made for the Japanese restaurant nearby. So I'd like to find out how much your company charges.

W Let me see. I could send someone to your store this afternoon to take some measurements and to give you a cost estimate and a catalog for a new sign. But I'm afraid our schedule is pretty full, so we won't be able to start right away. We could have it designed for you by next month though.

M Sure, that sounds fine. I'd just like to have it finished by the end of this year.

50 Where does the conversation take place?
(A) At a café
(B) At a hardware store
(C) At a restaurant
(D) At a sign-making company

51 What does the man request?
(A) A price estimate
(B) A discount
(C) A catalog
(D) A contact number

52 What concern does the woman mention?
(A) She won't be here until next month.
(B) An item is out of stock.
(C) Some work cannot be started immediately.
(D) A catalog is missing.

Questions 53-55 refer to the following conversation.

M Did you see the sales report? It says our printer sales went down by two percent last month.

W Really? That's strange. The Marketing Department was so busy promoting the new printers last month, weren't they?

M That's right. We have increased budgets for more advertisements and promotional events.

W And we were so glad to hear that our new printers received the highest scores in the quality evaluation. What do you think the problem is?

M Well, I'm afraid the printers may be priced too high. I think we'd better discuss this issue with the sales team as soon as possible.

W That's a good idea. How about this afternoon?

53 What are the speakers discussing?
(A) Developing a new product
(B) Sales performance
(C) Negotiating a contract
(D) Work assignments

54 What does the man say the problem is?
(A) The wrong address was given.
(B) The price of products is not reasonable.
(C) The workload is increasing in the marketing team.
(D) The quality of products needs to be improved.

55 What does the woman imply when she says, "That's a good idea"?
(A) She wants to hold a meeting.
(B) She needs to buy a new computer.
(C) She plans to make a plane reservation.
(D) She hopes to hire a sales representative.

Questions 56-58 refer to the following conversation.

M We received a lot of résumés for the legal assistant position we posted last month. I've been trying to narrow them down to a few applicants.

W The Legal Department is pretty short-handed right now. They really do need someone soon. When will you start the interview process?

M I plan to start contacting candidates today so that I can schedule the interviews this week. But with all the other projects I have to work on, I don't know if I can get through all the applications in time.

W Don't worry. I can give you a hand, so if you need help, let me know anytime.

56 What does the woman indicate about the Legal Department?
(A) It is understaffed.
(B) It recently hired some employees.
(C) It is being relocated.
(D) It requested more funds.

57 What does the man intend to do this week?
(A) Revise his résumé
(B) Arrange some interviews
(C) Apply for a license
(D) Ask for legal advice

58 Why is the man concerned?
(A) He has lost some documents.
(B) The applicants do not seem to be qualified.
(C) He may not be able to meet a deadline.
(D) He will soon run short of cash.

Questions 59-61 refer to the following conversation.

W Hi, Tom. This is Joanna. Would it be possible to give me a ride to work today?

M Unfortunately, my car is being fixed, and it won't be ready until tomorrow. By the way, what's wrong with your brother's car?

W He usually drops me off on his way to his office, but today, he had to leave early to meet a client.

M Well, I'm just going to take a taxi to work. Do you want to share one?

W That'd be nice. I'll be ready in ten minutes. Thank you, Tom.

M You're welcome. But you'd better make it in fifteen minutes. I still have a few things to do for my presentation today before I can leave.

59 What are the speakers mainly discussing?
(A) Meeting a client
(B) Sharing a ride
(C) Fixing a technical problem
(D) Leaving for a business trip

60 What does the woman mean when she says, "That'd be nice"?
(A) She wants to stop by a repair shop.
(B) She will contact a client.
(C) She agrees to take a taxi.
(D) She has to go to work early.

61 What will the man most likely do next?
(A) Book a taxi service
(B) Prepare for his presentation
(C) Contact a car repair shop
(D) Go to his office immediately

Questions 62-64 refer to the following conversation with three speakers.

M1 Look at the long line outside the window!

W This place must be popular with people around here.

M1 It was a good thing we hurried to have lunch before noon.

M2 You know, our firm did all the interior design work in this Italian restaurant.

W I know! I can't believe it! Even though I worked on the project, I have never eaten here.

M2 Neither have I, but I read a newspaper review about it. It said the chef is excellent.

M1 That's why I decided to bring our clients here tomorrow for lunch before we tour the building.

W Great choice. Not only will our clients have a nice lunch, but they'll also get to see our interior design work.

M1 That way, they may get some ideas about what they want for their own building.

62 Who most likely are the speakers?
(A) Tour guides
(B) Newspaper reporters
(C) Event planners
(D) Interior designers

63 What does the woman imply when she says, "I can't believe it"?
(A) She thinks the restaurant is not that good.
(B) She feels sorry for the men.
(C) She is pleased that the restaurant is popular.
(D) She disagrees with the men's opinion.

64 What will the clients do tomorrow after lunch?
(A) Sign a contract
(B) Choose a design
(C) Visit a building
(D) Provide opinions

Questions 65-67 refer to the following conversation and list.

W Good morning! Thank you for calling Comfort House Rental. How may I help you?

M I am looking for a furnished studio apartment.

W We have one studio apartment left for rent. We just finished renovating the kitchen and the bathroom a couple of weeks ago. The beds and the tables have also been purchased recently.

M That's great! I have a dog, and I also need a garage. How much is the monthly rate?

W It costs 2,500 U.S. dollars a month.

M Hmm... That's a little pricey. Could you let me think about it? I'll call you at the end of this week.

65 Look at the graphic. Which is the ideal place for the man?
(A) Syracuse (B) Bronx
(C) Bayside (D) Medford

66 What is the man concerned about the apartment?
(A) The rent is expensive.
(B) The garage needs repairing.
(C) The bathroom doesn't have enough space.
(D) The furniture is too old-fashioned.

67 When does the man say he will call the woman?
(A) This Friday
(B) Next Friday
(C) Next weekend
(D) In a couple of weeks

Questions 68-70 refer to the following conversation and timetable.

M Linda, have you seen the new film directed by Tomas Burton?

W No, I haven't seen it yet. But I saw an advertisement for it in a magazine and read some of the reviews. It is supposed to be wonderful.

M Actually, my sister and I wanted to see it last weekend, but the tickets were all sold out.

W You should have made a reservation in advance.

M Right! So I am going to surf the Internet to get some tickets for tonight. I can't wait! Would you like to join us? I could get a ticket for you if you want.

W Thanks for asking. But I have a lot of work to do tonight to prepare for tomorrow's company banquet. In fact, I'm on my way to meet with the company president now to discuss some final details.

68 Look at the graphic. Which movie will the man most likely see tonight?
(A) *Great Banquet* (B) *Sisters*
(C) *Heartbreak* (D) *Forever Love*

69 What does the man offer to do?
(A) Purchase a ticket
(B) Make dinner reservations
(C) Review a meeting agenda
(D) Create an advertisement

70 What does the woman say she will do tonight?
(A) Organize a company event
(B) Attend a formal banquet
(C) Watch a movie at home
(D) Meet with Tomas Burton

Part 4

Questions 71-73 refer to the following announcement.

The new school year is approaching fast, which means it's time to start thinking about buying a yearly membership. If you purchase before August fifteenth, you will receive thirty percent off your membership. Membership includes access to regular exhibitions, a fifty percent discount on special exhibits, and twenty percent off all merchandise in the gift shop. Annual memberships go on sale on August first. Check out our Web site in the coming weeks to see the list of exhibitions between September and May.

71 Why is the announcement being made?
(A) To introduce a staff member
(B) To announce a new system
(C) To promote a special offer
(D) To evaluate a project

72 When can people first purchase annual memberships?
(A) In January (B) In May
(C) In August (D) In September

73 What type of benefits can members enjoy?
(A) Discounts
(B) Free gifts
(C) Advance reservation
(D) Admission to all exhibitions

Questions 74-76 refer to the following advertisement.

Sometimes when we travel, we are embarrassed that we can't keep up with everything. Now, the new High-Tech Traveler's Watch will solve all your problems. By gathering data from a lot of other wristwatches, we were able to combine the best features of all of them. The watches were subjected to various events suffered during people's trips. They were dropped onto concrete, stuck between elevator doors, scratched, and dropped in water. Yet they not only function perfectly, but their surfaces also retain their perfect shine. The High-Tech Traveler's Watch is for the business, recreational, or adventure traveler. Before the end of this month, you can save up to twenty percent by making a purchase of our high-quality products.

74 What product is being advertised?
(A) A wristwatch
(B) A suitcase
(C) A map
(D) A compass

75 What is true about the product?
(A) It can be purchased in different sizes.
(B) It has been inspected by experts.
(C) It is available in many colors.
(D) It is rugged and waterproof.

76 What special offer is mentioned?
(A) A free coupon with every purchase
(B) A twenty-percent reduction in price
(C) A discount on a traveler's bag
(D) A two-year warranty

Questions 77-79 refer to the following talk.

The finance director of Russel Oil Refineries, James Moore, announced his retirement yesterday, creating an opening for someone new to move into his prestigious position. He has worked for Russel for over thirty-five years, and his colleagues will miss him a lot. The company is currently accepting applications for the position. The position requires not only a four-year degree in finance or economics but also at least ten years of experience in a senior management position. Preference will be given to bilingual candidates, especially those fluent in Russian. The salary range is 100,000~110,000 dollars. Please contact Human Resources for detailed information.

77 What is the purpose of the talk?
(A) To discuss Mr. Moore's promotion
(B) To advertise a new product
(C) To announce a job opening
(D) To review salary increases

78 What is James Moore's previous position?
(A) Economics professor
(B) Director of finance
(C) Director of Human Resources
(D) Senior manager

79 How long has Mr. Moore worked for Russel?
(A) For over 4 years
(B) For over 10 years
(C) For over 20 years
(D) For over 35 years

Questions 80-82 refer to the following telephone message.

Hello, Ms. Graves. This is Gary McMillan, the manager of Green Outdoor Planning. Thank you for your inquiry regarding employment at our firm. At this time, all our positions are filled. I will keep your application on file for review in August for possible openings at the Hampton and Baxter branch offices. Our local branches are sure to need extra help at that time, which could possibly lead to something more permanent. During the fall season, Green Outdoor Planning more than doubles in activity. We plan outdoor events such as weddings, picnics, and family reunions for our valuable customers. If you are still interested in a position with Green Outdoor Planning by the end of August, please contact our regional offices. Best of luck in your career, and I hope to hear from you again. Thank you.

80 Who most likely is the listener?
(A) A job applicant
(B) An event planner
(C) A recruiting manager
(D) An entertainer

81 What is the purpose of the message?
(A) To give some feedback
(B) To provide a schedule
(C) To explain a process
(D) To describe an event

82 What does the speaker want the listener to do?
(A) Review her application
(B) Get more qualifications
(C) Contact the headquarters
(D) Apply again later

Questions 83-85 refer to the following announcement.

Attention, all library patrons. My name is Rina Donnell, and I am from the Riverbend County Library. As you know, the sidewalk to the main entrance of the library has been in need of repairs for some time. The repair work for the entrance to the building will be done during the week of June tenth to sixteenth. During the repairs, patrons will not be able to access the main entrance, so you are asked to utilize the south entrance on eighth Avenue. Please make sure to do that. Parking near the main entrance will also be limited by construction, so you are encouraged to use the parking facilities at the post office, which is directly across from the library. Thank you for your patience. We apologize for any inconvenience.

83 Where is the announcement probably being made?
(A) In a post office
(B) In a library
(C) In a repair shop
(D) In a construction company

84 What will take place beginning on June 10?
(A) A main entrance will be closed.
(B) A parking lot will be renovated.
(C) A post office will reopen.
(D) The south entrance will be inaccessible.

85 What does the speaker mean when she says, "make sure to do that"?
(A) Patrons should understand why the library was built.
(B) Employees should find out the name of construction company.
(C) She has to check who built the post office.
(D) Patrons should know which alternate entrance to use.

Questions 86-88 refer to the following talk.

Welcome, everyone, to this year's global conference on community health. We're thrilled that there will be presentations by more than 200 professionals working for various community health programs all around the world. Our presenters will be sharing their experiences, research results, and ideas for providing medical treatment to patients. Before I introduce our plenary speakers, I have an important reminder about the small group sessions in the program. Due to limited space, advanced registration was required to participate in these sessions. You should have found tickets for every event you registered for in your welcome packet. If you were expecting tickets but didn't receive any, be sure to check our Web site to confirm that you are registered.

86 What is the main topic of the conference?
(A) Community health
(B) Research methods
(C) Web site design
(D) Medical products

87 What does the speaker say about the small group sessions?
(A) They will be held in several locations.
(B) They are not listed in the program.
(C) They require preregistration.
(D) They feature product demonstrations.

88 According to the speaker, what can the listeners find on the Web site?
(A) Research reports
(B) An evaluation form
(C) Registration confirmation
(D) A program schedule

Questions 89-91 refer to the following telephone message.

This is a message from Brian Martin with Human Publishers. Our offices in New Orleans were damaged by a hurricane over the weekend, and all of the factory pictures you sent us last week were destroyed. Here's the thing. I realize this is short notice, but we desperately need them by tomorrow to meet our printing deadline. Would it be possible for you to have a second set printed and sent to me by express mail? I will pay to have the items delivered. Please contact me as soon as possible to discuss this urgent matter. Thank you, Chris.

89 Where does the speaker probably work?
(A) At a delivery company
(B) At a factory
(C) At a photo studio
(D) At a publishing company

90 What does the speaker imply when he says, "Here's the thing"?
(A) He has to replace copies of some photographs quickly.
(B) He needs to have some pictures taken again.
(C) He wants some books reprinted.
(D) He will visit New Orleans tomorrow.

91 What does the speaker offer to do?
(A) Work overtime
(B) Pay a fee
(C) Send pictures by e-mail
(D) Extend a deadline

Questions 92-94 refer to the following recorded message and list.

Hello. This is Andrea Gordon. I'm calling from Discovery Scientific Instruments. This message is for Dr. Robert Williamson. You placed an order for five microscopes, fifteen test tubes, and ten pairs of protective gloves on our Web site the day before yesterday. I want to ask you something about the specifications for the products you want, and I'd like to check on them before shipping your order. Could you please call me back today before six or tomorrow between nine and six? My phone number is 012-234-9011. I will be waiting to hear from you.

92 What is the purpose of the message?
(A) To change an order
(B) To announce a special event
(C) To confirm an order of supplies
(D) To request a delivery address

93 Look at the graphic. What item should be removed from the list?
(A) Item 1 (B) Item 2
(C) Item 3 (D) Item 4

94 What does the speaker ask the listener to do?
(A) Mail a signed contract
(B) Provide a telephone number
(C) Return a phone call
(D) Gather information

Questions 95-97 refer to the following announcement and program.

Attention, all staffers. I would like to announce an upcoming training seminar that I encourage everyone to attend. It is not mandatory, but I believe everyone would benefit from participating in it. It will be held in the auditorium on January tenth from 9 A.M. to 12 P.M. If you are interested in attending, you must register before January eighth. From what I understand, seating is limited, so you should register as early as possible. I'd also like to mention that a senior engineer of ours, Ken Shelton, will be speaking during the seminar. I hope many of you support him and listen to his presentation. Thank you.

95 What is the purpose of the announcement?
(A) To notify employees of an upcoming event
(B) To report a schedule change
(C) To highlight a company's success
(D) To promote a conference that Mr. Shelton is hosting

96 By when should the listeners register for the seminar?
(A) Before January 8
(B) After January 8
(C) After January 10
(D) On January 10

97 Look at the graphic. Which presentation are the listeners especially encouraged to attend?
(A) Opening address
(B) Dynamic Shifts
(C) Overseas Markets
(D) The Global Economy

Questions 98-100 refer to the following excerpt from a meeting and chart.

Welcome to our weekly sales meeting today. As you know, we recently developed our new product, Bright Cleanette Sweeper. This new vacuum cleaner is proven to eliminate dirt ninety-nine percent on carpets more effectively than other models. Even hard-to-clean stains are removed easily by using its special feature. During the last month, we conducted a customer survey on the appliance, and I'd like to discuss the results with all of you. Now, let's look at the graph results. How surprising they are! The results are not what we had expected. Mr. Dalton, one of our sales representatives, will talk about why this age group is the most satisfied with our product. Okay. Mr. Dalton, are you ready?

98 Where does the speaker most likely work?
(A) At an electronics company
(B) At an office supply store
(C) At a car manufacturer
(D) At an Internet-service provider

99 What is one advantage of the Bright Cleanette Sweeper?
(A) It is recommended by experts.
(B) It is economical to buy.
(C) It removes stains easily.
(D) It is lightweight.

100 Look at the graphic. What age group will Mr. Dalton talk about?
(A) 21-30
(B) 41-50
(C) 51-60
(D) Over 61

TEST 05

| p.70

1	(B)	2	(C)	3	(A)	4	(B)	5	(B)
6	(D)	7	(B)	8	(C)	9	(B)	10	(C)
11	(C)	12	(B)	13	(A)	14	(A)	15	(C)
16	(B)	17	(C)	18	(A)	19	(A)	20	(B)
21	(B)	22	(B)	23	(A)	24	(B)	25	(C)
26	(A)	27	(C)	28	(C)	29	(A)	30	(C)
31	(C)	32	(C)	33	(C)	34	(A)	35	(C)
36	(B)	37	(A)	38	(A)	39	(C)	40	(B)
41	(B)	42	(A)	43	(C)	44	(D)	45	(D)
46	(C)	47	(B)	48	(B)	49	(D)	50	(D)
51	(B)	52	(C)	53	(C)	54	(D)	55	(A)
56	(B)	57	(A)	58	(C)	59	(A)	60	(B)
61	(D)	62	(B)	63	(D)	64	(D)	65	(C)
66	(A)	67	(B)	68	(D)	69	(C)	70	(D)
71	(B)	72	(A)	73	(C)	74	(C)	75	(B)
76	(D)	77	(B)	78	(D)	79	(A)	80	(B)
81	(C)	82	(D)	83	(B)	84	(C)	85	(D)
86	(D)	87	(A)	88	(D)	89	(A)	90	(C)
91	(D)	92	(A)	93	(D)	94	(C)	95	(C)
96	(C)	97	(B)	98	(C)	99	(D)	100	(A)

Part 1

1 (A) He is spraying some paint.
(B) He is hammering a nail.
(C) He is writing on the board.
(D) He is lifting some wood.

2 (A) Both of them are riding on horseback.
(B) The woman is putting on a straw hat.
(C) The man is walking ahead of the woman.
(D) They are feeding the horse together.

3 (A) The lawn is divided by a fence.
(B) The lawn is being mowed.
(C) The grass is being watered.
(D) They are walking under the shade.

4 (A) The man is resting near the bridge.
(B) The man is crossing over a stream.
(C) The man is filling his backpack.
(D) The man is walking along the beach.

5 (A) A box is being delivered to the owner.
(B) A box is being carried outdoors.
(C) They are opening some crates.
(D) They are wrapping some packages.

6 (A) The table is being set for a dinner party.
(B) They are picking some flowers for customers.
(C) They are sitting around the table.
(D) There is a floral centerpiece on the table.

Part 2

7 Where is the convention center?
(A) I need to attend a conference.
(B) Right across from the hospital.
(C) At seven o'clock in the morning.

8 Who delivered this package?
(A) The shipment was delayed.
(B) I needed some stamps.
(C) Someone from the mailroom.

9 Can you help me find my seat?
(A) That's okay. I'm fine.
(B) Of course. Please follow me.
(C) Sorry. All our tables are booked.

10 When will the shipment arrive?
(A) Probably by ship.
(B) I already ordered it last week.
(C) Tomorrow morning.

11 Why didn't you buy the smaller bag?
(A) The smaller, the better.
(B) I put the receipt in the bag.
(C) Because I didn't like the design.

12 How often should we change the engine oil?
(A) We should change it first.
(B) Why don't we check the manual?
(C) The repair shop is down the street.

13 Do you think you could close the window behind you?
(A) Sure, no problem.
(B) No, I think it's in front of you.
(C) Don't worry. We'll reopen tomorrow morning.

14 What's the problem with the annual report?
(A) It has a few spelling mistakes.
(B) The market doesn't open until next Monday.
(C) She's probably on a business trip today.

15 When is Jessica going to order office supplies for the whole department?
(A) I'm afraid the department store is closed today.
(B) She's not going to the party.
(C) She already did it yesterday.

16 The company picnic has been postponed.
(A) It should be held outside if the weather permits.
(B) Too bad. You were looking forward to it.
(C) Actually, today is better for me.

17 Which Web site is your favorite?
(A) I like vanilla ice cream the most.
(B) You could register online.
(C) This one looks more professional.

18 This form is difficult to fill out, isn't it?
(A) Yes, I'm not sure what to do with it.
(B) I found the exam is rather easy.
(C) Yes, the due date is tomorrow.

19 Did you make it to the annual conference?
(A) No, but I'll definitely go next year.
(B) No, but we also take monthly installments.
(C) Yes, she wants to go to the concert with you.

20 Do you prefer black and white film or color film for your camera?
(A) The picture is a little blurry.
(B) Actually, I use both.
(C) It comes in three different colors.

21 How do you like your new laptop computer?
(A) The printer is working fine so far.
(B) It's very convenient.
(C) That's a good idea. I'd love to buy one, too.

22 Are we having a meeting in their office or ours?
(A) I'm glad to meet you.
(B) Ours, I think.
(C) Put them over here.

23 Would you like it to be gift-wrapped?
(A) That's unnecessary. Thank you.
(B) We need to use another form.
(C) We have more than fifty guests coming.

24 Do you know who will take over Ms. Lim's position?
(A) Let's take it apart one by one.
(B) Our new section chief will.
(C) Yes, we should be there by seven.

25 Mr. Wilson will be attending tomorrow's meeting, won't he?
(A) No, he didn't send the product.
(B) It will be about the new product campaign.
(C) He'll be visiting one of his clients in Albany.

26 May I ask who's calling, please?
(A) This is Robert Kim from Smartlearn.
(B) Do you want me to take a message?
(C) Sure, I'll give you a call later.

27 What does the newspaper say about the election results?
(A) No, the mayor was not elected again.
(B) The sales figures fell by ten percent.
(C) The candidate I voted for lost.

28 Why hasn't the budget proposal been finished yet?
(A) Because it has a paper jam.
(B) Sure, I'd be glad to help you.
(C) Mr. Cullen was busy with another project.

29 Didn't you already mail the contract?
(A) Yes, but this one is revised.
(B) Let's keep in touch with each other.
(C) No, it's right next to the post office.

30 The first step is to have the blueprints drawn.
(A) You can withdraw money at any time.
(B) The painting should look great on this wall.
(C) Okay, I'll contact the chief architect.

31 Shouldn't we put these files in the back?
(A) Put it in the right order.
(B) Let's take the back roads.
(C) We might need them again soon.

Part 3

Questions 32-34 refer to the following conversation.

M Hi, Linda. I missed the first part of this morning's staff meeting, so I wonder if you can fill me in. What did the sales manager say about the Sydney office?

W He said that the Sydney group is doing really well. They've increased their sales considerably by targeting small families with young kids.

M Really? So does the sales manager think we should focus our advertising efforts on small families as well?

W I think so. He said we're supposed to have a workshop to talk about all of the details very soon.

M That's a good idea. Our employees need some systemized training.

32 What does the man ask the woman for?
(A) Help with a presentation
(B) Directions to another office
(C) Information about a meeting
(D) Traveling to Sydney together

33 What did the employees at the Sydney office do?
(A) They completed their training.
(B) They designed a new product.
(C) They increased their sales.
(D) They decreased their costs.

34 What will probably happen soon?
(A) A workshop will be held.
(B) A new sales manager will be hired.
(C) A trip to Sydney will be arranged.
(D) A new advertisement will be released.

Questions 35-37 refer to the following conversation.

M Did you hear that the company catalog is going to be redesigned? I got an e-mail about it yesterday.

W Yeah, I actually heard about it at the sales meeting last week. In the middle of the meeting, the director of the Marketing Department told us about his new ideas for the catalog and also asked for our suggestions. He is planning to start working on it next week after reviewing all the ideas he gathers.

M That's exactly why he e-mailed the rest of the staff yesterday. He wants new ideas. Did he say why he decided to change it? I thought the old catalog was quite good.

W Well, people did think it was simple, but the manager is concerned about the old layout. He wants a new layout with a more modern look in order to attract more clients.

35 What are the speakers discussing?
(A) Reviewing a movie
(B) Distributing catalogs
(C) Improving a catalog
(D) Planning a business trip

36 How did the woman find out about the change?
(A) From a newsletter
(B) From a meeting
(C) From an e-mail
(D) From a bulletin board

37 According to the woman, why will the change be made?
(A) To draw more clients
(B) To market a new product
(C) To lower printing costs
(D) To increase production

Questions 38-40 refer to the following conversation with three speakers.

W Hi. Do you both know anything about the new restaurant near the concert hall? I'm organizing the annual department luncheon, and I'm looking for a place to hold it.

M1 The place is called Bourgeois. Actually, I had lunch there a few days ago, and the food was excellent, but it took such a long time to be ready.

M2 I know. I had the same experience. The place is understaffed, and I heard that the owner is trying to find more employees.

W That's too bad. Then that might not be a good option after all.

M1 All the other restaurants around here are either too small or already booked that day.

W I guess we need to have our get-together here in our company dining room again this year.

M2 I think that's fine. That way, people won't have to waste their time going back and forth between places.

38 What event are the speakers discussing?
(A) A luncheon
(B) A workshop
(C) A concert
(D) A retirement party

39 What problem do the men mention about the Bourgeois?
(A) There are not enough seats.
(B) The price is too expensive.
(C) More staff members are needed.
(D) The menu needs to be revised.

40 What does the woman decide to do?
(A) Postpone an event
(B) Use a company facility
(C) Prepare an agenda
(D) Contact some other agencies

Questions 41-43 refer to the following conversation.

M Good morning. I have a ten o'clock appointment with George Winston. Could you tell me where his office is?

W Sure. It's down this hall and to the left. I'll show you the way. Follow me. Are you here about the new marketing position?

M No, I actually just hired your firm to do the Web design for my real estate company. Mr. Winston and I are going to discuss the design and features that I'd like today.

W Oh, you must be Mr. Newton. I am Catherine Whitaker, Mr. Winston's assistant. I will be working with him to create your Web site. It's nice to meet you, and I look forward to working with you.

41 Where most likely are the speakers?
(A) In a medical clinic
(B) In an office building
(C) On a street
(D) At a construction site

42 Who is George Winston?
(A) A Web designer
(B) A lawyer
(C) A receptionist
(D) A security guard

43 Why did the man come to see Mr. Winston?
(A) To interview for a marketing position
(B) To explain his upcoming court case
(C) To discuss a design for his Web site
(D) To purchase a piece of real estate

Questions 44-46 refer to the following conversation.

W Thank you for coming, Mr. Wiley. I'm Andrea McNeil, the maintenance manager of this museum. Here is the wall with the hole that needs to be repaired.

M Hmm... it'll probably take a few trips to repair completely since I'll have to apply a few layers of drywall mud and then sand it and paint it more than two times.

W Unfortunately, you will only be able to work during the evenings after the museum closes at six o'clock. How long do you think the work will take?

M I think I can probably do it in three days. I should be finished by Thursday. I'll let you know if there are any changes in terms of the schedule.

44 Where most likely does the conversation take place?
(A) At a furniture store
(B) At an art gallery
(C) At a hardware store
(D) At a museum

45 When does the man have to do the repair work?
(A) During the weekend
(B) During the hours of operation
(C) Early in the mornings
(D) Late in the evenings

46 What does the man mean when he says, "I'll let you know if there are any changes"?
(A) He thinks that the place might close early that day.
(B) He is happy that the facility is finally being renovated.
(C) He thinks there might be some unexpected problems.
(D) He is not sure who should be hired for the position.

Questions 47-49 refer to the following conversation.

W Mark, the front window display looks great. I really like the outfits you chose for the mannequins and decoration display. So is everything ready for next weekend's sale?

M Almost, but I have a question to ask you. I'd like to run an advertisement in the newspaper, but I'm not sure how many days it should be run. Do you think we should run the advertisement for one or two days?

W Can you find out the difference in cost? I think we ran it for one day last year, and that brought us a lot of business.

47 What does the woman say she likes?
(A) A newspaper article
(B) The appearance of display
(C) The weekend get-away plan
(D) The sale signs on the window

48 What will happen next weekend?
(A) A new store will open.
(B) A sale will take place.
(C) New merchandise will arrive.
(D) A reporter will visit the store.

49 What does the man ask about the advertisement?
(A) Where it should be placed
(B) How much he should spend on it
(C) When it should be run
(D) How many days it should appear

Questions 50-52 refer to the following conversation.

M Today's going to be a busy day. We received a lot of orders from our promotional ads this week.

W I'm not surprised. Our promotional ads have always worked well. I also thought a lot of people would be ordering food for the holiday weekend.

M We've got that wedding banquet this weekend to get ready for. We have to deliver all of the food by 11 A.M. on Saturday. So that's going to take some time, too.

W That probably means we'll have to work overtime on Friday to make sure everything is ready for the banquet. Let's start working on them in the order that they are going to be delivered.

50 What does the woman imply when she says, "I'm not surprised"?
(A) They have spent a lot of money on advertisements.
(B) There is a seasonal effect regarding ads.
(C) She has seen the advertisements before.
(D) She expected the ads would increase the business.

51 Where do the speakers probably work?
(A) At a department store
(B) At a caterer
(C) At a photo studio
(D) At an advertising agency

52 What might the speakers do on Friday?
(A) Shop for holiday gifts
(B) Make some wedding cakes
(C) Put in extra hours
(D) Do some painting

Questions 53-55 refer to the following conversation.

W Hello. Technical Support Department. Michelle speaking. How may I help you?

M Hi, Michelle. This is Kevin Johnson in the Accounting Department. I am having a problem with my computer. Yesterday, I created a spreadsheet document and saved it on the hard drive before I went home. But today, I can't get the document to open. I keep getting an error message that I'm not familiar with. It is very important that I retrieve this document. Could you send someone over here to help me access it this morning?

W I'm afraid I can't this morning. Several new computers have just arrived, so all the technicians are busy installing them at the moment. But I'll be happy to submit a service request form to get someone over to you early in the afternoon.

53 Which department does the woman work in?
(A) Accounting (B) Marketing
(C) Technical Support (D) Personnel

54 What are the speakers discussing?
(A) Scheduling a software installation
(B) Getting rid of computer viruses
(C) Purchasing a new computer
(D) Solving a technical problem

55 What does the woman say she will do?
(A) Fill out a request form
(B) Fix the problem herself
(C) Install a new program
(D) Cancel an installation

Questions 56-58 refer to the following conversation.

W Hello. One of my friends told me that your sign shop is having a special promotion for first-time customers. Could you tell me more, please?

M Certainly. New customers can receive their first sign order the day after they place it.

W I need the sign as soon as possible, so this is a great offer.

M Yes, ma'am. We can accommodate any of your requests. What kind of sign are you interested in?

W Well, I own a clothing store and recently opened a branch on Oak Street, which is crowded with shops and stores. I want a sign that will direct people to my space.

M Of course. I think one of our large exterior banners will be great to help people find your store.

W Hmm... That sounds good. Is there anything I should be aware of before I place an order?

M Well, given the rainy weather we get here, you might like one made out of waterproof material.

56 What special offer is available for new customers?
(A) Customized designs
(B) Overnight delivery
(C) An extended warranty
(D) Price discounts

57 Why does the woman want to put a sign?
(A) To indicate a location
(B) To promote a special sale
(C) To announce a relocation
(D) To show a parking area

58 What does the man recommend doing?
(A) Increasing the advertising expenses
(B) Visiting another store on Oak Street
(C) Using waterproof material
(D) Collecting client feedback

Questions 59-61 refer to the following conversation with three speakers.

M Hey, Lydia. Do you know what's going on with the color photocopier? There's been a sign on it for a few weeks that it needs new toner.

W1 Yes, the company has a new supplier for toner, but our office wasn't notified.

M Hmm, that's news to me. Mindy, do you know when I can use the color copier? I need to make copies for my presentation for the meeting tomorrow.

W2 Well, I just found out about the new supplier. I didn't send in the order until yesterday, so it should be here tomorrow morning.

W1 Just to be safe, why don't you e-mail the file to the copy store downstairs and have it printed there?

W2 Good idea. Just keep the receipt for the cost so that you can be reimbursed.

M Thanks a lot. I'll do that.

59 What is the man concerned about?
(A) Copying a document
(B) Finding a contract
(C) Being late for a meeting
(D) Contacting a person in charge

60 According to Mindy, what most likely is the problem?
(A) A cost has increased.
(B) An order was submitted late.
(C) An invoice was not paid.
(D) A file was deleted.

61 What does the man agree to do?
(A) Order a new photocopier
(B) Use another conference room
(C) Call a repair person
(D) Print the file at a nearby business

Questions 62-64 refer to the following conversation and list.

W Good afternoon. I'm looking for a new camera.

M Okay. What features are you looking for?

W Well, I'm a news reporter, and I carry my laptop and camera at all times. So I'd like something compact with a good zoom lens. I also need something that is easy to transfer photos to my computer.

M Then I would recommend a camera made by Censtar. The recently released Z3000 series would fit your needs perfectly. These cameras are easy to use and vary in color, and all of them come with a powerful zoom lens.

W Okay. I'd like this one in white then. I've never had a camera in white, and I'd like to try one this time.

62 What is the woman's job?
(A) Photographer
(B) Reporter
(C) Musician
(D) Sales person

63 What does the man say about the Z3000 series cameras?
(A) They are durable.
(B) Their prices are reasonable.
(C) They have a lot of memory.
(D) They have a powerful zoom lens.

64 Look at the graphic. What model does the woman probably purchase?
(A) Z2000
(B) Z2000 plus
(C) Z3000
(D) Z3000 plus

Questions 65-67 refer to the following conversation and floor plan.

W Elliot, I know you're heading to the conference room to deliver a speech at the training session, but do you have a minute to approve the room assignment for our renovation?

M Sure. So what am I looking at here?

W Offices three and four have been assigned to our new sales managers. And you've got the office next to the conference room.

M That should work well. So that leaves the office next to the copy room for you, right?

W Yes, I thought it would be good for me to be close to you, and I would also like to help the new managers.

M It looks fine. I think everyone on the staff will be excited to hear about the room assignments at the meeting this afternoon.

65 According to the woman, what is the man going to do?
(A) Contact the maintenance crew
(B) Apply for a loan for renovation
(C) Speak at a training workshop
(D) Meet with company executives

66 Look at the graphic. Which office has been assigned to the man?
(A) Office 1
(B) Office 2
(C) Office 3
(D) Office 4

67 What does the man say will take place this afternoon?
(A) A job interview
(B) A staff meeting
(C) A product demonstration
(D) Office renovations

Questions 68-70 refer to the following conversation and itinerary.

W Hi, Scott! Have you checked your plane reservations for the trade show in London? I was just looking at mine. We could travel there together if you want.

M Hey, Morgan. I just got mine, too. I am planning to go on Monday and stay until Friday. How about you?

W I can't stay the whole time. I have to leave a little early because I've got meetings with some of my international clients in Madrid and Paris later in the week.

M We can still try to go to London on Monday though.

W Great. Actually, my meetings all finish on Friday, but I decided to stay over the weekend to meet some of my relatives.

M I didn't know you have relatives in Europe. That is interesting.

68 What are the speakers mainly discussing?
(A) Taking a vacation
(B) Scheduling a relocation
(C) Visiting international clients
(D) Going on a business trip

69 What does the woman need to do?
(A) Make an appointment
(B) Give a presentation
(C) Leave a trade show early
(D) Reschedule a meeting

70 Look at the graphic. Where will the woman meet her relatives?
(A) In London (B) In Madrid
(C) In Paris (D) In Munich

Part 4

Questions 71-73 refer to the following announcement.

Ladies and gentlemen, we have just entered the recently renovated section of the convention hall. As you can see, this place is spacious enough to hold all kinds of private and business events, such as business meetings, awards ceremonies, and concerts. This room can hold up to a thousand people. As a part of the renovations, we newly installed removable walls with soundproof materials. Now you can have meetings and group activities in the same place simply by moving a few walls in the corner. And during the months of January and February, we have a special offer. We provide shuttle bus services to and from major hotels and airports in the area. You can arrange a shuttle for your own group by calling us at least two hours in advance. So let's take a look around, and we'll talk about rental fees after we go back to the hall.

71 Where does the talk take place?
(A) At a real estate agency
(B) At a convention hall
(C) In a hotel lobby
(D) At a job fair

72 What does the speaker say was recently installed?
(A) Movable walls
(B) Soundproof equipment
(C) A security system
(D) An information counter

73 What is offered in January and February?
(A) Free hotel rooms
(B) Guided tours of the area
(C) Shuttle bus service
(D) Reduced rental prices

Questions 74-76 refer to the following telephone message.

Hi. This message is for Mr. Wright. This is Paula calling from Hometown Motors. I'm calling to let you know that we've completed your vehicle inspection. However, there are two problems that must be fixed in order to pass the inspection. First, you need new tires because they do not have a sufficient amount of tread remaining to meet the guidelines. There is also a rear brake light that has burned out. These items must be taken care of before we can approve the inspection. Both of these items can be fixed here at Hometown Motors. Please call us back at 360-4500 to let us know if you would like us to complete these repairs. We need your permission to start the job. Thank you and have a nice day.

74 What kind of business does the speaker probably work for?
(A) A home inspection company
(B) A package delivery service
(C) An automobile repair shop
(D) A lighting store

75 What is the purpose of the message?
(A) To conduct a survey
(B) To provide inspection results
(C) To file an insurance claim
(D) To advertise a new service

76 What does the speaker ask the listener to do?
(A) Pay for the repairs in advance
(B) Give a credit card number
(C) Schedule a delivery date
(D) Authorize a repair service

Questions 77-79 refer to the following talk.

Let me explain how things work here at Martin's Fruit Farm. The fruit we have in season right now is apples, which you can pick on your own. Before you head out to the field this morning, make sure you get a special bag from the farm store, which is located on your left next to the main entrance. You'll definitely need one of them to put the apples in as you harvest them. And if you need any assistance while you're in the field, just ask one of our farm workers. You'll be able to spot them easily by the bright red aprons they're wearing. So now, let me show you the correct technique for harvesting apples.

77 According to the speaker, where can the listeners get bags?
(A) From the speaker
(B) From a store
(C) From a truck
(D) From a farmer

78 What should a person who needs help in a field do?
(A) Contact the farm supervisor
(B) Go back to the main building
(C) Go to the information desk
(D) Talk to a farm worker

79 What will the speaker most likely do next?
(A) Give a demonstration
(B) Explain a recent study
(C) Weigh the fruit the listeners picked
(D) Collect admission fees

Questions 80-82 refer to the following advertisement.

How would you like to learn the cooking secrets of a world-class chef? This summer, the Wyndham Culinary Institute is offering a French cooking class taught by award-winning chef Jean-Michel Roux. Chef Roux is famous for his passion for recreating traditional French cuisine in his own creative way. The class will meet once a week for eight weeks and is offered on both Tuesday and Thursday evenings. Don't miss your opportunity to learn from someone who has been the head chef for fifteen years at one of the top French restaurants in all of Europe! For more details and enrollment information, visit the institute's Web site at www.wyndhamculinary.com. Don't delay as class sizes are limited.

80 What is the advertisement for?
(A) Summer vacation packages
(B) Cuisine classes
(C) French language classes
(D) A recently opened restaurant

81 Why does the speaker say, "someone who has been the head chef for fifteen years"?
(A) To advertise a vacant position
(B) To ask people to buy his books
(C) To encourage people to sign up
(D) To propose an alternate solution

82 What should listeners do to get more information?
(A) Visit an institute
(B) Call a toll-free number
(C) Attend an informational meeting
(D) Go to an online page

Questions 83-85 refer to the following announcement.

Good evening, everyone, and welcome to the Laugh Zone Comedy Club. Before the show begins, I would like to inform you of our club rules. First, smoking is not permitted in the club. Please go out front to our designated smoking area. You can order food and beverages from our wait staff, but please do so quietly during the show. We ask that you please silence your mobile phones. In addition, photographs should not be taken at any time during the show. The entertainers will be available afterward for photographs and autographs. We appreciate your cooperation. And don't forget to pick up the schedule of the upcoming performances at the Laugh Zone Comedy Club on your way out. Thank you very much and enjoy the show!

83 Where is the announcement most likely taking place?
(A) At a movie theater
(B) At a comedy show
(C) At a sporting event
(D) At a music performance

84 What is the main purpose of the announcement?
(A) To advertise upcoming events
(B) To ask for volunteers for a show
(C) To request proper behavior
(D) To introduce the performers

85 What does the speaker mean when he says, "The entertainers will be available afterward"?
(A) He wants the audience to have a discussion with them in person.
(B) He predicts that the show will be a great success.
(C) He thinks that they would hold a signing event for audience.
(D) He acknowledges people want to spend some time with them.

Questions 86-88 refer to the following talk.

Thank you all for attending this meeting in spite of your busy schedules. As you know, we have been searching for a new editor-in-chief ever since Mr. Watson announced his retirement in March. We interviewed several qualified candidates, and one stood out as a perfect fit for our newspaper. I'm very pleased to introduce Carla Diaz as the new editor-in-chief of the *Seattle Tribune*. She has a lot of experience in journalism and will be a perfect addition to our staff. She is coming to us from San Francisco, where she was the assistant editor at the *San Francisco Daily* for eight years. Prior to that, she worked as a news editor in Miami and Atlanta. I will turn the microphone over to Ms. Diaz now. She would like to share some of her ideas on the future of our organization. Please help me welcome Ms. Carla Diaz.

86 What is the purpose of the talk?
(A) To report a job opening
(B) To recommend a former employee
(C) To honor an award winner
(D) To introduce a new employee

87 In which city did Ms. Diaz most recently work?
(A) San Francisco
(B) Atlanta
(C) Miami
(D) Seattle

88 What will the listeners probably do next?
(A) Travel to San Francisco
(B) Set up an interview
(C) Meet with the president
(D) Listen to Ms. Diaz's speech

Questions 89-91 refer to the following announcement.

Due to the overwhelming response for tickets for the Broadway musical *Forever Love*, the Jackson Theater is pleased to announce the addition of two afternoon shows for the November schedule. These shows will take place on November sixth and seventh at 1 P.M. Because this is a last-minute addition, tickets are only available for purchase at the theater box office. There will be no online sales. The box office is open Monday through Friday from 9 A.M. to 5 P.M. and on weekends from 11 A.M. to 6 P.M. If you are a member of the Jackson Theater's Premium Membership Club, you are eligible for a ten percent discount as usual. Just show your membership card at the ticket counter. These shows are sure to sell out quickly, so purchase your tickets as soon as possible.

89 What is the announcement mainly about?
(A) A change in a schedule
(B) The opening of a new theater
(C) The casting for a new play
(D) A show cancelation

90 How should listeners purchase tickets for the additional performance?
(A) By reserving them on a Web site
(B) By sending an e-mail to a dealer
(C) By visiting the theater in person
(D) By contacting a performance director

91 What does the speaker imply when she says, "this is a last-minute addition"?
(A) A discount will be given to the customers.
(B) Ticket prices won't be that expensive.
(C) The number of spectators will decrease.
(D) Tickets can be purchased only at a designated area.

Questions 92-94 refer to the following radio broadcast.

Good evening and welcome to KSG Sports Roundup. I am Harry Kenwood, and I will be on the air for the next two hours for this evening's Carling Cup football matches. We have a great prize for one lucky winner tonight. If you correctly guess the first player to score in all of tonight's games, you will win a pair of tickets to the grand final to be held at the Millennium Stadium in two weeks. It couldn't be simpler, so pick a player and get ready to call the station with your predictions. Lines will be open after the commercials.

92 Who most likely is the speaker?
(A) A sports presenter (B) A radio journalist
(C) A football player (D) A match referee

93 What prize will be awarded to a winner?
(A) Dinner with an athlete
(B) An autographed football shirt
(C) A two-week trip
(D) Tickets for the final

94 What information are listeners asked to provide?
(A) The title to a game
(B) The date of an event
(C) The name of the first scorer
(D) The total score of a team

Questions 95-97 refer to the following announcement and schedule.

Attention, customers. It's eight forty-five, and the Wellington Department Store will be closing in fifteen minutes. Please make your final selections and proceed to the checkout counter nearest to you. We will reopen tomorrow morning at ten o'clock. Don't forget that a Wellington gift card is always a great present for your special ones. It's a perfect way to make sure your loved ones get what they want this holiday season. Gift cards can be purchased at any cash register, and they are available in a variety of amounts of your choice from fifty to five hundred dollars. Once again, we'll be closing in fifteen minutes. Thank you for shopping at Wellington's.

95 What will probably happen after the announcement?
(A) Customers will start shopping.
(B) Free gifts will be distributed to the customers.
(C) Some customers will pay for their purchases.
(D) Employees will take inventory.

96 Look at the graphic. Which day of the week is tomorrow?
(A) Monday (B) Friday
(C) Saturday (D) Sunday

97 What is stated about gift cards?
(A) They can be redeemed online.
(B) They are available at every register.
(C) They can be purchased with cash only.
(D) They are available at other stores in the mall.

Questions 98-100 refer to the following telephone message and list.

Hi, Lisa. It's Henry from Accounting. I'm going through the expense report you submitted for your recent sales trip to Las Vegas from May third to seventh. It looks like one of the receipts is missing from your report. I see you're requesting the reimbursement of an expense of fifty dollars on May seventh, but I can't find the receipt for it. I'll need that to process the payment you requested. If you don't have it with you or cannot find a way to get a new one, please give me a call. Then, I'll explain what the procedure is for requesting reimbursement without a receipt. I know it sounds like a nuisance, but this is a necessary step to follow. Thank you.

98 What is the purpose of the message?
(A) To change a reservation
(B) To cancel a trip to Las Vegas
(C) To request a missing document
(D) To correct a mistake the speaker made

99 Look at the graphic. Which expense needs to be confirmed?
(A) Hotel (B) Restaurant
(C) Car Rental (D) Parking

100 What does the speaker offer to do?
(A) Describe a process
(B) Handle a complaint
(C) Reschedule an appointment
(D) Contact a hotel for the listener

TEST 06

| p.84

1	(B)	2	(B)	3	(A)	4	(C)	5	(D)
6	(D)	7	(C)	8	(A)	9	(B)	10	(C)
11	(A)	12	(B)	13	(C)	14	(A)	15	(C)
16	(A)	17	(C)	18	(C)	19	(B)	20	(B)
21	(C)	22	(A)	23	(A)	24	(A)	25	(B)
26	(A)	27	(B)	28	(C)	29	(A)	30	(C)
31	(B)	32	(D)	33	(B)	34	(A)	35	(B)
36	(B)	37	(A)	38	(C)	39	(A)	40	(D)
41	(D)	42	(C)	43	(B)	44	(D)	45	(B)
46	(C)	47	(D)	48	(C)	49	(A)	50	(D)
51	(A)	52	(B)	53	(A)	54	(A)	55	(B)
56	(A)	57	(B)	58	(D)	59	(D)	60	(A)
61	(C)	62	(D)	63	(C)	64	(A)	65	(A)
66	(D)	67	(C)	68	(A)	69	(C)	70	(D)
71	(C)	72	(B)	73	(A)	74	(A)	75	(A)
76	(B)	77	(C)	78	(D)	79	(B)	80	(B)
81	(A)	82	(B)	83	(C)	84	(D)	85	(B)
86	(C)	87	(A)	88	(C)	89	(D)	90	(C)
91	(B)	92	(C)	93	(B)	94	(A)	95	(B)
96	(C)	97	(D)	98	(D)	99	(C)	100	(A)

Part 1

1 (A) The man is unplugging a keyboard.
(B) The man is facing the monitor.
(C) The man is checking into a hotel.
(D) The man is filling out some papers.

2 (A) They are getting in the taxi.
(B) They are standing near a vehicle.
(C) They are going back to the office.
(D) They are crossing the road.

3 (A) Some boats are docked in a harbor.
(B) Swimmers are floating in a pool.
(C) Some trees are being planted in pots.
(D) Cars are parked alongside the river.

4 (A) A woman is serving some food.
(B) A woman is shopping for some groceries.
(C) A woman is stirring something in a pan.
(D) A woman is preparing for a party.

5 (A) A man is pushing a cart to a register.
(B) A woman is walking up some stairs.
(C) Some merchandise is being loaded into a truck.
(D) Some shoppers are browsing in a store.

6 (A) Some chairs are being carried into the hallway.
(B) The dinner table is being set.
(C) A lamp has been placed in the corner of the room.
(D) Some decorations have been mounted on the wall.

Part 2

7 When should I call you?
(A) All right. Thank you.
(B) That sounds fine.
(C) Tomorrow would be good.

8 What products does your company make?
(A) Perfumes and cosmetics.
(B) The Production Department.
(C) Yes, I tried that sample.

9 How much did that nice shirt cost?
(A) Inside the store.
(B) Forty dollars.
(C) No, thanks. I have enough shirts.

10 Do you know why the TV is on in the conference room?
(A) Yes, I went to New York for a conference.
(B) A thirty-percent discount will be applied to the TV set.
(C) Sorry. I forgot to turn it off.

11 Will Mr. Berkley travel by plane or train?
(A) He usually flies.
(B) He is a financial consultant.
(C) He is always in a hurry.

12 Who's going to review the sales data before it is submitted to the director?
(A) No, page 9.
(B) I can do that.
(C) We have a great view.

13 Could you take this to the service center?
(A) Stand in line, please.
(B) It's not far from the center.
(C) Sure, no problem.

14 Which office is yours, Tom?
(A) The one in the middle.
(B) You can reach me anytime.
(C) It's official now.

15 Have you heard about Jack's promotion to senior manager?
(A) I can manage it by myself.
(B) It takes a long time to get there.
(C) No, I haven't.

16 What documents do I need to bring on the first day?
(A) The ones in the package I sent you.
(B) Yes, I'll be back then.
(C) I haven't had time to read them.

17 I would really like to listen to the new singer perform.
(A) There is something you should hear.
(B) I need to fill out this form.
(C) I'm afraid the tickets are all sold out.

18 You ordered some new desks and chairs, didn't you?
(A) We should call someone on the maintenance staff.
(B) Yes, we can still use the old ones.
(C) Yes, we need them for the new office.

19 You should attend the meeting with us.
(A) She intended to order some.
(B) I'll be there in a minute.
(C) Yes, they are very similar.

20 Didn't you finish the proofreading?
(A) Yes, it was.
(B) No, not yet.
(C) I have the correct one.

21 Where is the guest list for the fundraising party?
(A) I don't think they've decided yet.
(B) A little earlier if possible.
(C) Maureen probably knows.

22 I'm afraid I won't be able to make it to the picnic on Saturday.
(A) I'm sorry to hear that.
(B) We are thinking of having it in the park.
(C) Games, prizes, and plenty of food.

23 I'd like to order some office furniture from your catalogue.
(A) Which items would you like?
(B) Usually on the first floor.
(C) Breakfast is no longer being served.

24 You remembered to lock the office door, didn't you?
(A) I'll double-check.
(B) The road was blocked.
(C) I can't remember his name.

25 Why don't you hire more temporary help?
(A) Yes, it was terrific.
(B) We've never considered that.
(C) On the upper shelf.

26 Do you think the new brochure gives enough information?
(A) I would have liked more pictures.
(B) Thank you. I've had enough.
(C) In the company directory.

27 Who wants to attend the annual convention?
(A) At the registration desk.
(B) I'll see who's interested.
(C) We can't meet the deadline.

28 Why do we have to complete so many documents?
(A) He will come in at any minute.
(B) Yes, they are our biggest competitors.
(C) Who knows? We seem to be drowning in paper.

29 Do you prefer the original catalog or the revised one?
(A) Definitely the new one.
(B) He sent a catalog and a price list.
(C) I prepared it for you.

30 When was the last time you watched a soccer game on TV?
(A) From the sporting goods store.
(B) It's going to take a little more time.
(C) I haven't watched since I was in university.

31 Haven't you already fixed the date for the company retreat?
(A) I can fix the flat tire now.
(B) Yes, but we don't have a venue yet.
(C) Twenty euros per ticket.

Part 3

Questions 32-34 refer to the following conversation.

M Hello. I'm calling from the Hilton Conference Center. A security officer found a laptop, and I called the phone number on the business card I found in the case. Are you missing a computer?

W As a matter of fact, I am. Thank you so much. I just realized it was missing a few minutes ago. Some of my colleagues might still be at the conference. Should I ask one of them to pick it up for me?

M Actually, it cannot be done that way. It's the center's policy to ship found items directly to the owner. I can send it to your work address or your home address depending on which you prefer.

W Hmm... I think the work address would be better. I spend more time at work anyway.

32 Where does the man work?
(A) At an electronics store
(B) At a shipping center
(C) At an airport
(D) At a conference center

33 Why is the man contacting the woman?
(A) A shipment has arrived.
(B) A computer was found.
(C) An event has been postponed.
(D) A reservation is canceled.

34 What does the man offer to do?
(A) Send an item
(B) Revise a meeting agenda
(C) Fix a computer
(D) Make an appointment

Questions 35-37 refer to the following conversation.

M Good morning. I'm not a customer here, but my cousin recommended one of your services. I'd like to open a new interest-bearing savings account at your bank.

W Of course. I'll need to see a form of photo identification. Do you have your driver's license or passport with you?

M Sure. Here's my passport.

W Thank you. Now, why don't you fill out this application form while I make a copy of your passport? I'll be back in a minute.

35 Where most likely are the speakers?
(A) At a police station
(B) At a financial institute
(C) At a photo studio
(D) At an airline check-in counter

36 What does the woman request?
(A) An account number
(B) An identification
(C) A credit card
(D) A billing statement

37 What will the man most likely do next?
(A) Complete a form
(B) Take a picture
(C) Apply for a driver's license
(D) Close an account

Questions 38-40 refer to the following conversation.

M Hi, Mary. I'd like to ask you a favor. Tomorrow afternoon, some important packages will arrive at my house, and I really need to be here. Do you mind if I work from home?

W Not at all, but what's the status of the construction budget you're working on for the new shopping center?

M I'm nearly finished with it.

W The closing date for the project is coming up quite soon, and I'm worried about sending in our work late.

M Don't worry about it. I should be able to send you the final version tomorrow.

W All right, as long as you can finish the budget by tomorrow, it should be okay. We aren't presenting the proposal to the clients until early next week.

38 What does the man want to do tomorrow?
(A) Leave work early
(B) Meet with a client
(C) Work from home
(D) Lead a presentation

39 What is the woman concerned about?
(A) Submitting the work on time
(B) Shopping for a present
(C) Organizing a committee
(D) Finding some documents

40 What does the woman say will happen next week?
(A) An office will be cleaned.
(B) Some equipment will be replaced.
(C) An employee will be unavailable.
(D) A proposal will be presented.

Questions 41-43 refer to the following conversation.

M Dr. Rose, I read the report about your research on bike materials last month, and it sounded really interesting.

W Yes. I led a research team in the development of a carbon fiber-reinforced material which is light in weight but very strong. It should be useful for making high-quality bike frames.

M When do you think the product will be available on the market?

W Well, the manufacturing agreements are complete. And the prototype has already been tested. You should see it in stores everywhere six months from now.

41 Who most likely is the woman?
(A) A cyclist
(B) A reporter
(C) A shop owner
(D) A researcher

42 What does the woman mention about the material?
(A) It is reasonably priced.
(B) It is easy to make.
(C) It is light and strong.
(D) It is environmentally friendly.

43 According to the woman, what will happen in 6 months?
(A) A new researcher will be hired.
(B) A product will be introduced to the market.
(C) A bike race will be held in town.
(D) An agreement will be signed.

Questions 44-46 refer to the following conversation.

M Hi. I'm looking for a car, and I'd really like to get something that is durable and reliable.

W Sure, many people are concerned about reliability when they buy a second-hand car. Let me show you what we have. Right here is a three-year-old Raven. It's in good condition. It looks like a brand-new car. It has an automatic transmission, seats five comfortably, and has an excellent fuel-efficiency rating. Plus, we give all our customers a six-month warranty.

M Hmm, it looks nice and comfortable, but do you have anything that isn't so big? There are just two of us, and we don't need all that room.

W Of course. Over here is a Raven Mini, ideal for small families.

44 What is the man mainly considering to choose a car?
(A) A discounted price
(B) Comfortable seating
(C) Brand name
(D) The reliability of a car

45 According to the woman, what is offered to customers?
(A) A ten-percent discount
(B) A six-month warranty
(C) A coupon for free fuel
(D) An extra set of tires

46 Why does the man ask to see another model?
(A) He saw it in an advertisement.
(B) He would like a newer car.
(C) He prefers something smaller.
(D) He wants a car in a different color.

Questions 47-49 refer to the following conversation with three speakers.

W1 Hi. I'd like a table for two, please. You're still serving dinner, right?

M I'm sorry. We're closing in a few minutes. We close at ten. You could try the fast-food restaurant around the corner. It's open until midnight.

W2 Well, it looks like it's quite a walk from here, but I guess we have to go there.

W1 By the way, do you close at ten every day? What are your weekend hours like?

W2 Good question. We might have to stay here until Sunday.

M We have the same hours on the weekends. We're open from eight in the morning to ten at night every day.

W2 We'll try to come back later then. Thank you.

47 When is the conversation taking place?
(A) In the morning
(B) At noon
(C) In the afternoon
(D) At night

48 What does the man imply when he says, "You could try the fast-food restaurant around the corner"?
(A) His restaurant doesn't serve vegetarian dishes.
(B) The food usually takes longer to be served at his restaurant.
(C) His restaurant is about to close for the day.
(D) It is open 24 hours a day.

49 What does the man say about his restaurant?
(A) It closes at the same time every day.
(B) It is usually crowded on weeknights.
(C) It is especially popular on weekends.
(D) It has daily specials during the week.

Questions 50-52 refer to the following conversation.

W I'm glad we could meet for lunch and talk about the marketing work I'm currently doing for your company. I've come up with a few great ideas for your company's advertising campaign. And I'd like to talk about them.

M Wonderful, but I only have an hour. Then, I have to get back to the office for a weekly staff meeting.

W Okay, we should order lunch first and talk while we're waiting.

M Good idea. I recommend the lunch special here. It comes quickly and is served with the drink of your choice.

W Let's order then. I'll just have whatever you get.

50 Who is the woman most likely talking to?
(A) A colleague
(B) A store manager
(C) A salesperson
(D) A client

51 According to the man, what is the advantage of the lunch special?
(A) It comes with a beverage.
(B) It is served with side dishes.
(C) It is cheaper with a coupon.
(D) It uses organic products.

52 What will the speakers probably do next?
(A) Schedule a meeting
(B) Order some food
(C) Go back to the office
(D) Postpone a staff meeting

Questions 53-55 refer to the following conversation.

W Please take a look over there. You can see how many robotic devices we use on our automated assembly line.

M That's pretty impressive. Not many factories are using these kinds of advanced robotic devices. This factory seems to be fully automated. But some of the wiring looks old and loose.

W That's why I asked you to come here today. We need to upgrade some of the cables and wires to increase productivity. I'd like you to decide how much electrical work should be done and then provide an estimate of how much your company would charge to do that work.

53 Where does this conversation take place?
(A) At a manufacturing plant
(B) At a repair shop
(C) In a research laboratory
(D) At an electric company

54 What is the man impressed with?
(A) The automation level of a factory
(B) The high price of some equipment
(C) The size of an assembly line
(D) The variety of goods on display

55 What does the woman ask the man to do?
(A) Repair some machines
(B) Provide a cost estimate
(C) Advertise a new product
(D) Join her company

Questions 56-58 refer to the following conversation.

M Hi. I'm looking for a birthday present for my wife. I think she'd like one of these sweaters, but do you have any in a smaller size?

W I'm pretty sure everything we have is out here on the display table. But I can check the stockroom in the back if you'd like.

M Thanks. That would be great. You know, they look perfect for early spring. They are light but warm.

W That's right. I got one for my friend, and she wears it a lot. So I'm sure your wife would love one. And we're selling them for thirty percent off this week.

M That's good to know. I hope you have one in my wife's size.

56 What is the man looking for?
(A) A gift for a family member
(B) A restaurant with outdoor seating
(C) A location for a new store
(D) A piece of luggage

57 What does the man ask the woman for?
(A) The address of a shop
(B) An item in a different size
(C) An additional discount
(D) A warm drink

58 What does the woman mean when she says, "I got one for my friend"?
(A) She would like the man to meet her friend.
(B) Her friend is the same size as the man's wife.
(C) She is willing to pay for a purchase.
(D) She is emphasizing how good a product is.

Questions 59-61 refer to the following conversation.

M Jessica, we're a little short of staff this evening since three waitresses are off today. So I'm hoping the trainees can help out. Could you work for Jane to serve food to guests in the Rose Room?

W Sure, no problem. But will there be enough people to help with everyone seated in the patio?

M I think Philippe can handle it with the rest of the staff, and I can help out if necessary. If you need me, let me know. I'll be supervising the reception down in Pacific Hall.

W Okay. I'll go and change into a uniform.

M Thank you, Jessica.

59 Where do the speakers probably work?
(A) At an employment agency
(B) At a caterer
(C) At a theater
(D) At a restaurant

60 Why does the man ask the woman to help?
(A) Some employees are off duty today.
(B) The food has not been prepared.
(C) Some guests did not make reservations.
(D) An event has to be rescheduled.

61 What will the woman probably do next?
(A) Go to the patio
(B) Work with Philippe
(C) Put on different clothing
(D) Wait for the man's call

Questions 62-64 refer to the following conversation and map.

W I heard you moved into a new house in Whitewood. Aren't you farther from work now?

M Yes, it's a little farther, but it's in a really good neighborhood, so it's very clean and quiet. I don't drive anymore because there is a quiet road I can bike to work on every day.

W That's great. You have no more traffic to worry about. And you can exercise by riding your bike to work. How long does it take to ride to Sherman Corporate Center? That's where you work, right?

M Yes. It only takes twenty-five to thirty minutes. If I take Parkway Avenue, I can avoid a busy intersection. Plus, I can stop at a great coffee place on my way to the office. I go there almost every day.

W Okay. I'll have to try that way, too.

62 What does the man say about his new house?
(A) It is in a heavily populated area.
(B) It is closer to his office.
(C) It is in a business district.
(D) It is in a good neighborhood.

63 How does the man get to work now?
(A) By car
(B) By train
(C) By bicycle
(D) By bus

64 Look at the graphic. Where does the man go for coffee on his way to work?
(A) Café Bianca
(B) Espresso Bar
(C) Whitewood Shopping Center
(D) Julie's Coffee Shop

Questions 65-67 refer to the following conversation and schedule.

W Mr. Quinn, the president of Dedham Industries just called. He is looking for a new law firm to represent his company, and he wants to come in on Wednesday at four to discuss our legal services.

M Wow. That's good news. Dedham Industries is a huge company in the publishing industry and would be our biggest client. Could you please reserve conference room A for the meeting? It's the nicest room.

W Actually, I already tried, but that meeting room is booked at four o'clock.

M Well, let me take a look. Ah, it's been reserved by Jason. I'm sure we can persuade him to use Room B instead. This could be big for the whole company.

W Yeah, that's true. I'll give him a call and ask him if he's willing to make that change.

65 Where do the speakers work?
(A) At a law firm
(B) At a newspaper
(C) At a manufacturing facility
(D) At a bookstore

66 Look at the graphic. According to the man, what event is Jason in charge of?
(A) The luncheon meeting
(B) The engineering forum
(C) The networking event
(D) The sales strategy workshop

67 What will the woman do next?
(A) Contact a client about a contract
(B) Conduct a job interview
(C) Ask a coworker to change rooms
(D) Revise a company policy

Questions 68-70 refer to the following conversation and sign.

W Do you know why the elevators will be out of service tomorrow?

M Last week, Ms. Yamada noticed the certificate of inspection for the elevators will expire at the end of March, and maintenance checks are required for a renewal.

W Oh, I see. But did you see the sign? The elevator closest to the entrance will close at 1 P.M. Why would a closure be scheduled at a time when the lobby is crowded right after lunch?

M You should mention this to the manager. I'm sure he'll want to cause the least amount of disturbance.

W I think I will. It might not be too late for him to call the technicians to reschedule.

68 What did Ms. Yamada realize last week?
(A) A certificate will be no longer valid.
(B) New equipment was installed.
(C) New tenants will move in.
(D) Some machines should be fixed.

69 Look at the graphic. Which elevator is closest to the entrance?
(A) North Elevator
(B) East Elevator
(C) South Elevator
(D) West Elevator

70 What does the man suggest the woman do?
(A) Reschedule a meeting
(B) Call a technician
(C) Display a new sign
(D) Speak to a supervisor

Part 4

Questions 71-73 refer to the following announcement.

Attention, all passengers waiting to board Rainbow Air Flight 681 to Chicago. Due to the current snowstorm, all outbound flights after 8 P.M. have been canceled. This includes the 8:30 P.M. flight to Chicago. The next available flight to Chicago will be tomorrow morning at 9 A.M. We will be providing hotel rooms and shuttle bus service for those in need. Please speak to a customer service representative at the rebooking desk for further assistance. We sincerely apologize for the inconvenience and thank you for your understanding.

71 Where is the announcement being made?
(A) At a travel agency
(B) At a train station
(C) At an airport
(D) At a bus terminal

72 What is the cause of the problem?
(A) Overbooked flights
(B) Weather conditions
(C) Mechanical problems
(D) Traffic congestion

73 What will be provided for some passengers?
(A) Hotel accommodations
(B) Complimentary beverages
(C) Full refunds for their tickets
(D) Seating upgrades

Questions 74-76 refer to the following advertisement.

This week only, E-Store is offering discounts on its entire range of electronic goods. E-Store is known not only for great deals but also for excellent customer service. For twenty years, you have been coming to our shop because of our commitment to great service. To thank our customers, we would like to invite you to our twentieth anniversary party on September twelfth. Come to see our remodeled store in the heart of the city's shopping district. Get the great service when you need it. Mark it on your calendar and bring your friends and family to our big celebration.

74 What type of business is being advertised?
(A) An electronics store
(B) A food market
(C) A furniture store
(D) A car repair center

75 According to the advertisement, why do customers like the business?
(A) It provides good customer service.
(B) It offers online shopping.
(C) It is conveniently located.
(D) It has a variety of products.

76 What will the business do on September 12?
(A) Close for remodeling
(B) Host a celebration
(C) Count its inventory
(D) Hire a new staff member

Questions 77-79 refer to the following telephone message.

Hello, Brian. It's Tracy Williams calling from the payroll office. You sent me an e-mail asking why last month's paycheck was less than usual. I apologize for that. There was a mistake in the calculations. One of our accountants calculated your working hours incorrectly. But the problem has been fixed, and we expect to be able to transfer the difference to your account this afternoon. Or if you'd like to pick it up at our office yourself, please let me know as soon as possible, and I'll have someone on my staff issue the check here for you. Once again, we apologize for the inconvenience. Have a nice day.

77 Why did the speaker leave the message?
(A) To ask for a refund
(B) To request technical assistance
(C) To respond to an inquiry
(D) To arrange an appointment

78 Why does the speaker say, "I apologize for that"?
(A) To express her regret for a delay in delivery
(B) To explain why an accountant was late for a meeting
(C) To report an accident on the road
(D) To acknowledge that there has been an error

79 What might happen this afternoon?
(A) An official announcement will be made.
(B) Some money will be transferred.
(C) A delivery will be made.
(D) A part will be ordered.

Questions 80-82 refer to the following news report.

Good morning. This is Jeff Thompson with your KLK Radio traffic report. Remember the construction in the Broadmore area began last spring? Well, the bad news is that exit five of the coastal highway is closed to commuters today so that heavy machinery can be brought in for final paving. The Highway Department expects to reopen exit five for commuters tomorrow morning. The good news for commuters and shoppers is that it looks like everything will be ready for the Broadmore Department Store to be open in March as planned. In other areas, all roadways are moving along well right now. I'll be back in twenty minutes with another KLK news update.

80 Who most likely is the report intended for?
(A) Traffic police officers
(B) Commuters
(C) Shopping center managers
(D) Construction supervisors

81 What problem is the speaker discussing?
(A) A road closure
(B) An equipment breakdown
(C) Construction delays
(D) An increase in traffic

82 According to the report, what will happen in March?
(A) A construction project will begin.
(B) A department store will open.
(C) A highway will be closed.
(D) A new road will be built.

Questions 83-85 refer to the following telephone message.

Hi, Mr. Waters. This is Tim Chang from International Freight Services. We received your request for a price estimate on a delivery, but we need some more information in order to quote you an accurate price. First, we need the weight as well as the size of the package. I also see you want to ship it by air, but we have two different air delivery options. Regular air is our most affordable option, but if you need to get it there quickly, express air is probably a better choice. Express air packages are delivered to any international location within 48 hours. As soon as we have this information, we can get an estimate to you. Thanks for choosing International Freight Services. We look forward to doing business with you.

83 What did Mr. Waters request?
(A) An airplane ticket
(B) A delivery schedule
(C) A price estimate
(D) A special warranty

84 What additional information does Mr. Waters have to provide?
(A) A telephone number
(B) A mailing address
(C) A payment option
(D) A delivery preference

85 What does the speaker mean when he says, "express air is probably a better choice"?
(A) Its price has been marked down.
(B) It is faster than the other option.
(C) He has used the service before.
(D) The other service is not available now.

Questions 86-88 refer to the following advertisement.

Do you like to learn about popular and unusual vacation destinations? Then don't miss *TV Tour World* with its hostess, Raquel Sylvia. Each week, Raquel Sylvia gives detailed information about famous must-see sights and many little-known places that are worth a visit. *TV Tour World* airs every Friday at 9 P.M. with a repeat show at 11 A.M. on Saturday here on Channel seven. For pictures taken by professional photographers and a complete schedule including upcoming destinations that will be featured, visit our Web site at www.tvtourworld.com.

86 What is being advertised?
(A) A nature course
(B) A travel book
(C) A TV show
(D) A holiday tour package

87 Who is Raquel Sylvia?
(A) A TV program host
(B) A university professor
(C) A tour guide
(D) An environmentalist

88 What can be found on the Web site?
(A) An application form
(B) The location of the station
(C) Some images
(D) A price list of packages

Questions 89-91 refer to the following news report.

And in business news, O'Malley's Office Supplies at 206 Adam Street has purchased a building next to it at 208 Adam Street. In a telephone interview yesterday, business owner Peter O'Malley noted that his office supplies company is growing steadily, so he needs more space for product displays and for putting together customer orders received through various channels. The ground floor of the new building has already been remodeled to contain a display area for office furniture. And the floor above will accommodate the new employees Mr. O'Malley plans to hire by the end of the year to fill the increasing number of orders placed online, by phone, and by fax. One interesting fact Mr. O'Malley said to his surprise is that most of his customers still place their orders by phone.

89 What type of business does Peter O'Malley own?
(A) An insurance company
(B) A building renovation company
(C) A furniture manufacturer
(D) A stationery store

90 What does the company plan to do by the end of the year?
(A) Renew a Web site
(B) Construct a building
(C) Hire some staff members
(D) Design a line of furniture

91 What does the speaker imply when she says, "most of his customers still place their orders by phone"?
(A) O'Malley's will increase its product prices soon.
(B) New employees will take customers' calls.
(C) Some new employees will get higher salaries.
(D) A store is moving to a new location.

Questions 92-94 refer to the following introduction.

And now we have an exclusive interview with renowned consultant Dr. Benita Covey. Dr. Covey's recent work with business strategy development is the subject of her new book, *Developing Your Strategy To Reach Your Goal*. Dr. Covey has taught business strategy and planning at the University of Lidon for fifteen years and has worked as a consultant in the business strategy industry for ten years. Her book addresses issues faced by businesses of all sizes from small family-owned stores to large corporations and how the strategy of a business can affect its success. I should also mention that Dr. Covey has recently redesigned her Web site to share insights gained from her vast experience. Now, Dr. Covey, I'd like to start by having you tell our listeners how you got started in business.

92 What is the subject of Dr. Covey's recent book?
(A) Designing a Web site
(B) Teaching at a university
(C) Developing business strategies
(D) Publishing a novel

93 For how long has Dr. Covey worked as a consultant?
(A) 5 years
(B) 10 years
(C) 15 years
(D) 20 years

94 According to the speaker, what will probably happen next?
(A) Dr. Covey will discuss her experience.
(B) The interviewer will describe a book.
(C) The radio program will end.
(D) There will be a commercial break.

Questions 95-97 refer to the following talk and flow chart.

Thank you for attending our companywide new product review. On behalf of the product development division, I'm pleased to have the chance to brief you on our ambitious ongoing project, our new concept bike, Yellowjeep. As you can see from this flowchart, our team has been working step by step to successfully introduce this product to the market. We have completed product testing and gained positive feedback from our potential customers. Participants in the field study seemed to like this new bike a lot, but there was some negative feedback, too. So the next step should be completed within the next month, and we'll initiate a full marketing campaign early next year. Now, let me start my presentation with the basic structure of Yellowjeep. Please look at the first slide.

95 Who most likely is the speaker?
(A) A corporate executive
(B) A product developer
(C) A customer service representative
(D) A field test participant

96 Look at the graphic. According to the speaker, which step should be completed within the next month?
(A) Build a model
(B) Conduct a field test
(C) Make design revisions
(D) Launch a marketing campaign

97 What will the listeners probably do next?
(A) Develop a prototype
(B) Fill out a document
(C) Test a new product
(D) Look at a slide

Questions 98-100 refer to the following talk and schedule.

Can I have everyone's attention here at the front of the bus? I hope you enjoyed your lunch at the restaurant Baron. As I mentioned earlier, it first opened in 1880 and has been operating longer than any other restaurant in Charlestown. Now, if you look out the window on your right, you'll see the national museum of history. According to our schedule, we're right on time. We'll be spending about two hours here. Let me pass out the brochures with the information about the permanent and temporary exhibits you'll be seeing today. We'll meet again at the main entrance at three thirty for our next schedule. Enjoy yourself.

98 What does the speaker say about the restaurant Baron?
(A) Its menu is updated daily.
(B) It has multiple locations nationwide.
(C) It recently won an award.
(D) It is the oldest restaurant in the city.

99 Look at the graphic. What time is the talk most likely being given?
(A) At 10:00 A.M.
(B) At 12:00 P.M.
(C) At 1:30 P.M.
(D) At 3:30 P.M.

100 What will the speaker distribute?
(A) Information booklets
(B) Admission tickets
(C) Bottles of water
(D) Local maps

TEST 07

| p.98

1	(C)	2	(A)	3	(D)	4	(C)	5	(C)
6	(B)	7	(A)	8	(B)	9	(C)	10	(A)
11	(B)	12	(A)	13	(B)	14	(B)	15	(A)
16	(B)	17	(C)	18	(B)	19	(A)	20	(B)
21	(B)	22	(B)	23	(C)	24	(B)	25	(C)
26	(C)	27	(B)	28	(A)	29	(A)	30	(A)
31	(B)	32	(D)	33	(B)	34	(A)	35	(A)
36	(C)	37	(D)	38	(C)	39	(A)	40	(B)
41	(D)	42	(A)	43	(B)	44	(A)	45	(D)
46	(C)	47	(C)	48	(B)	49	(C)	50	(C)
51	(D)	52	(A)	53	(B)	54	(A)	55	(C)
56	(C)	57	(D)	58	(A)	59	(C)	60	(D)
61	(B)	62	(B)	63	(D)	64	(C)	65	(C)
66	(C)	67	(B)	68	(D)	69	(A)	70	(C)
71	(B)	72	(C)	73	(A)	74	(C)	75	(D)
76	(A)	77	(D)	78	(A)	79	(C)	80	(A)
81	(B)	82	(C)	83	(D)	84	(D)	85	(B)
86	(C)	87	(D)	88	(A)	89	(B)	90	(D)
91	(A)	92	(C)	93	(A)	94	(D)	95	(D)
96	(B)	97	(B)	98	(B)	99	(B)	100	(D)

Part 1

1 (A) The woman is washing her hands.
(B) The woman is leaning against the wall.
(C) The woman is picking up something.
(D) The woman is cleaning the floor.

2 (A) Some tires have been removed from a vehicle.
(B) A man is fixing an engine.
(C) A pile of tires is being moved to the warehouse.
(D) A man is relaxing in a repair shop.

3 (A) A woman is giving a presentation.
(B) A man is handing out some papers.
(C) They are all facing the same direction.
(D) They are gathered around the conference table.

4 (A) A woman is cleaning a window.
(B) A woman is walking along the street.
(C) The floor is being swept.
(D) The building is being constructed.

5 (A) They are stepping onto a stage.
(B) They are marching in a parade.
(C) They are all dressed alike.
(D) They are putting on their hats.

6 (A) Trucks are parked by a fence.
(B) Dirt has been gathered into a pile.
(C) A road is being resurfaced.
(D) A hole is being covered with plastic sheets.

Part 2

7 How is the cake?
(A) It tastes quite good.
(B) Put it there on the table.
(C) I'm feeling much better. Thanks.

8 Where is he going?
(A) Sunday morning.
(B) To the pharmacy.
(C) At the store.

9 Why was Scott late for the meeting?
(A) The second door on the right.
(B) Yes, I'll meet him.
(C) He lost his car keys.

10 What kind of tea would you like?
(A) I'll have some green tea.
(B) Yes, I'd love to.
(C) After I finish eating.

11 The photocopier should be fixed right away.
(A) You should take a picture of it.
(B) I'll call the maintenance office.
(C) The interest rate is fixed for three months.

12 When will the shipment of fabric samples get in?
(A) Later this week.
(B) In the warehouse.
(C) Since last week.

13 Should we revise the memo before or after lunch?
(A) Lunch was delicious.
(B) Let's take care of it now.
(C) We should peel it first.

14 Would you like some help setting up the computer?
(A) Yes, you're going to set the table.
(B) Thanks. I'd appreciate that.
(C) I usually take the commuter train.

15 Isn't Ms. Patel out of town?
(A) Actually, her trip was canceled.
(B) She's from Rome.
(C) No, she still has some.

16 Do you want to use this colored paper to print the birthday cards?
(A) In the newspaper this morning.
(B) Will it fit in the printer?
(C) Because it's out of print.

17 Your name is Michael Peters, isn't it?
(A) No, I've never met him.
(B) He should be in the conference room.
(C) No, I'm Michael Taylor.

18 Where is the company's party going to be?
(A) At ten o'clock.
(B) At the Murano Hotel.
(C) For the weekend.

19 I didn't know you were back in town.
(A) I got back yesterday.
(B) I stayed in a downtown hotel.
(C) I'll call back later.

20 Excuse me. Can you tell me when the next train leaves for Denver?
(A) The training session is set for next week.
(B) You should check the schedule board.
(C) I'm sorry. I'm too busy to go with you.

21 What plan does the company have to mark its twentieth anniversary?
(A) Yes, that's still the plan.
(B) There will be a big celebration.
(C) Please make twenty more.

22 Who's handling the book design?
(A) That's an elegant design.
(B) It's been assigned to George.
(C) Mine has a black handle.

23 Shouldn't we consult with a lawyer before we sign the contract?
(A) We shouldn't be here now.
(B) I signed up for it.
(C) Yes, you're probably right.

24 You only design women's clothing, don't you?
(A) The total is 580 dollars.
(B) Actually, I have a children's line as well.
(C) Okay, we'll check if it's in stock.

25 When will Mr. Takashi be returning from New York?
(A) I'll return his call this afternoon.
(B) Yes, I have been there.
(C) Sometime next week.

26 How often do you visit the manufacturing facility?
(A) Miguel Castano, the floor manager.
(B) I think it's in Liverpool.
(C) I haven't had time lately.

27 Could you pick out a paint color for the walls?
(A) Hang it with other paintings.
(B) Okay, let's go to the store in the afternoon.
(C) I'll pick up the groceries on my way home.

28 But I thought you were interested in the position.
(A) They told me I have to work late a lot.
(B) Those are for Mr. Stone.
(C) Twenty résumés and applications.

29 Can we listen to music at our desks while we're working in the office?
(A) As long as you wear headphones.
(B) Yes, a new work desk.
(C) No, we didn't hear about it.

30 Why haven't they received the payment?
(A) Sorry. I forgot to send it.
(B) The Billing Department.
(C) After July 1st.

31 I just heard a news report on the radio about seasonal part-time work.
(A) These are homegrown vegetables.
(B) Which station was it on?
(C) The National Weather Bureau's announcement.

Part 3

Questions 32-34 refer to the following conversation.

M Hello. I need to see Mr. Edwards, please.

W I'm afraid Mr. Edwards isn't available at this time. Is there anything I can help you with?

M Actually, I'm supposed to get his signature on these documents. It's very time-sensitive.

W He is in a meeting with the board of directors now. You're more than welcome to wait until he's done. He should be out in ten to fifteen minutes or so. Would you like some water or anything to drink?

32 What is the purpose of the man's visit?
(A) To schedule a meeting
(B) To review some contracts
(C) To pick up some documents
(D) To get a signature

33 According to the woman, where is Mr. Edwards?
(A) In a cafeteria
(B) In a meeting room
(C) In a staff lounge
(D) In his office

34 What does the woman say the man can do?
(A) Wait until Mr. Edwards is available
(B) Come back in 10 minutes
(C) Call Mr. Edwards later
(D) Leave the documents with her

Questions 35-37 refer to the following conversation.

W Paul, do you think Gene will be back from San Francisco in time for our sales meeting this afternoon?

M No, I'm afraid he won't be back by then. He called earlier this morning to say that his connecting flight in Chicago was delayed because of bad weather. He won't arrive until late this evening.

W Oh, then we should postpone the meeting until tomorrow or early next week.

M That'd be great, but you and I should still get together to go over the monthly sales report before we leave today.

W Good idea. That way, there won't be any surprises during the meeting.

35 When was the meeting supposed to take place?
(A) This afternoon
(B) This evening
(C) Tomorrow
(D) Next week

36 Why will the meeting be postponed?
(A) All meeting rooms are booked.
(B) Some information is not available yet.
(C) One participant cannot attend.
(D) The office is closing early.

37 What does the man suggest doing?
(A) Going to an airport
(B) Holding a teleconference
(C) Listening to a weather forecast
(D) Looking over a report

Questions 38-40 refer to the following conversation.

W Good morning. Welcome to the Baker's Dozen Bakery. How can I help you?

M I'm here to pick up a birthday cake. I called a few days ago and ordered a large ice cream cake with chocolate icing. My last name is Jones.

W I have your cake right here, Mr. Jones. We made it first thing this morning, and it turned out great. Now, would you like to have anything written on it?

M Yes, please. Could you write "Happy Birthday Cindy"? My sister is celebrating her 22nd birthday today, and we're having a surprise party for her.

38 Where are the speakers?
(A) At a reception desk
(B) At a restaurant
(C) At a store
(D) At a party

39 What does the man say he did a few days ago?
(A) Ordered a cake
(B) Canceled an order
(C) Met with his sister
(D) Made dinner reservations

40 According to the man, what will probably happen today?
(A) He will send out some invitations.
(B) He will attend a birthday party.
(C) He will bake some special cakes.
(D) He will get an extra discount.

Questions 41-43 refer to the following conversation.

W Good morning! May I see your passport and ticket?

M Here you go. I'm a little worried about my connection. I noticed that the flight to New York arrives at a different terminal from my connecting flight to Paris. And I'll only have twenty minutes to get from one terminal to the other. Would you be able to arrange a shuttle bus to take me to the other terminal once I arrive in New York? I have a very important meeting in Paris, and I can't miss it.

W That's not a problem. I'll arrange for a shuttle bus to be waiting for you upon arrival. I've also printed both of your boarding passes, so you won't have to check in again in New York.

41 Where does this conversation probably take place?
(A) At a travel agency
(B) In a governmental office
(C) On a bus
(D) At an airport

42 Why is the man concerned about his trip?
(A) He might miss a flight.
(B) His luggage might be delayed.
(C) His passport has expired.
(D) His meeting might be canceled.

43 What does the woman offer to do?
(A) Talk to the flight attendant
(B) Arrange some transportation
(C) Postpone a meeting
(D) Confirm a reservation

Questions 44-46 refer to the following conversation.

W Are you planning to go to the conference in Boston next month?

M I haven't decided yet. It depends on whether I can find a reasonably priced flight. I wanted to book a flight last week, but the prices were too expensive.

W Well, I just booked my flight through my travel agent yesterday, and I got a pretty good deal. Let me give you his phone number so that you can see if he can book the same flight for you.

44 What are the speakers discussing?
(A) Booking an airline ticket
(B) Organizing a conference
(C) Reserving a hotel room
(D) Planning a vacation

45 What does the man imply when he says, "the prices were too expensive"?
(A) He wants to receive a membership discount.
(B) The hotel doesn't offer a special rate.
(C) He wants the company to cover a cost.
(D) He couldn't get the flight he wanted.

46 What information will the woman give the man?
(A) A colleague's e-mail address
(B) A travel guide for a trip
(C) A travel agent's contact number
(D) A brochure about a conference

Questions 47-49 refer to the following conversation.

M I think it's great that the company is obtaining so many new contracts. Just this month, we've landed three new commercial building projects. Management says they are expecting to get at least one more big construction contract by the end of the quarter.

W That sounds good, but we'll need to hire some more employees soon. We're already understaffed, and we need some help to finish the job.

M I'm not sure how many new employees we can afford to hire, but we definitely need more people in the Engineering Department. We could also use more people in Accounting Department, but I don't think we can afford to hire for both departments.

W I think we should just hire people in the Engineering Department for now. We have to get these projects started soon so that we don't miss our deadlines.

47 What are the speakers mainly talking about?
(A) A television commercial
(B) A lack of space
(C) A need for more employees
(D) A surplus in the budget

48 Where do the speakers most likely work?
(A) At a real estate agency
(B) At a construction company
(C) At an advertising agency
(D) At an accounting firm

49 According to the woman, which department has the highest priority?
(A) Management
(B) Accounting
(C) Engineering
(D) Marketing

Questions 50-52 refer to the following conversation with three speakers.

W1 Thank you for coming in for this interview on such short notice, Mr. Batista. I'm Maria Hoffman, the head of Human Resources at Channel Seven.

W2 And I am Abby Thompson. I produce the nightly news program.

M Nice to meet you, Ms. Hoffman and Ms. Thompson.

W2 We've looked over your résumé and are very impressed with your qualifications. You'll be a good fit for the camera operator's position for our station.

W1 One thing we're curious about is your availability since our crews often go out on assignments with little warning.

M I understand that I would need to be available on short notice once I become a member of a news group. That is not a problem.

W2 Great. Now, why don't we have a look at some of your work? You said you brought a video. Can you show us?

M Sure, the file's right here on my laptop.

50 Where do the women most likely work?
(A) At an electronics store
(B) At an employment agency
(C) At a TV station
(D) At a movie theater

51 What job requirement do the speakers discuss?
(A) Being professionally certified
(B) Holding relevant degrees
(C) Having management experience
(D) Having a flexible schedule

52 What will the man do next?
(A) Show a video
(B) Provide references
(C) Tour a facility
(D) Submit some documents

Questions 53-55 refer to the following conversation.

W Hello. Thank you for calling the Skyline Hotel. How may I help you?

M Hi. My name is Paul Horowitz. I'm from BNT Publishing, and I'd like to reserve a conference room for a meeting on Tuesday around noon. Do you have a room large enough for twenty-five people?

W Let me check. Our regular conference room is free at noon, but it can accommodate only up to twenty people. Our largest conference room will be available if you're willing to wait until twelve thirty.

M I guess twelve thirty is okay. Some members of our group have flights out of town later that afternoon, so the meeting has to be done by three thirty at the latest.

W Okay, Mr. Horowitz. I'll make a note of it on my calendar.

53 What type of business is the man calling?
(A) A publisher
(B) A hotel
(C) A restaurant
(D) A bookstore

54 Why is the man calling?
(A) To reserve a venue for an event
(B) To book hotel rooms for his employees
(C) To cancel a reservation he made earlier
(D) To purchase airline tickets for participants

55 What does the woman say she will do?
(A) Prepare some equipment
(B) Clean up the conference rooms
(C) Write down some information
(D) Call a travel agency

Questions 56-58 refer to the following conversation.

W Good morning, Allen. How was the seminar yesterday? It was about consumer behavior, right?

M Yes, and it was really informative. I was quite impressed with the instructor, Keith. He covered a lot in just a half day.

W Oh, I know him. He's very knowledgeable. What kinds of things did he talk about?

M He shared a lot about his sales experience in the auto industry. I think I'll incorporate some of the things I learned when we start developing our new marketing strategy next week.

56 What was the main topic of the seminar?
(A) Managing time more efficiently
(B) Running a responsible corporation
(C) Understanding consumer behavior
(D) Becoming a great instructor

57 What does the man mean when he says, "I was quite impressed with the instructor"?
(A) He thinks the instructor looks good.
(B) He has met the instructor before.
(C) He wants to be like the instructor.
(D) He thinks the instructor was efficient.

58 What will the man do next week?
(A) Work on a marketing strategy
(B) Buy a new car for his family
(C) Meet with corporate lawyers
(D) Train new employees

Questions 59-61 refer to the following conversation.

M Hello. How can I help you?

W Hi. I just noticed this stain on my blouse, and I need it for an important meeting tomorrow. How long will it take to clean it? Can you do it today?

M It looks like a food spill, and it won't take a long time, but I won't be able to get to it until later today because we're really backed up at the moment.

W As long as it's done today, I'm willing to wait. Should I leave the blouse and come back for it later?

M Yes, that should work. Why don't I give you a call once I'm finished with it? Could you write down your name and phone number?

W Sure, just give me one second.

59 Where is the conversation taking place?
(A) At a paint store
(B) At a clothing store
(C) At a dry cleaner's
(D) At a dentist's office

60 What does the woman ask the man about?
(A) Contacting a different store
(B) Changing a meeting time
(C) Altering her blouse
(D) Removing a stain from clothing

61 What will the woman probably do next?
(A) Pay for her purchase
(B) Provide her contact information
(C) Return an item for a refund
(D) Wait for gift-wrapping

Questions 62-64 refer to the following conversation.

M Paula, why are you still at your office? Aren't you volunteering at the company fundraising event today?

W Well, I volunteered last year, and I have to deal with so many problems with my new packaging design project this month.

M Oh, that's too bad. What happened?

W Some customers are upset the packaging was defective and their products were ruined because of it. We've already sent the new ones, but I'm actually nervous because I'm not sure how to make up for the inconvenience.

M I see. Well, I'm sure you'll do fine. You've dealt with this type of issue before. I need to get to the fundraiser now, but I'll bring this problem up at our staff meeting tomorrow so that this doesn't happen again.

W Thank you, Mr. McNealy.

62 What is the main topic of the conversation?
(A) Giving a big presentation
(B) Responding to client complaints
(C) Launching a new product
(D) Holding a charity event

63 What does the woman imply when she says, "I volunteered last year"?
(A) She is able to train other volunteers.
(B) She is proud of doing volunteer work.
(C) She met someone at last year's event.
(D) She doesn't plan to attend an event today.

64 What does the man say he will do tomorrow?
(A) Raise some funds for an event
(B) Prepare a marketing questionnaire
(C) Discuss an issue at a meeting
(D) Conduct some product testing

Questions 65-67 refer to the following conversation and invoice.

W Oh, no! We ordered two hundred invitations for the company party, but only received one hundred and seventy from the stationery store. We have to do something about this.

M Well, the party isn't until the end of the month, so we have a little time. I got an e-mail from them, and they promised to send us the rest of the invitations and catalogues by the end of the week. They said they will also issue a shipping refund to make up for the inconvenience.

W Great, but I'm going to call the store right away and let the person there know how important it is for us to get our entire order in time.

M Well, you should definitely give the store a call. We want to make sure all of our employees receive an invitation as soon as possible.

65 What is the purpose of the conversation?
(A) To negotiate a price
(B) To explain a process
(C) To discuss a problem
(D) To review customer feedback

66 Look at the graphic. How much money will the speakers be refunded?
(A) $800
(B) $900
(C) $30
(D) $1,730

67 What does the woman want the store to do?
(A) Refund some money
(B) Expedite the rest of an order
(C) Change a delivery time
(D) Send an invoice via e-mail

Questions 68-70 refer to the following conversation and list.

W Hey, James. Is the Internet working on your computer?

M Yeah, I'm not having any problems with it.

W Well, I can't connect to it, so I can't see any of my e-mails. Did the one with the latest travel itinerary come yet?

M Hmm... let me see. Yes, here it is. Do you want me to send a response?

W That won't be necessary for now, but could you print it for me? I need a copy of the itinerary before I confirm my flight reservation.

68 Why is the woman unable to access her e-mail?
(A) Her password has expired.
(B) She forgot to update some software.
(C) Her computer needs some repairs.
(D) Her Internet connection is not working.

69 Look at the graphic. Who sent the e-mail the speakers are referring to?
(A) Ilene Rosenthal
(B) David Choi
(C) Adrian Harris
(D) Helen Edmond

70 What does the woman ask the man to do?
(A) Call for technical assistance
(B) Prepare for a conference
(C) Print a document
(D) Review some sales figures

Part 4

Questions 71-73 refer to the following news report.

This is Pamela Cox with the WLW morning forecast. We are expecting some changes to the unseasonably warm weather we've had recently. A cold front is moving in, and we'll be experiencing some frigid temperatures today. We only expect the high for the day to reach minus three degrees Celsius. I recommend that you wear warm clothes such as padding or wool coats. In addition, don't forget your hats and gloves, especially if you are spending more than a few minutes outdoors. These temperatures will likely stick around for a few days. I will have details on what the rest of the week's forecast looks like after this message from our sponsor, Food Club Grocery.

71 What is the report about?
(A) Health
(B) Weather
(C) Sports
(D) Traffic

72 What does the speaker suggest the listeners do?
(A) Spend some time outside
(B) Drive carefully
(C) Dress warmly
(D) Stack up some groceries

73 What will the listeners hear next?
(A) An advertisement
(B) A music program
(C) An emergency report
(D) An interview with a guest speaker

Questions 74-76 refer to the following telephone message.

Good evening, Mr. Burgess. This is Felix Martinez at the Pro Care Auto Shop. I've just finished replacing the brakes on your car, so it's ready to be picked up. However, we are about to close for the day, so you can come by tomorrow between nine and six to pick it up. I also noticed that your wiper fluid was low, so I refilled it for you. There's no charge for that. If you have any questions, feel free to give me a call. Otherwise, I'll see you sometime tomorrow. Thanks.

74 What is the purpose of the message?
(A) To request some contact information
(B) To suggest some future repairs
(C) To report the completion of a job
(D) To advertise an auto product

75 What does the speaker mean when he says, "we are about to close for the day"?
(A) His place will be closed during the weekend.
(B) He thinks the work might be delayed.
(C) He wants the customer to hurry up.
(D) He doesn't want the customer to come today.

76 What did the speaker notice about the car?
(A) The wiper fluid needed to be refilled.
(B) The air conditioning was broken.
(C) The brake lights weren't working.
(D) The oil needed to be changed.

Questions 77-79 refer to the following introduction.

Good afternoon, everyone. I'd like to introduce Elaine Perkins, our new receptionist. Since our customer base has been expanding rapidly for the past two years, we are really happy to have her join our company. Elaine has had experience working in smaller offices, but this is her first time she has worked for an operation as large as ours. So please take the time to help her to get to know her way around. I'll give her a tour of the offices and boardroom this morning before she begins her training with Cathy.

77 What is Elaine Perkins' profession?
(A) A board member
(B) An operator
(C) A tour guide
(D) A desk clerk

78 What are the listeners asked to do?
(A) Help a new employee
(B) Make a seating plan
(C) Put their names on a waiting list
(D) Greet some customers

79 What does the speaker say he will do this morning?
(A) Give a job interview
(B) Hire a trainer
(C) Give a tour
(D) Revise a manual

Questions 80-82 refer to the following excerpt from a meeting.

Before we get to today's managers' meeting, I have an important announcement to make. I just found out that Michael Santos, our chief executive officer, will be visiting us next Thursday. As you know, the large remodeling project we've just completed was part of a corporate program to update all of the department stores in our chain. The CEO has been visiting some of the renovated stores, and we're next on his list. Now, this isn't a formal inspection, so no special preparations are required. There'll be a luncheon for Mr. Santos that day, and it would be great if you could come and give him a warm welcome. Please let me know your availability by the end of the day.

80 Why is Mr. Santos coming for a visit?
(A) A project has been completed.
(B) A new branch has opened.
(C) A sales record has been achieved.
(D) A new manager has been hired.

81 Why does the speaker say, "this isn't a formal inspection"?
(A) To remind the listeners of an event
(B) To reassure employees
(C) To dispute a claim
(D) To express disagreement

82 What event have the listeners been invited to?
(A) A retirement party
(B) A fashion show
(C) A welcome luncheon
(D) A product demonstration

Questions 83-85 refer to the following telephone message.

Hello, Stanley. This is Maggie from the Accounting Department. I've been working on finalizing some expense reports so that the reimbursement checks can be issued to employees. In your case, I have the documentation you provided for your client dinner in Hong Kong last month. Unfortunately, I noticed that you didn't include the receipt from the restaurant. I would appreciate it if you could fax a copy of it to me as soon as possible. If I get your fax by Wednesday morning, I can issue your payment before the end of the week. My fax number is 555-8181. Thanks.

83 Why did the speaker leave a message?
(A) To request a client list
(B) To report on a budgeting change
(C) To provide an update on travel plans
(D) To request missing documentation

84 What does the speaker ask the listener to do?
(A) Mail a package
(B) Send an e-mail
(C) Provide a forwarding address
(D) Fax a copy of a receipt

85 When does the speaker hope to receive a reply?
(A) By Tuesday
(B) By Wednesday
(C) By this week
(D) By this month

Questions 86-88 refer to the following talk.

I'd like to begin today's meeting with some great news. The final sales report of the year was completed this morning, and I just had a chance to read over it. I am pleased to inform you that we not only achieved our yearly sales goal, but exceeded it by ten percent. I am extremely proud of all of you for your hard work this year to help the company achieve this goal. Management has decided to reward your efforts with an end-of-the-year bonus check. The checks will be issued at the end of the month and mailed to your home addresses. For those of you who would like to view the final sales report, a copy will be available to download from the company Web site by the end of the week. Congratulations again. Now, let's proceed with the remaining items on today's agenda.

86 Where is the talk probably being given?
(A) At a company picnic
(B) At an awards ceremony
(C) At a company meeting
(D) At a job fair

87 What was completed this morning?
(A) An office renovation
(B) A meeting agenda
(C) A new Web site
(D) A sales report

88 What will happen later this month?
(A) Financial bonuses will be awarded.
(B) A revised agenda will be sent by e-mail.
(C) A celebration will be held.
(D) A new president will be named.

Questions 89-91 refer to the following advertisement.

If you're looking for the most affordable furniture for your home or office, Easton's Furniture is the place to go. We have everything you need from beds and bookshelves to tables and office furniture. We've recently upgraded our Web site, so now you can browse our wide selection of merchandise without even leaving your home. You can also place your order online and benefit from free home or office delivery on orders over 900 dollars. Just go to www.eastonsfurniture.com to view every item in our showroom. We look forward to being of service.

89 What kind of business is being advertised?
(A) A paint store
(B) A furniture store
(C) An office supply store
(D) A graphic design company

90 What does the upgraded Web site offer?
(A) Coupons for discounts on office furniture
(B) Faster speed to access information
(C) Clear directions to the store
(D) The convenience of online shopping

91 How can customers receive free delivery?
(A) By spending over a certain amount
(B) By making a purchase by credit card
(C) By applying for a membership card
(D) By completing a customer survey

Questions 92-94 refer to the following telephone message and map.

Good morning, Steven. This is Samantha calling from Dr. Brady's office. I'm calling to remind you about your appointment for a medical checkup this week. The appointment is at eleven o'clock on Friday morning. However, I suggest you leave your place earlier than normal as the traffic around our building has been bad because of road construction. You might also want to park your car in the annex building at the corner of Forest Road and Oakland Avenue and walk to our office to avoid any further delays. If, for any reason, you need to cancel or reschedule your appointment, please call me right away. I look forward to seeing you on Friday.

92 What is the purpose of the message?
(A) To cancel a meeting
(B) To schedule some repairs
(C) To confirm an appointment
(D) To ask for an address

93 What does the speaker recommend the listener do?
(A) Leave earlier than usual
(B) Use public transportation
(C) Come back later
(D) Bring some medical records

94 Look at the graphic. Which number shows where the annex building is?
(A) 1 (B) 2
(C) 3 (D) 4

Questions 95-97 refer to the following excerpt from a meeting and list.

Before we talk about our sales results from last quarter, let me say how pleased I am with the success that Jessie's Café has been having. When I started this business last year, I was not sure how well it would do. But the results show that we've exceeded our goals. Of course, there's always room for improvement. As you know, our biggest rival is All Flavors. This list compares features of the two restaurants so that we can see where we can do better. If we want to be competitive, we'll have to offer all the same services. So, let's talk about what we can add so that we can keep up with All Flavors.

95 What is the main topic of the talk?
(A) Relocation plans
(B) A potential acquisition
(C) Software upgrades
(D) A business performance

96 Who most likely is the speaker?
(A) A marketing researcher
(B) A business owner
(C) A news reporter
(D) A store clerk

97 Look at the graphic. What will the speaker most likely discuss next?
(A) Prices
(B) Atmosphere
(C) Menus
(D) Customer Service

Questions 98-100 refer to the following talk and brochure.

Thank you all for coming to Digit-Tech's first conference for software developers. If you haven't received a gift bag filled with pens and notebooks yet, please make sure to pick one up from the front desk where you got your conference badge. Please be aware that there is one change made to today's schedule in the brochure, though. Our first speaker this morning had a plane delay because of the heavy fog, so he will switch his presentation time with that of the next speaker of the day at 2 P.M. Until the first presentation starts at 10 A.M., everyone is invited to the Reedsburg Ballroom for an informal networking session to get to know your colleagues in the industry.

98 What is offered to the listeners?
(A) A visitor's badge
(B) A bag of supplies
(C) A presentation ticket
(D) A complimentary drink

99 Look at the graphic. According to the speaker, who will make the first presentation?
(A) Chris Appleton
(B) Mark Elliot
(C) Lorena Kim
(D) Jennifer Lock

100 Why are the listeners invited to the Reedsburg Ballroom?
(A) To eat breakfast
(B) To attend a presentation
(C) To register for the event
(D) To meet people

TEST 08

| p.112

1	(C)	2	(C)	3	(A)	4	(D)	5	(B)
6	(C)	7	(B)	8	(A)	9	(C)	10	(C)
11	(A)	12	(B)	13	(C)	14	(B)	15	(B)
16	(B)	17	(C)	18	(A)	19	(A)	20	(B)
21	(B)	22	(C)	23	(B)	24	(C)	25	(C)
26	(C)	27	(C)	28	(A)	29	(C)	30	(A)
31	(B)	32	(B)	33	(A)	34	(C)	35	(B)
36	(B)	37	(C)	38	(A)	39	(B)	40	(C)
41	(D)	42	(B)	43	(C)	44	(B)	45	(C)
46	(D)	47	(B)	48	(A)	49	(C)	50	(C)
51	(B)	52	(D)	53	(B)	54	(D)	55	(C)
56	(B)	57	(D)	58	(C)	59	(A)	60	(C)
61	(D)	62	(D)	63	(C)	64	(A)	65	(B)
66	(C)	67	(D)	68	(A)	69	(B)	70	(B)
71	(C)	72	(D)	73	(A)	74	(A)	75	(A)
76	(B)	77	(B)	78	(A)	79	(D)	80	(A)
81	(A)	82	(B)	83	(C)	84	(B)	85	(D)
86	(C)	87	(A)	88	(D)	89	(D)	90	(B)
91	(C)	92	(C)	93	(D)	94	(A)	95	(B)
96	(B)	97	(D)	98	(B)	99	(C)	100	(D)

Part 1

1 (A) A man is talking to a friend.
(B) A man is walking through a park.
(C) A man is sitting at a desk.
(D) A man is watching a performance.

2 (A) People are parading around a square.
(B) A flag is fluttering in the wind.
(C) A fence surrounds some sculptures.
(D) Workers are cleaning a hallway.

3 (A) A man is reading something outdoors.
(B) A man is serving a meal.
(C) A man is pouring coffee into a cup.
(D) A man is reaching for a bag under a chair.

4 (A) One of the men is driving a car.
(B) The men are leaning against a wall.
(C) Tires have been dropped on the floor.
(D) The hood of a car has been opened.

5 (A) They are looking at the view through a window.
(B) Some people are listening to a presentation.
(C) One of them is setting up a meeting room.
(D) They are distributing notepads.

6 (A) Some customers are entering a store.
(B) One of the cars is being towed.
(C) Some vehicles are facing the front of a building.
(D) The parking lot is almost empty.

Part 2

7 Who asked for the monthly financial report?
(A) Eleven o'clock tomorrow.
(B) I believe it was Mr. Harden.
(C) Yes, the bill came this week.

8 When is the next available appointment with Dr. Kimball?
(A) On Friday at three.
(B) Yes, he's available.
(C) At the hospital.

9 What plans do you have for our clients tonight?
(A) A group of five executives from Korea.
(B) Yes, that's a good idea.
(C) I'm going to take them to a nice restaurant.

10 How is your newsletter article coming along?
(A) To the art museum.
(B) He's coming soon.
(C) I'm almost finished with it.

11 Are you planning to go shopping tomorrow?
(A) No, I have to work.
(B) It's an architectural plan.
(C) Yes, I heard that, too.

12 Our manager will be retiring in August.
(A) A two-year contract.
(B) She'll certainly be missed.
(C) We already reserved it.

13 Is a 10 A.M. flight okay, or should I book you on a later one?
(A) I'm not usually late for meetings.
(B) Sorry. We're fully booked.
(C) Earlier would be better.

14 Why did Lynette call?
(A) Yes, I think that's her name.
(B) She needed help finding a document.
(C) Approximately an hour ago.

15 What kind of ticket would you like?
(A) The plane arrives on time.
(B) One in the first row.
(C) It's a different kind of fabric.

16 Could you please show Mr. Ishida my office?
(A) It starts at three.
(B) Sure, I will get him.
(C) Thank you. It's very kind of you.

17 You're from Japan, aren't you?
(A) He's never been to Tokyo.
(B) No, all the international flights have been canceled.
(C) Yes, from the northern part of the country.

18 How soon can you start scanning these forms?
(A) I'll start this afternoon.
(B) At the registration desk.
(C) Beginning on page seventeen.

19 Should I open the window?
(A) I'll turn on the air conditioning.
(B) The weekly weather forecast.
(C) I'd like that one, please.

20 Didn't Kelly order office supplies last week?
(A) Put them in her office.
(B) Yes, they'll be delivered today.
(C) They'll revise it by tomorrow.

21 Where is the copy of this month's fashion magazine?
(A) Several popular summer colors.
(B) Did it arrive already?
(C) An old version of the photocopier.

22 Did Samantha give you the key to the warehouse?
(A) They work in the womenswear section.
(B) She is on her way to Singapore.
(C) I thought you had it.

23 Do you think anyone will have trouble understanding this point?
(A) Some more people should be arriving soon.
(B) Yes, the terms seem too technical.
(C) It hasn't been sharpened recently.

24 Why do they want to meet at eleven instead of in the afternoon?
(A) After a one-hour break.
(B) Thank you for your suggestion.
(C) You should ask Ms. Chen.

25 We should review our presentation for tomorrow's meeting.
(A) She already sent them.
(B) Actually, it was yesterday.
(C) Sure. When should we meet?

26 Who's in charge of testing the new software?
(A) By September tenth.
(B) Yes, you're right.
(C) I'm handling that.

27 Which of the interns is working today?
(A) Erin repaired it yesterday.
(B) Turn at the end of the hall.
(C) Janice will be here in thirty minutes.

28 Didn't you just contact maintenance about the fax machine?
(A) Don't tell me it's broken again.
(B) Twenty copies printed and bound.
(C) No, my office is on the second floor.

29 We'd like you to present your research at the next directors' meeting.
(A) Conference room B.
(B) Yes, yesterday after lunch.
(C) Sure. I would be happy to give you an update.

30 Will the office party be catered, or do you want me to reserve a restaurant?
(A) Louise hired a caterer.
(B) Until the end of the month.
(C) I'm afraid they're running late.

31 You haven't taken inventory of the RX series, have you?
(A) You can take as many as you want.
(B) Was I supposed to?
(C) Yes, this is a new invention for children.

Part 3

Questions 32-34 refer to the following conversation.

M Hello. I am here for the New Technology Convention. Am I in the right place?

W You sure are. Will you give me your name so I can check the registration list and give you the pass that you'll need when entering the facility?

M Of course. My name is Jason Lamez. Oh, and can you tell me where the lecture on the micro-electronic industry is going to be held?

W Let me check. Here it is. It'll be in the main auditorium in this building at 6 P.M.

32 Where most likely is the conversation taking place?
(A) In an office meeting
(B) At a convention center
(C) At an airport
(D) In a university lecture room

33 What will the man receive?
(A) An entry pass
(B) An information booklet
(C) A registration form
(D) A free lecture

34 What does the man want to know?
(A) The attendees at an event
(B) The room where he will be staying
(C) The location of an event
(D) The fee for registration

Questions 35-37 refer to the following conversation.

W Hello, this is Sinead Callaghan calling from the press office of the Paint Association. I have been asked about a new stain remover, Anchor Effect, which I understand your company manufactures. However, I have not heard of this product before.

M I'm delighted that our product is proving popular. Anchor Effect is fast becoming a great favorite with our clients. Would you like me to arrange one of our sales representatives to visit you to describe it in detail?

W Yes, I would like to find out more about the product, in particular the way it was formulated and the performance test results.

M Sure. Let me organize a visit from one of our sales team to demonstrate the product and answer any questions you may have.

35 Who is the woman?
(A) A researcher
(B) A press officer
(C) A decorator
(D) A market analyst

36 Why is the woman calling?
(A) To reorder some equipment
(B) To request product information
(C) To ask for advice on a project
(D) To report an invoice error

37 What does the man offer to do?
(A) Arrange for a house to be painted
(B) Change the amount of products ordered
(C) Organize a visit from a representative
(D) Mail some samples

Questions 38-40 refer to the following conversation.

M Sandra, when will you be back from Boston?

W Probably next Monday if all the meetings go especially well. Otherwise, I'll have to stay the entire week and come back next weekend. Why?

M Well, Chelsie's leaving for a new position in Korea, so we're planning to throw her a farewell party at a downtown restaurant next Tuesday. I was hoping you could go.

W Oh, that's a shame because I don't think I'll be able to make it on Tuesday. Anyway, thanks for telling me about Chelsie. I should stop by her office before I leave. She has been such a great colleague, so I must say goodbye to her.

38 What does the man want to know?
(A) The woman's schedule
(B) The reason for the woman's trip
(C) Directions to a downtown area
(D) The location of Chelsie's office

39 What will happen next Tuesday?
(A) A promotion of an employee
(B) A party for a coworker
(C) A business investment
(D) A staff meeting

40 What will the woman do before her trip?
(A) Stop by a gas station to fill up the tank
(B) Move to Korea to open a business
(C) Meet her colleague in person
(D) Visit the downtown office

Questions 41-43 refer to the following conversation.

M Have you seen the figures for our computer game sales nationwide? I'm talking about the ones from last quarter. *Quest West* is responsible for the entire increase.

W That's very exciting. You know, it's been a long time since we released a game that had such a tremendous impact. How are international sales doing?

M Actually, they've been kind of slow because the versions in other languages are not on the market yet. But I understand several versions will be in stores in Asia and Europe by the end of the month.

W Well, as soon as they are, I'm sure we'll see similar results. *Quest West* will be popular with gamers worldwide.

41 What are the speakers discussing?
(A) The renovation of a building
(B) Promoting a new branch
(C) Reimbursement for expenses
(D) A sales performance

42 What is *Quest West*?
(A) A television program (B) A computer game
(C) A guidebook (D) A magazine

43 What will probably happen at the end of the month?
(A) A publicity campaign will begin.
(B) Overseas branches will be open.
(C) Some versions of a product will be available.
(D) A product will be popular with younger consumers.

Questions 44-46 refer to the following conversation.

W Hi. I saw a jacket that I like on display, but I don't know how much it costs. Can you help me?

M Sure, which one are you interested in?

W Over here. See? This jacket looks great, but I can't find the price tag.

M Okay, let me take a look. It must be hidden inside.

W Actually, I already checked the inside for a tag, and there wasn't one.

M All right, I need to find the price on our Web site. Just give me a minute, and I'll be right back.

44 What problem does the woman mention?
(A) A receipt is missing.
(B) Some information can't be found.
(C) A popular item is out of stock.
(D) The price is higher than expected.

45 Why does the woman say, "This jacket looks great"?
(A) To explain the quality of an item
(B) To convince the man to buy a product
(C) To show interest in making a purchase
(D) To ask the man to check an inventory list

46 What does the man say he will do?
(A) Expand a product line
(B) Look for discount offers
(C) Print a receipt
(D) Check a Web site

Questions 47-49 refer to the following conversation with three speakers.

M Welcome to Yamada Printing company.

W1 Hi. I'd like to have some fliers printed for a charity event that I'm organizing.

M All right, here's a book of designs for you to choose from.

W1 Actually, we already have a hard copy of our design and logo, so we'd like to use those.

M Oh, our shop's policy is that customers must use one of our design templates because it's easier for us to work with. But let me ask the manager. Ms. Yumi, this customer has her own design for her printing job. Is that okay?

W2 It's okay, but it will cost a bit more because the design will have to be manually entered and modified for our machine.

W1 Oh, in that case, can I get an estimate of how much extra that will cost? I want to make sure it's worth the money.

47 What are the speakers mainly discussing?
(A) A computer upgrade
(B) A printing order
(C) A store refund
(D) An advance payment

48 What store policy is mentioned?
(A) Customers must use a shop design.
(B) Customers must place an order two weeks in advance.
(C) Services must be paid in full when ordering.
(D) Deliveries could cost extra depending on the location.

49 What does Ms. Yumi explain to the customer?
(A) A warranty cannot be extended.
(B) A replacement part should be ordered.
(C) An extra charge will be added.
(D) An account has been suspended.

Questions 50-52 refer to the following conversation.

M Emily, how's the development of the payroll software coming along?

W We gave the latest version to some of our clients so they could test it.

M Did you have a chance to review their feedback about it?

W I did review their comments. Apparently, some clients thought it was too hard to navigate the system. So I'm making some adjustments to make the software more user-friendly.

M Okay. By the way, the vice president asked me when the final version of the program will be available.

W We're right on schedule. We should be ready to launch it in March.

50 What is the conversation mainly about?
(A) A payroll error
(B) A department reorganization
(C) Software development
(D) Decreased sales

51 According to the woman, what did the feedback show?
(A) The company should hire more employees.
(B) Some clients were dissatisfied with a program.
(C) Employees made some mistakes.
(D) Management communicated with employees well.

52 What will happen in March?
(A) Salaries will be increased.
(B) A workshop will be scheduled.
(C) Some customers will be interviewed.
(D) A product will be released.

Questions 53-55 refer to the following conversation.

M Hey, Lisa. Thank you for giving me that book on contemporary art. Not only was it interesting, but it also gave me insights into how art history has changed over the years.

W I figured you'd like it.

M Do you know any other good books on that subject?

W Hmm... Try *History Tours through Art*. It offers diverse perspectives of art over the past few centuries.

M Great. I'll order it online right away.

W I think the bookshop on Main Street has a big sale going on right now. If I were you, I would check that place out first to get it for a lower price.

M Oh, okay! I'll go there tonight after work. Thanks again.

53 What has the man been reading about?
(A) Personal relationships
(B) Art history
(C) Web design
(D) Architecture

54 What does the man ask the woman to do?
(A) Change a deadline
(B) Discuss a project
(C) Offer a lower price
(D) Provide a recommendation

55 Where does the man say he will go tonight?
(A) To a museum
(B) To a library
(C) To a bookstore
(D) To a gallery

Questions 56-58 refer to the following conversation with three speakers.

W1 Hi, Andy. I have a question about how things work here at the magazine.

M Sure, Becky. What is it?

W1 Well, a former colleague of mine would be a good fit for our team. He is looking for a new editorial position, and we've got an opening in our department. How can I recommend him for the job?

M Good question. Oh, let's see... Junko has been here a long time.

W2 Did I just hear my name?

M Yes. Do you know how to refer job candidates to the Hiring Department? Becky wants to make a recommendation.

W2 Sure. Go to the company Web site, find the Human Resources link, select "Referrals," and you can find a form to fill out.

W1 Thanks, Junko, I really appreciate it.

56 What does Becky want to do?
(A) Change a work shift
(B) Refer a friend for employment
(C) Attend an employee training session
(D) Request a transfer to another department

57 What does the man mean when he says, "Junko has been here a long time"?
(A) Junko plans to retire soon.
(B) He was surprised about a mistake that Junko made.
(C) He thinks Junko should be promoted.
(D) Junko can answer a question instead.

58 What does Junko recommend doing?
(A) Consulting a professional counselor
(B) Picking up extra materials
(C) Visiting a Web site
(D) Talking to a manager in person

Questions 59-61 refer to the following conversation.

M Hello, Ms. Lim. I heard you'd like my agency to design a new advertising campaign for your moving company.

W Yes, we're concerned because another moving company just opened nearby, and we're starting to feel the effects of the competition.

M I see. I'm sure with the help of well-targeted advertisements, you should be able to gain the upper hand back. Now, it would help if I had a better sense of what customers like about your company.

W Well, people say they appreciate our top-notch customer service and the effort we make to meet customers' expectations.

M I think that could be something we emphasize in the campaign.

W That's a good point. I think so, too.

59 What type of business does the woman work for?
(A) A moving company
(B) A real estate agency
(C) A delivery company
(D) An advertising agency

60 What is the woman concerned about?
(A) Shipping delays
(B) New government regulations
(C) An increase in competition
(D) A staff shortage

61 What does the woman emphasize about the company?
(A) The affordable prices
(B) The design of Web site
(C) The speedy delivery service
(D) The customer service

Questions 62-64 refer to the following conversation and directory.

W Raj, it's a really good idea to stop by the grocery store before we leave for the team hike. What are we going to buy for everyone?

M I'm sure we'll all get thirsty after a couple of hours of walking. So let's get a case of bottled water. I think it will be a good team-building exercise to spend the afternoon hiking with the rest of the team.

W Yes, I couldn't agree more. By the way, don't forget to fill out the reimbursement form after we're done shopping. The company reimburses expenses for department outings like this.

M Good point. Hmm... I've never been in this store, and I'm not sure where we can find bottled water.

W I'm not sure either. Let's take a look at the directory.

62 What are the speakers planning to do?
(A) Organize a business dinner
(B) Attend a professional conference
(C) Participate in a sports competition
(D) Go hiking with employees

63 Look at the graphic. Which aisle should the speakers go to?
(A) Aisle 1
(B) Aisle 2
(C) Aisle 3
(D) Aisle 4

64 What does the woman remind the man to do?
(A) Fill out a form
(B) Ask for a discount
(C) Check a price online
(D) Present a membership card

Questions 65-67 refer to the following conversation and review.

M Vera, did you see the article in *Food & Wine Magazine* with the list of the best restaurants in the area? The article gave our restaurant five stars in the category of food quality. As the head chef, you must be so proud.

W Yes, I saw that article, and I'm glad I decided to change the suppliers for our main dishes. It shows that customers are satisfied with the quality of our fresh ingredients.

M True, but I'm disappointed that some of our ratings weren't better. I'm not surprised that we scored low in the pricing category, but I am surprised by this one, where we only received three stars.

W We'll definitely work on improving that area next year.

M Yes, that's why I think it may be a good idea to discuss this issue with the staff. They may have some ideas for some changes we can make to improve the situation.

65 Who most likely is the woman?
(A) A waitress
(B) A chef
(C) A restaurant owner
(D) A food critic

66 Look at the graphic. What do the speakers want the restaurant to improve in?
(A) Atmosphere
(B) Prices
(C) Customer service
(D) Food quality

67 What does the man suggest doing?
(A) Lowering the prices of some dishes
(B) Offering cooking classes during the day
(C) Providing food samples for customers
(D) Asking employees for suggestions

Questions 68-70 refer to the following conversation and weather forecast.

M Maria, I heard it's going to rain all day next Tuesday. So we might have to change the date of our company picnic.

W Well, here's the weather forecast. Later next week seems okay.

M You're right. Twenty-five degrees is nice, and there's nothing about rain either. So let's reschedule it for then.

W I better call the caterer to let them know about the date change.

M That's a good idea. Hopefully, we won't be charged extra for delaying our food order by a few days.

68 What event are the speakers discussing?
(A) A company picnic
(B) An outdoor concert
(C) An awards ceremony
(D) A retirement party

69 Look at the graphic. Which day do the speakers choose?
(A) Wednesday
(B) Thursday
(C) Friday
(D) Saturday

70 What will the woman do next?
(A) Mail some invitations to participants
(B) Contact a food preparation company
(C) Book a venue for an event
(D) Call the weather bureau for more details

Part 4

Questions 71-73 refer to the following excerpt from a meeting.

Good morning, everyone. To start today's meeting, I'd like you all to meet Christina Hanson, the newest member of our team here at Future Tech Incorporated. Ms. Hanson majored in international relations, and she is bilingual, with strong English and Korean language skills. As you all know, we'll soon be opening our latest branch in Seoul, and Ms. Hanson's going to be integral to that process. On a personal note, she enjoys playing sports in her free time. So I'd like to encourage her to join our company's softball team this fall. Now, let's give her a warm welcome to our company.

71 What is the purpose of the talk?
(A) To announce an award winner
(B) To notify listeners of a company move
(C) To introduce a new employee
(D) To publicize a sports competition

72 What does the speaker indicate about Ms. Hanson?
(A) She used to work for a competing company.
(B) She has an advanced degree in accounting.
(C) She has been a good leader of her team.
(D) She can speak two languages.

73 What does the speaker invite Ms. Hanson to do?
(A) Join a sports team
(B) Review an employment contract
(C) Demonstrate her language skills
(D) Participate in a training session

Questions 74-76 refer to the following telephone message.

Hello, this is Joy Walton from Rox Management Corporation. We are holding a two-day sales meeting, and I would like to check out your room prices and availability. On your Web site, it states that you have a number of seminar rooms that can accommodate the number of people we anticipate to be in attendance. The sales meeting is planned for the third week in March although the dates are quite flexible at the moment. We are expecting approximately one hundred people over the two days, and I would like to make an appointment to view the facilities. Please call me as soon as possible to discuss this matter. Thank you.

74 Why is the speaker calling?
(A) To make inquiries about a gathering
(B) To book a dinner reservation
(C) To confirm an appointment
(D) To inform of a change in plans

75 What information did the speaker find on a Web site?
(A) Room sizes
(B) Options for meals
(C) Opening hours
(D) Large group discounts

76 What does the speaker want to do?
(A) Negotiate with a manager
(B) Visit the venue
(C) Receive an estimate
(D) Put down a deposit

Questions 77-79 refer to the following tour information.

Hello and welcome to Kingstar Motors. You'll see every step of the assembly process of our LX-5000 truck model on this guided tour. Now, it's almost a three-hour tour, so as we walk around the factory, we'll try to stop at areas with benches when we can. In addition, our automobile museum is currently under renovation and closed to the public. However, if you save your tickets from today's tour, you can come back to see the museum when it reopens without being charged again. Now, let's start the tour by putting on hard hats and goggles for your safety.

77 Where does the talk most likely take place?
(A) At a science museum
(B) At a manufacturing plant
(C) At a trade convention
(D) At an electronics store

78 Why does the speaker say, "it's almost a three-hour tour"?
(A) To caution the listeners
(B) To announce a delay
(C) To correct some mistakes
(D) To express satisfaction with a situation

79 What does the speaker recommend the listeners do?
(A) Buy the safety equipment
(B) Create order forms
(C) Review the brochures
(D) Keep their tickets

Questions 80-82 refer to the following announcement.

Attention, please. The new security system will be in operation beginning next Monday after the installation is completed over the weekend. All employees will need their identification cards to enter or exit the building. On each door, there will be a security panel into which you will have to place your card before the door will open. Be sure to have your card with you at all times. Beginning next Monday morning, guests will be required to stop by the security office before entering the building. There, they will be issued a temporary card. If you do not receive your new identification pass by early Friday afternoon, contact your supervisor to make sure that you get it before the day ends.

80 What is the main topic of the announcement?
(A) A security system
(B) A new club membership
(C) A maintenance job
(D) A personal credit card

81 When will the new change go into effect?
(A) On Monday
(B) On Tuesday
(C) On Friday
(D) On Sunday

82 What should the listeners do if they don't receive their pass?
(A) Contact the security office
(B) Talk to a supervisor
(C) Register for one online
(D) Complete a request form

Questions 83-85 refer to the following telephone message.

Hello, Frank. It's Jamie. Thanks again for preparing for our Japanese clients' visit. I've looked at the Web sites for the hotel and restaurants you chose, and they look great. We have one thing to change, however. I was just told that Mr. Matsuda will be added to the visiting group. Would you please call the hotel and reserve another room for him? I think he would prefer a room on his own. Oh, one last thing: in your e-mail, you mentioned taking the visitors to the photography exhibition at the art museum. That exhibition received negative reviews. So what do you think about a musical concert instead?

83 What is the speaker mainly discussing?
(A) Conference arrangements
(B) A vacation itinerary
(C) Some visiting clients
(D) A restaurant opening

84 What change does the speaker mention?
(A) The menu at a restaurant
(B) The number of guests
(C) A price of admission
(D) The time of an appointment

85 What does the speaker imply when she says, "That exhibition received negative reviews"?
(A) She disagrees with the reviews.
(B) She wants some additional information.
(C) She assumes a place will not be crowded.
(D) She thinks a plan should be changed.

Questions 86-88 refer to the following advertisement.

Do you need to get your bathroom cleaned but just don't want to begin the tiring work? Then it's time for Wash & Flush, which is used by thousands of people all over the world. This revolutionary cleaning system will help you make your bathroom as clean as new with little or no effort. Wash & Flush is easy to use and finishes the job in no time. You don't need to keep all your heavy, old cleaning tools anymore. Wash & Flush will do the entire bathroom for you. If you place an order right now, the shipping and handling will be free. But you need to hurry. This offer only lasts until midnight tonight. Don't hesitate. Call 275-555-9800 now!

86 What is being advertised?
(A) A cleaning tool for offices
(B) A fabric stain remover
(C) A system for cleaning bathrooms
(D) A washing machine

87 What is mentioned about the product?
(A) It is simple to use.
(B) It takes a long time to make.
(C) It is cheaper than other brands.
(D) It is not sold at other stores.

88 What is the benefit of ordering now?
(A) Receiving an additional product for free
(B) Getting a product at half price
(C) Getting a discount voucher for future use
(D) Receiving complimentary shipping

Questions 89-91 refer to the following announcement.

As most of you already know, our company has been facing intense competition in recent months since other businesses have been establishing strong presences in the field. In order to keep our place as the leader in the market, it is vital that everyone in this department strengthen their sales and marketing skills. So I've specially scheduled a professional development seminar for next Tuesday at two o'clock. Some of you may have other appointments at that time, but this is very important to our company's success. I'd like detailed feedback from you following the seminar, so I'll send you a form afterward. Please be sure to complete it and send it to me within twenty-four hours of receiving it.

89 According to the speaker, what has happened in recent months?
(A) A product release has been delayed.
(B) Customer complaints have increased.
(C) Employees have reported low satisfaction.
(D) Competition from other companies has increased.

90 What does the speaker imply when he says, "this is very important to our company's success"?
(A) He wants to change the terms of a contract.
(B) He expects employees to attend a seminar.
(C) He hopes to find an alternative solution.
(D) He acknowledges the listeners' effort.

91 What should the listeners send to the speaker?
(A) Training materials
(B) An expense report
(C) A feedback form
(D) A list of client contacts

Questions 92-94 refer to the following radio broadcast.

Good morning. I'm Chad Vallone, and I'm thankful to EBC Radio's Econo-morning for giving me the chance to speak today. I've been a financial consultant for more than two decades now, and I would like to share some of what I've learned about financial planning. Let's begin with an easy method to control expenses and to reduce credit card debt. The first thing you have to do is create a budget. Always remember to work within your budget, especially when you plan to go shopping. Write down a list of things you need to buy and how much you expect to spend for each item. This small bit of extra planning will surprise you by how much money you can save.

92 Who is the speaker?
(A) A bank manager
(B) A radio producer
(C) A financial adviser
(D) A professional salesman

93 What is the speaker mainly discussing?
(A) How to purchase discounted goods
(B) How to be prepared for retirement
(C) How to become a financial counselor
(D) How to control spending

94 What does the speaker recommend?
(A) Making a budget for spending
(B) Going shopping less often
(C) Getting rid of unnecessary credit cards
(D) Visiting a Web site for further information

Questions 95-97 refer to the following telephone message and table.

Hello, Ms. Simpson. I'm calling from the Western Electric Company to remind you that your electricity bill was due on Friday, August eleventh. Since your payment is ten days overdue, a late fee has been added to your account balance. Please pay the bill plus the ten-day late fee on our Web site at www.westernelectric.com. For your convenience, we also offer an auto payment feature on our Web site. If you want to sign up for this service, you will need a valid credit card or bank account number. Once you do that, your future bills will be paid automatically on the day they are due. This way, you won't miss the date and be charged extra. If you have any questions about this option, please call us at 555-2453. Thank you.

95 Where does the speaker most likely work?
(A) At a financial institution
(B) At a utility company
(C) At a library
(D) At a customer service center

96 Look at the graphic. How much is the listener's late fee?
(A) $4.00
(B) $10.00
(C) $20.00
(D) $30.00

97 What should the listener provide to sign up for the service?
(A) Some contact information
(B) An invoice number
(C) A valid identification card
(D) Some payment details

Questions 98-100 refer to the following announcement and list.

Thank you all for coming to today's meeting. As you know, we're now in the process of launching our clinic's Health Pro mobile application. This new technology will allow us to monitor our patients closely and offer them better medical assistance through their mobile phones. So what I would like you all to do now is try the app yourselves on your own mobile phones. The first thing you'll see is a list of features that Health Pro offers. For example, the medication tracker will help the doctors at our clinic write a prescription. The appointment history section will show how frequently patients needed our services. But the feature I think patients will find most useful is at the bottom of your screens. It gives patients access to our health professionals anywhere, anytime.

98 Where is the talk most likely taking place?
(A) At a community center
(B) At a medical clinic
(C) At a pharmacy
(D) At a fitness center

99 What are the listeners asked to do?
(A) Purchase some new software
(B) Give a product demonstration
(C) Try some new technology
(D) Read an instruction manual

100 Look at the graphic. What feature does the speaker think will be most useful?
(A) Medication Tracker
(B) Nutrition Evaluation
(C) Appointment History
(D) Instant Messenger

TEST 08

TEST 09

| p.126

1	(A)	2	(D)	3	(B)	4	(A)	5	(D)
6	(C)	7	(C)	8	(A)	9	(B)	10	(C)
11	(C)	12	(A)	13	(B)	14	(A)	15	(A)
16	(A)	17	(A)	18	(B)	19	(C)	20	(C)
21	(B)	22	(C)	23	(B)	24	(A)	25	(C)
26	(B)	27	(C)	28	(A)	29	(A)	30	(A)
31	(B)	32	(A)	33	(B)	34	(A)	35	(C)
36	(B)	37	(B)	38	(B)	39	(C)	40	(D)
41	(D)	42	(A)	43	(A)	44	(A)	45	(C)
46	(B)	47	(B)	48	(A)	49	(D)	50	(D)
51	(A)	52	(C)	53	(A)	54	(B)	55	(D)
56	(C)	57	(A)	58	(A)	59	(B)	60	(A)
61	(D)	62	(A)	63	(D)	64	(A)	65	(B)
66	(D)	67	(D)	68	(A)	69	(C)	70	(A)
71	(A)	72	(D)	73	(B)	74	(D)	75	(D)
76	(C)	77	(C)	78	(A)	79	(B)	80	(B)
81	(C)	82	(D)	83	(A)	84	(D)	85	(C)
86	(D)	87	(A)	88	(B)	89	(A)	90	(B)
91	(D)	92	(C)	93	(B)	94	(A)	95	(C)
96	(A)	97	(D)	98	(C)	99	(A)	100	(D)

Part 1

1 (A) A woman is looking in a window.
(B) A woman is waiting to make a purchase.
(C) A woman is putting something in a bag.
(D) A woman is folding some clothes.

2 (A) A man is staring at the computer.
(B) A man is holding a book.
(C) A woman is handing out some materials.
(D) A woman is resting her hands on the table.

3 (A) A train is stopped at a crowded platform.
(B) Passengers are waiting for a train.
(C) Passengers are getting on a train.
(D) Some trains have been delayed.

4 (A) They are taking a stroll on a beach.
(B) They are throwing a ball to each other.
(C) They are sitting near the lake.
(D) They are swimming in the ocean.

5 (A) A woman is speaking on the phone.
(B) A woman is arranging her desk.
(C) A woman is reading some magazines.
(D) A woman is sitting on a chair at the desk.

6 (A) Dishes are being served in a restaurant.
(B) All seats are occupied.
(C) A flower arrangement has been placed on the table.
(D) There are paintings hanging on the wall.

Part 2

7 How many people participated in the seminar for sales managers?
(A) Let's do this immediately.
(B) They are qualified managers.
(C) Approximately fifteen.

8 What kinds of products does your company sell?
(A) Office supplies.
(B) The Sales Department.
(C) Yes, I sold them all.

9 Could you pass me the quarterly earnings report?
(A) Of course. I'll do that again.
(B) Yes, here it is.
(C) It's a new report.

10 You don't even know how to get to the hospital, do you?
(A) My monthly premium.
(B) From 9 A.M. to 6 P.M.
(C) I should buy a city map.

11 When do you think the best time to call Ms. Lohan is?
(A) I think it's not good.
(B) On the phone.
(C) Anytime after work.

12 Who asked for the revised version of the manual?
(A) Mr. Atkins did.
(B) Thank you. You helped me a lot.
(C) By tomorrow morning.

13 Do you prefer to work independently or in a group?
(A) It became independent.
(B) I like both ways.
(C) I'll be back to work.

14 Why did you recommend express delivery instead of standard shipping?
(A) Because it guarantees fast delivery.
(B) You could drive on the expressway.
(C) By cruise ship.

15 Could you tell me the way to the nearest vending machine?
(A) It's right next to the elevator.
(B) Yes, we are there.
(C) That's too early.

16 Where can I find Ms. Jillian?
(A) I'm afraid she's out of town for a meeting.
(B) Have you met her before?
(C) Friday between one and three.

17 I would really like to go to the concert.
(A) Unfortunately, the tickets are all sold out.
(B) I need to cancel the concert.
(C) You shouldn't speak like that.

18 Can we check this report tomorrow?
(A) Yes, three days a week.
(B) Actually, I'm going to go to headquarters then.
(C) I want to check out some books.

19 Why did the Italian restaurant go out of business?
(A) I'm in the wrong place.
(B) It is close to the subway station.
(C) Due to the economic downturn.

20 Do you want to rehearse your presentation here or in the conference room?
(A) Yes, I need it.
(B) He wants to speak about it tomorrow.
(C) Let's get started here.

21 Let's get more chairs so that people can sit more comfortably.
(A) I will put this on the chair.
(B) Do we need some help?
(C) Fifty dollars, please.

22 Do you think we can meet the deadline for registration?
(A) At the registration desk.
(B) We will meet our client this weekend.
(C) I hope so.

23 You can attend the next conference, can't you?
(A) At the conference hall.
(B) I'm going on vacation.
(C) The meeting went too long.

24 Don't you have a copy of the itinerary for our trip to London?
(A) Yes, but not the updated one.
(B) I can copy that.
(C) The proposal is quite impressive.

25 How often do you drop by each branch office?
(A) David Marshall, the sales manager.
(B) San Diego, I believe.
(C) I haven't done that yet.

26 Has the software engineer's flight been delayed?
(A) Has he approved the deal?
(B) I will check on the status on the Web site.
(C) He recently developed some new software.

27 Who is the contact person for the manufacturing plant?
(A) By September 1st.
(B) Yes, you're right.
(C) I'm in charge.

28 I was sure that you would be able to finish the report today.
(A) Isn't it postponed?
(B) No, it was scheduled for last week.
(C) I suppose you don't have to update it.

29 Sales of our new mobile phone increased significantly this quarter, right?
(A) Yes, by twenty percent.
(B) About the quarterly advertising report.
(C) We had a board meeting.

30 Why didn't anyone in the Accounting Department receive the e-mail?
(A) I forgot to send it.
(B) Please send a message by e-mail.
(C) Before April 2nd.

31 Please let Mr. Gibson know that I'm coming.
(A) The schedule for my upcoming vacation.
(B) I told him to expect you.
(C) He's our new boss.

Part 3

Questions 32-34 refer to the following conversation.

W Hello, Mr. Jackson. I know that you made an appointment with Dr. James at ten thirty. Please have a seat. He will be available in a moment.

M Thanks. I was wondering if you could copy my test results while I wait. Two weeks ago, I had a blood test done here, and I would appreciate it if you checked that out.

W Well, I'm afraid I can't gain access to the computer files right now because we are examining the security and backup systems. But that will be done soon, so I can have it ready for you after you see the doctor.

32 Where most likely are the speakers?
(A) At a doctor's office
(B) At a department store
(C) In a security office
(D) At a computer shop

33 What does the man ask for?
(A) A product manual
(B) A copy of some results
(C) A prescription
(D) A receipt of payment

34 Why is the woman unable to deal with the man's request immediately?
(A) Some systems are being examined.
(B) The office will close soon.
(C) The information has not come out yet.
(D) She is not good at using computers.

Questions 35-37 refer to the following conversation.

M Hi. My name is Joshua Bell, and I'm from Freddie Designs. I'm calling to confirm that the closing time at your store is 9 P.M. I'm curious because I would like to go there and install a signboard outside your building.

W Yes, you're right. You can start hanging it up immediately after closing time. How long does it take to do that? I want everything ready by tomorrow morning.

M Oh, there will be enough time for the installation. My team should be able to finish it by then.

W Excellent. Our security guard will help you do the work and lock the door after you complete setting it up.

35 What is the man calling to confirm?
(A) An address
(B) A list of staff members
(C) A closing time
(D) An inventory

36 What does the woman ask about?
(A) Which items will be on sale
(B) How long a task will take
(C) How many workers will be coming
(D) What options can be selected

37 What does the woman say a security guard will do?
(A) Give a receipt
(B) Lock up a store
(C) Provide materials
(D) Issue a parking permit

Questions 38-40 refer to the following conversation.

W Excuse me. I've just arrived on Flight 172 from Sydney, but I couldn't find my suitcase in the baggage claim area. Could you check on that for me? Here's the information on my baggage.

M Hmm... The database says that your bag wasn't put on your flight. Unfortunately, you won't get it until tomorrow evening at the earliest.

W Oh, no! I really need my bag because I have to give a presentation at a conference tomorrow morning. What's your airline's policy on delayed baggage?

M We'll provide reasonable compensation, but if you want more details, please read this pamphlet to know what is covered.

38 What is the conversation mainly about?
(A) A flight cancelation
(B) Missing luggage
(C) Airfare
(D) Seat changes

39 What does the woman say she will do tomorrow?
(A) Move to a different city
(B) Check out a hotel
(C) Make a presentation
(D) Sign a contract

40 What does the man recommend the woman do?
(A) Check her passport
(B) Book a flight
(C) Use another form of transportation
(D) Read about a policy

Questions 41-43 refer to the following conversation with three speakers.

M Do either of you know why the copying machine is down again? It is not working at all, so I can't print copies of the report for a meeting.

W1 Is it still broken? I thought it was already fixed.

W2 Oh, I called the maintenance staff, and he will come to our office to fix it tomorrow.

W1 I see. As you know, it is important for us to get everything ready for the meeting.

M Actually, I'm a little bit worried about the tight deadline. Is there any place near here where I can make copies?

W2 Yes, the Zet Supplies. It's right across from our office.

M Good, I'll head up there now.

41 What are the speakers discussing?
(A) Expanding a client base
(B) Hiring a new staff member
(C) Purchasing office supplies
(D) Preparing for a meeting

42 What has caused a problem?
(A) Some equipment is malfunctioning.
(B) Some data did not arrive.
(C) Their company is understaffed.
(D) A particular item is out of stock.

43 What does the man say he will do?
(A) Make copies at a store
(B) Reserve a meeting room
(C) Meet the maintenance staff
(D) Notify colleagues of a new deadline

Questions 44-46 refer to the following conversation.

M Good afternoon, I'm Robert Grayson in Room 205. I am supposed to check out tomorrow morning, but something urgent came up, so now I need to stay here in New York for one more night. Is it possible to extend my stay here?

W Let me check it for you. Fortunately, there is a room available, but you'll have to upgrade to a double for tomorrow. In that case, you have to pay twenty dollars more.

M That's fine, it's within my budget. One more thing: I'm attending the Global Business conference, and I'm not sure where the convention hall is.

W This brochure shows where it is located.

44 What does the man want to do?
(A) Stay an extra night
(B) Upgrade a room
(C) Take a city tour
(D) Receive a brochure

45 What does the man mean when he says, "That's fine, it's within my budget"?
(A) He doesn't need to cancel his reservation.
(B) He wants to try another place.
(C) He does not care about cost.
(D) He thinks the room rate is inexpensive.

46 What most likely will the man do next?
(A) Attend a workshop
(B) Review information
(C) Investigate a location
(D) Print out a document

Questions 47-49 refer to the following conversation.

W Hi, Mr. Ford. I heard there is a problem with the training session schedules we printed for the interns.

M Right. We got a sample copy from the printing office earlier today. I realized that some of the interns' names were misspelled, so I called the office. The person there made an apology and said he will send the revised ones by Thursday.

W Hmm... I think that's not going to work. The reason is that the interns are expected to come in on Wednesday, and I want to hand out the schedules then. Would you mind calling the printing office back and asking to have the schedules delivered no later than Tuesday?

47 What was printed?
(A) Sales promotions
(B) Training schedules
(C) Conference materials
(D) Invitation cards

48 What was the problem with the sample item?
(A) Some information was incorrect.
(B) Some pages were torn out.
(C) It was the wrong size.
(D) It was only printed in black.

49 What does the woman ask the man to do?
(A) Rearrange a meeting
(B) Revise a report
(C) Use a different printer
(D) Change a delivery date

Questions 50-52 refer to the following conversation.

W Welcome back to *The Interviews* on SMP radio. We're now with our special guest, Richard Wilson, an expert on creative thinking. Mr. Wilson, can you give us some advice on thinking creatively?

M Yes, I'd love to. One of the simplest things you can do is take notes frequently. This will help you organize your thoughts.

W Great. Now, I heard that you plan to write a book about this. Can you tell us the features of your book?

M Well, that's hard to say. At the moment, the only thing I can say is it will have a lot of reliable information.

50 What suggestion does the man make?
(A) Complying with regulations
(B) Prioritizing work assignments
(C) Making a list of goals
(D) Writing something to remember

51 What is the man planning to do?
(A) Write a book
(B) Arrange an interview
(C) Design a book
(D) Organize a meeting

52 What does the man mean when he says, "that's hard to say"?
(A) He is eager to talk about his future schedule.
(B) He doesn't understand what the woman said.
(C) He is reluctant to provide an answer.
(D) He wants to hear the question again.

Questions 53-55 refer to the following conversation.

W Hi, Mr. Robinson. I've been trying to log on to my computer, but it keeps blocking me and saying that my password is not correct. Have you had this problem before?

M No, I've had no problem with it. The IT Department carried out a regular system check yesterday though, so I think that might be the cause of your trouble.

W Oh, I see. I should talk to someone on the IT staff. Who's the contact person in the IT Department?

M I don't know, but I recommend submitting a service request. Let me do that for you.

53 What is the woman unable to do?
(A) Sign in to a computer
(B) Revise a document
(C) Print a report
(D) Find a place for a meeting

54 According to the man, what happened yesterday?
(A) A building had a power failure.
(B) A system was checked.
(C) An office was moved.
(D) A computer virus was detected.

55 What does the man offer to do?
(A) Call one of his colleagues
(B) Install some programs
(C) Restart a computer
(D) Submit a help request

Questions 56-58 refer to the following conversation.

W Hi, Mr. Barkley. You must be exhausted after your long trip to Australia. How was the trip? I know that you visited some companies we do business with. You also tried to find a new supplier for our shoes. Do you have any good news?

M Yes, I found one called Milestone Footwear. It has very high-quality products. The only concern we have to think about is that the products cost twice as much as those of other suppliers.

W If its products are as good as you say, we can pay the extra cost. Why don't we request some samples to see how well made they are?

56 What did the man do in Australia?
(A) Bought some souvenirs
(B) Attended some forums
(C) Visited some businesses
(D) Met some coworkers

57 What problem does the man mention?
(A) Some items are high-priced.
(B) A product is defective.
(C) Some clients complained about a contract.
(D) A schedule is too tight.

58 What does the woman suggest?
(A) Requesting some samples
(B) Refunding some money
(C) Placing an advertisement
(D) Renting a new office

Questions 59-61 refer to the following conversation.

M Hi. I'm planning to hold a special dinner for General Manufacturing. Is there a room available for a banquet at your hotel on September fifteenth?

W Yes, but before that, could you give me information on how many people will participate? I want to confirm that the room is big enough to accommodate your group.

M Sure. Roughly two hundred people will be there.

W In that case, I would suggest the Ocean View Room. It's big enough to hold the event. The view of the sunset from there is so beautiful. So it's perfect for your dinner. If you want to make a reservation, the next step is to draw up a contract. Why don't I send it by e-mail, and then you can take a look at it?

59 Why is the man calling?
(A) To accept a proposal
(B) To inquire about a venue
(C) To negotiate a contract
(D) To change a schedule

60 What information does the woman request?
(A) The number of attendees
(B) The amount of money due
(C) The type of event
(D) The location of a hotel

61 What does the woman offer to do?
(A) Decorate a banquet hall
(B) Set up an alternative schedule
(C) Call the man back later
(D) Send the man a document

Questions 62-64 refer to the following conversation and list.

W Hello. I recently purchased a desktop from your store, but I have a problem getting access to Web sites. It worked perfectly yesterday, but it is not working well today.

M It might not be the computer's fault. It could be caused by a bad Internet connection. Have you checked it?

W I tried a number of things—restarting the computer, reinstalling the operating system, changing the cables...

M Okay, I will check it for you. Hmm... you're right. It's a common LAN card problem. If you replace it, the error will be solved. It will only take about ten minutes.

W Great. I'm glad it's not the hard drive.

62 Where does the conversation take place?
(A) At an electronics store
(B) At a computer class
(C) At a manufacturing facility
(D) At an Internet service company

63 According to the woman, what seems to be the problem?
(A) Some parts are out of stock.
(B) A system needs to be installed.
(C) An item is too old to use.
(D) A product is not working properly.

64 Look at the graphic. How much will the woman pay?
(A) $50
(B) $80
(C) $100
(D) $250

Questions 65-67 refer to the following conversation and itinerary.

M I'd like to talk about our city cycle tour. According to a local magazine, we ranked second last month. By removing the most distant area from our agency, we should revise our itinerary to attract new customers.

W Right, a one-hour cycle tour is too long for our customers. If they visit there, they don't have enough time to see other attractions.

M I totally agree. However, I just want our customers to know that the place is good for cycling. I am sure they would like it once they get there.

W So why don't we come up with a route for it and post it on our Web site? If we do so, more customers would visit there.

65 Why does the man want to adjust the itinerary?
(A) A tour didn't receive favorable reviews.
(B) A place is far from the travel agency.
(C) Customers didn't like to visit a place.
(D) Some places need to be renovated.

66 Look at the graphic. Which place will be removed from the itinerary?
(A) National Museum
(B) Art Gallery
(C) Flea Market
(D) Theme Park

67 What does the woman suggest?
(A) Hiring more staff
(B) Buying additional bicycles
(C) Searching for a new manager
(D) Posting some information on the Internet

Questions 68-70 refer to the following conversation and list.

M I'm really thrilled to hear that our company is sponsoring the race. Many people will be participating in it. So it will help promote our company.

W That's true. And we are now looking for a firm to design the race T-shirts. Have you checked this list of graphic design firms that I sent you by e-mail? We have to hire one quickly to make sure that they are ready on time.

M Oh, I see. I can look it over right away. Hmm... Polypony is the best option we can select, but its prices are too high as we have a tight budget for this event.

W Good point. Let's go with the one located in London. It offers reasonable prices and has a good reputation as well.

68 What type of event is the company sponsoring?
(A) A race
(B) A music concert
(C) A fundraiser
(D) A fashion show

69 What is the man concerned about?
(A) Inclement weather conditions
(B) A customer complaint
(C) A limited budget
(D) A defective product

70 Look at the graphic. Which company will the speakers most likely choose?
(A) Forza (B) Sunrise
(C) Polypony (D) Cardine

Part 4

Questions 71-73 refer to the following announcement.

Attention, all passengers. This is your captain speaking. I'd like to welcome you all on Flight F428 to Beijing. However, I'm afraid that there will be a slight departure delay due to a few missing passengers. To allow the passengers to board our airplane, we will leave in ten minutes or so. Despite these circumstances, we expect to arrive on time in Beijing. We apologize for any inconvenience and confusion this may cause you. Thank you for choosing Royal Airlines, and I appreciate your patience and understanding.

71 Where most likely are the listeners?
(A) On an airplane (B) On a subway
(C) On an airport shuttle (D) At a bus stop

72 What is the cause of the delay?
(A) A reservation has been canceled.
(B) A vehicle has broken down.
(C) There is an unexpected weather change.
(D) Some passengers have not yet arrived.

73 What does the speaker say will happen?
(A) The weather will be getting worse.
(B) The listeners will arrive as scheduled.
(C) Some refreshments will be provided.
(D) Some seats will not be available.

Questions 74-76 refer to the following telephone message.

Hi, Mr. Oscar. I was pleased to meet with you today to talk about your company's new sportswear advertisement. Our designers will create the initial design of the printed version of the advertisement, which will be based on your comments. In addition, we are currently offering a discount on online advertisements that you may want to use. Please let me know by Friday if you're interested in this promotion. The reason is that the deadline for this offer is the end of this week.

74 Why did the speaker meet with Mr. Oscar?
(A) To introduce a product
(B) To make a contract
(C) To review a sales report
(D) To discuss a design

75 What does the speaker offer Mr. Oscar?
(A) A company tour
(B) A job opportunity
(C) A free coupon
(D) A special discount

76 According to the speaker, what should Mr. Oscar do before Friday?
(A) Complete some paperwork
(B) Submit an application
(C) Make a decision
(D) Take a photograph

Questions 77-79 refer to the following introduction.

I'd like to thank you all for participating in today's cooking class demonstrated by chef Jean Jarre. He will be showing us tonight how to prepare real French cuisine. Chef Jarre is the head chef at La Cinq. He has been working there for more than thirty years and recently designed a new menu that features authentic French dishes. He also holds a cooking class at the restaurant every Wednesday night. Those interested in learning some of Mr. Jarre's secret recipes for classic French cooking should see him after class. Now, please welcome chef Jean Jarre.

77 What event is being introduced?
(A) A restaurant reopening
(B) A cooking competition
(C) A cooking class
(D) An international food fair

78 What did Mr. Jarre recently do?
(A) Designed a menu
(B) Renovated a restaurant
(C) Published a cookbook
(D) Opened a new restaurant

79 According to the speaker, why should some listeners see Mr. Jarre after the event?
(A) To taste new dishes
(B) To obtain cooking information
(C) To register for another cooking class
(D) To buy his cookbook

Questions 80-82 refer to the following instruction.

Good afternoon. My name is Brian Falcon, and I work for the Save the Earth organization. Your president has invited me here today to introduce you to a new program that will help you protect the environment and reduce costs at the same time. There will be many changes in company's recycling policies, but among them, let's start with the simplest one that you can all do easily. You can reduce paper waste by making copies on both sides of the paper. We also need one volunteer from each department who will help manage this program. Now, I will be handing out a piece of paper, so please write your name on it if you are interested.

80 What is the talk mainly about?
(A) Holding a charity event
(B) Being environmentally friendly
(C) Revising the company policies
(D) Reducing electricity use

81 Why does the speaker say, "let's start with the simplest one"?
(A) To express concerns about an event
(B) To ask for more effort to succeed
(C) To relieve the listeners from the burden of a change
(D) To invite the listeners to make a decision

82 What are the listeners asked to do?
(A) Order paper in different size
(B) Print in black and white
(C) Replace a part of the copy machine
(D) Make full use of paper

Questions 83-85 refer to the following telephone message.

Hi, Jenny. It's Ryan from Lowe Furniture. I'm calling with regard to the order you placed. We received your order for stools yesterday. I just want to let you know that one thousand units is a lot for us. We haven't received that kind of number before. Plus, I must remind you that we couldn't make the entire order in just two weeks even if our factory were working at full capacity. Please call me as soon as possible to discuss your order. Thank you.

83 What does the factory produce?
(A) Furniture
(B) Stationery
(C) Computer parts
(D) Automobiles

84 What does the speaker imply when he says, "one thousand units is a lot for us"?
(A) He needs to hire additional employees.
(B) The order is too expensive.
(C) He is delighted to receive such a big order.
(D) The order may have to be changed.

85 What does the speaker say about the factory?
(A) It will discontinue production.
(B) It is moving to a new location.
(C) It has a limited production capacity.
(D) It can manufacture different types of products.

Questions 86-88 refer to the following announcement.

I'll tell you briefly about the company's upcoming winter internship program. We once again succeeded in recruiting some of the top students majoring in journalism and communications from all over the country. They will help our journalists over the next three months. This year, however, interns will help and learn with them in a different way, which means the company will make our journalists constantly supervise the interns to teach them how to write articles. Frequent feedback from the supervisors will help streamline the process of preparing the interns for full-time positions in the spring next year.

86 Where does the speaker most likely work?
(A) At a university
(B) At an employment agency
(C) At an advertising agency
(D) At a newspaper

87 What change to a program does the speaker mention?
(A) Staff members will provide more feedback.
(B) The internships will be postponed.
(C) Students will receive other assignments.
(D) The company will hire more staffers to train the interns.

88 What is the purpose of the change?
(A) To provide more benefits for journalists
(B) To simplify the hiring process
(C) To decrease the program cost
(D) To store records efficiently

Questions 89-91 refer to the following excerpt from a meeting.

Let's move on to the next item on the agenda. I'm delighted to announce that there will be a change in the shipping process. Starting next month, we will ship products to international customers in addition to the domestic customers we already serve. Over the past few years, our products have gotten a lot of attention, especially from people in foreign countries. So we have created the infrastructure to meet our customers' needs. I will keep an eye on our profits over the next few months to see if this change is beneficial to our company.

89 According to the speaker, what service will the company be offering?
(A) International shipping
(B) Customized designs
(C) Free installation
(D) Online orders

90 Why has the company decided to offer the service?
(A) Competition has been fierce.
(B) Demand has increased.
(C) Cost-cutting programs have been introduced.
(D) Customers are not satisfied with the ongoing service.

91 What does the speaker say he will do over the next few months?
(A) Develop new products
(B) Deal with customer complaints
(C) Conduct a survey
(D) Monitor company profits

Questions 92-94 refer to the following advertisement.

Are you tired of ironing shirts? Maybe you've spent a lot of time looking for a true non-iron shirt. Even if you find what you want, you have to pay a lot of money for it. So if you want to save money, you don't have any option other than doing it by yourself. Imagine being able just to sit on the sofa to watch TV or spending your valuable time with your family instead of ironing out wrinkles. If this sounds good, then look no further than Albion Shirts. We guarantee high quality and reasonable prices. Our non-iron shirts are still crisp at the end of the day. If you would like more information on what we have, please visit our Web site at www.albionshirts.com.

92 What is being advertised?
(A) Sporting goods
(B) Laundry detergent
(C) Apparel
(D) Home appliances

93 What does the speaker mean when she says, "then look no further"?
(A) A product is on sale.
(B) Customers will like the product.
(C) Some merchandise has poor quality.
(D) There is no option to consider.

94 Why does the speaker suggest that listeners visit a Web site?
(A) To check some information
(B) To post a product review
(C) To request a free sample
(D) To make an online purchase

Questions 95-97 refer to the following announcement and schedule.

Ladies and gentlemen, thank you for participating in the seminar this afternoon despite your busy schedules. If you're one of those individuals who were unable to join us during the morning session, your information packets are waiting for you at the registration desk. Before starting the next session, I have an important announcement to make. Dr. Ramirez, our last speaker, is not able to give a lecture due to another commitment. Luckily, Dr. Diane will share her insights and knowledge instead. We are sorry for the inconvenience this may cause you. Please enjoy the rest of the event.

95 What is the purpose of the announcement?
(A) To introduce a new staff member
(B) To select the most popular lecturer
(C) To inform listeners of a change in a schedule
(D) To review the agenda for a meeting

96 What are some listeners asked to do?
(A) Pick up some materials
(B) Remain seated
(C) Turn off their phones
(D) Submit their reports

97 Look at the graphic. What time will Dr. Diane be speaking?
(A) 1:00 P.M.
(B) 2:00 P.M.
(C) 4:00 P.M.
(D) 5:00 P.M.

Questions 98-100 refer to the following announcement and list.

Hello, HS Grocery shoppers. As we mark our tenth anniversary, we're happy to offer you a special promotion. This week only, you'll find discounted items ranging from fruits to meat and fish. You won't want to miss it! You can check the full list of promotional items on the bulletin board at the store's entrance. And please don't forget to stop by our bakery, where you can find our featured item today: French bread. We hope to continue serving you. Thank you for your strong support during the last decade.

98 Why is the store having a sale?
(A) To help revive the local economy
(B) To introduce some new items
(C) To celebrate an anniversary
(D) To raise additional funds

99 Where is a full list of discounts available?
(A) By the doorway
(B) On the Web site
(C) Near the bakery
(D) On a flyer

100 Look at the graphic. What is the discount rate on today's special item?
(A) 15%
(B) 20%
(C) 30%
(D) 40%

TEST 10

| p.140

1	(C)	2	(A)	3	(C)	4	(B)	5	(A)
6	(D)	7	(C)	8	(A)	9	(C)	10	(B)
11	(C)	12	(A)	13	(B)	14	(C)	15	(B)
16	(C)	17	(C)	18	(A)	19	(A)	20	(B)
21	(A)	22	(C)	23	(B)	24	(B)	25	(A)
26	(C)	27	(A)	28	(B)	29	(A)	30	(A)
31	(B)	32	(B)	33	(D)	34	(D)	35	(B)
36	(B)	37	(A)	38	(C)	39	(B)	40	(A)
41	(C)	42	(D)	43	(A)	44	(B)	45	(A)
46	(D)	47	(C)	48	(A)	49	(D)	50	(C)
51	(D)	52	(A)	53	(C)	54	(C)	55	(A)
56	(C)	57	(A)	58	(B)	59	(D)	60	(A)
61	(C)	62	(A)	63	(B)	64	(D)	65	(A)
66	(C)	67	(D)	68	(D)	69	(C)	70	(C)
71	(A)	72	(B)	73	(D)	74	(C)	75	(D)
76	(B)	77	(A)	78	(C)	79	(D)	80	(A)
81	(C)	82	(C)	83	(D)	84	(B)	85	(A)
86	(B)	87	(A)	88	(D)	89	(C)	90	(D)
91	(C)	92	(B)	93	(D)	94	(D)	95	(D)
96	(A)	97	(C)	98	(C)	99	(C)	100	(B)

Part 1

1 (A) A woman is pushing a shopping cart.
(B) A woman is opening her handbag.
(C) A woman is holding some merchandise.
(D) A woman is assembling some shelves.

2 (A) Some clothing is being displayed.
(B) Some windows are being washed.
(C) One of the women is trying on skirts.
(D) One of the women is picking up packages.

3 (A) Some people are admiring a sculpture.
(B) One of the men is painting a picture.
(C) Some artwork is hanging on the wall.
(D) A hallway is being swept.

4 (A) A woman is baking some bread.
(B) A woman is leaning over a table.
(C) A woman is closing the curtains.
(D) Some flowers are being picked in a garden.

5 (A) A file drawer has been opened.
(B) A man is placing some documents on a machine.
(C) A man is delivering some furniture.
(D) Some doorknobs are being installed.

6 (A) Some business cards are being handed out.
(B) Some cabinets are being moved into a room.
(C) A computer is being used by a clerk.
(D) A plant has been put on top of a cabinet.

Part 2

7 Who offered you the job?
(A) She did it already.
(B) I prefer an olive.
(C) Mr. Olsen did.

8 Where is the calculator?
(A) Look in the drawer.
(B) It's about fifty dollars.
(C) I'll do it later.

9 When will you meet Mr. Riviera?
(A) I'll take a taxi.
(B) In the city.
(C) The day after tomorrow.

10 Why can't we use the second-floor conference room?
(A) It's my first time.
(B) It's being painted.
(C) The third door on the right.

11 He's worked here for a while, hasn't he?
(A) He didn't meet the requirements.
(B) No, he won't.
(C) Yes, for about a year.

12 Which computer would you like?
(A) Whichever costs less.
(B) Not really.
(C) Turn on the power switch.

13 Do you prefer to travel alone or with a group?
(A) A group of twelve visitors.
(B) I enjoy both.
(C) I usually travel by car.

14 Would you like to join us for dinner at seven o'clock this evening?
(A) I arrived at ten to nine this morning.
(B) No, I didn't see anything.
(C) I'd be delighted.

15 Do you know who ordered more stationery?
(A) No, I'm staying with a friend.
(B) That would be Ms. Margaret.
(C) I'd like some ice cream.

16 Why are you the only one working on the project?
(A) No, I prefer to do it on Friday.
(B) The projector is making a slight noise.
(C) Because no one else is available.

17 Shouldn't we leave for the airport soon?
(A) His flight departed this morning.
(B) I flew in yesterday.
(C) Yes, we don't want to be late.

18 What do you do with the extra time each day?
(A) I exercise at the gym.
(B) Yes, I usually do.
(C) That should be enough time.

19 Would you like me to make you some coffee?
(A) Yes, please. I drink it black without sugar.
(B) Mary said she'd copy it.
(C) He likes to set it there.

20 Which lamp do you think will go well with the colors in my office?
(A) The light has turned red.
(B) I think either would be fine.
(C) I'll see you there.

21 The reception staff members weren't very helpful, were they?
(A) I didn't think so.
(B) There weren't any speeches.
(C) Thanks, but I'm all right.

22 Tim is quite pleased about his promotion to supervisor.
(A) Yes, please do.
(B) Yes, the supervisor has it.
(C) He's worked hard for it.

23 Will the printer be replaced soon?
(A) No, it's beside the bookcase.
(B) Yes, Janet has placed the order.
(C) It's been turned on.

24 How did you build this model?
(A) No, it should take three months.
(B) Actually, Michael made it.
(C) By the side of the road.

25 Should I buy a new car or a used one?
(A) I didn't know you got your driver's license.
(B) I'm used to this city.
(C) There's parking right next to that building.

26 Our flight has been delayed again.
(A) Paris is nice this time of the year.
(B) I left it in the airport lounge.
(C) We should get something to eat while we wait.

27 There's so much to learn about this marketing strategy.
(A) How do you like it so far?
(B) Yes, it'll take less time to learn.
(C) The class is boring sometimes.

28 What brand of paper should I order?
(A) By Thursday at the latest.
(B) I've never ordered supplies before.
(C) That's where it is.

29 Haven't you found the key to the filing cabinet yet?
(A) No, and I've looked everywhere.
(B) You have to file the application before the deadline.
(C) No, we have a reservation.

30 Have they already started the road construction?
(A) They almost finished it.
(B) It's too far from the major roadways.
(C) His instructions weren't very clear.

31 Aren't you going to give him a good review?
(A) A few employees have expressed interest.
(B) Let's see how this deal turns out first.
(C) Put it on my desk as soon as you're done with it.

Part 3

Questions 32-34 refer to the following conversation.

W Hello, Professor Anderson. This is Erica Kutcher calling. I'm the organizer for the City Tourism Convention. Our theme this year is diverse cultures, and since you're an expert in this area, we'd like to invite you to be the keynote speaker.

M Well, I'd be happy to do that, but it would depend on the date. My calendar is already pretty full.

W The convention is from May third to fifth, and your speech will be on May third. It's a Friday, by the way.

M Let me see... Yes, I'm available then. I'd be glad to speak.

W That's great. One more thing: would you mind if we made a recording of your presentation available online for the tourism association's members?

32 What does the woman invite the man to do?
(A) Go on a tour
(B) Give a talk
(C) Conduct some research
(D) Register for a class

33 What information does the woman provide?
(A) The length of a document
(B) Directions to a location
(C) The number of participants
(D) The date of an event

34 What does the woman ask for permission to do?
(A) Invite city officials
(B) Select a conference site
(C) Change a travel itinerary
(D) Put some materials online

Questions 35-37 refer to the following conversation.

M Excuse me. We've been waiting for this ride for about ten minutes now. Do you know the approximate waiting time to ride this roller coaster?

W Well, from the end of the line, right now, the wait is about an hour or so. So I would actually recommend coming back after 5 P.M. when the park is less crowded. The wait will probably only be about fifteen to twenty minutes then.

M That sounds like a good idea. We'll play some video games for a while and then come back. Thanks for your help.

W No problem.

35 What is the man asking about?
(A) The rules of a game
(B) The length of a wait
(C) The cost of a ticket
(D) The time of a show

36 What does the woman tell the man?
(A) The game costs ten dollars to play.
(B) The line will be shorter later in the day.
(C) The park closes at five in the evening.
(D) The show is sold out for the day.

37 What will the man probably do next?
(A) Play some games
(B) Wait in line
(C) Eat some lunch
(D) Attend a show

Questions 38-40 refer to the following conversation with three speakers.

W1 Thanks for meeting us, Mr. Aspen. I have the estimate for your new office, and I brought our architect, Michelle Meyers, in case you have questions.

M It's wonderful to meet you both. I'm glad my accounting firm is moving to a bigger office building. We don't have enough room in our current office.

W2 And you'd like to add a small employee fitness center?

M Yes, we'd like to have one next to the breakroom.

W1 Well, there's certainly room for one at this new place.

M Great. Do you think the project will take longer if we add that? It's important that the construction be finished by the end of August. That's when the lease on our current office space ends.

W2 I think it should be okay. But let me double-check the schedule and get back to you on that.

38 According to the man, why is the accounting firm moving to a new office?
(A) The rent is high.
(B) The current location is far from downtown.
(C) The space is small.
(D) The transportation is inconvenient.

39 What does the man want to add to his office?
(A) A breakroom
(B) A fitness center
(C) A storage area
(D) Extra parking spaces

40 What will most likely happen at the end of August?
(A) A lease will expire.
(B) An inspection will take place.
(C) A conference will be held.
(D) Some executives will visit the premises.

Questions 41-43 refer to the following conversation.

M Thank you for calling the Rocky Top Grill. How may I help you?

W Hi. I'm calling to make a reservation for a dinner party this Friday.

M I'm afraid we don't accept reservations at the Rocky Top Grill, but we do offer call-ahead seating.

W Oh, I didn't know that. Could you tell me how that works?

M It's simple. Just call in after 5 P.M. on that day and tell us how many are in your party and what time you will be arriving. As soon as we receive this information, we will place your name on the list and attempt to get you a table within thirty minutes of your arrival.

41 What is the purpose of the woman's call?
(A) To ask about a bill
(B) To order some groceries
(C) To make a reservation
(D) To invite the man to an event

42 According to the man, what is the problem?
(A) No seats are available.
(B) A restaurant went out of business.
(C) There are no vegetarian options.
(D) A place does not take reservations.

43 What does the man suggest?
(A) Trying another option
(B) Going to a waiting area
(C) Visiting another location
(D) Coming back another day

Questions 44-46 refer to the following conversation.

M Hi, Rachel. Gina will be back from the Las Vegas trade show tomorrow, won't she?

W Actually, she met some potential clients at the trade show and will be staying a couple of extra days to conduct meetings and to try to land some more business. She said she'll be back in the office by Thursday.

M Oh, okay. That's great news. I was going to ask her to help me interview some candidates for the summer internship program on Friday, but if she's coming back on Thursday, she'll probably have too much other stuff to catch up on.

W Why don't you ask Phillip to help you with it? Phillip has some experience with that kind of work.

44 According to the woman, what is Gina most likely doing?
(A) Recruiting internship candidates
(B) Meeting with potential clients
(C) Enjoying her vacation
(D) Attending a press conference

45 What does the man want Gina to do?
(A) Interview some people
(B) Lead a training session
(C) Make travel arrangements
(D) Postpone a business trip

46 What does the woman mean when she says, "Phillip has some experience with that kind of work"?
(A) The speakers should hire Phillip for a position.
(B) Gina and Phillip used to work in the same department.
(C) Phillip organized an internship program last year.
(D) Phillip should be able to assist the man.

Questions 47-49 refer to the following conversation.

M Hey, Amy. Do you know anything about downloading pictures from a memory card? I've tried using the default software on this computer, but I'm not having much luck.

W I'd love to help you out, but I have to dial into a conference call in five minutes. I can give you a hand in about two hours when I'm finished with the call.

M Thanks, but I don't think I can wait that long. I need to e-mail these property photos to a potential customer in the next hour so she can make a final decision.

W You know, there's a print shop on the first floor. Why don't you go there to see if someone there can help you? I heard that other employees use its services quite often.

M That's actually a good idea. Thanks, Amy.

47 What does the man need help with?
(A) Installing a new computer program
(B) Downloading anti-virus software
(C) Transferring photos to a computer
(D) Dialing into a conference call

48 Why is the woman unable to help the man right now?
(A) She has to participate in a meeting.
(B) She has to show a client a property.
(C) She has to visit a print shop.
(D) She has too many e-mails to send.

49 What will the man probably do next?
(A) Contact another colleague
(B) Look for help online
(C) Wait until tomorrow
(D) Visit a store

Questions 50-52 refer to the following conversation with three speakers.

M Hey, Jennifer. I wonder if you can attend the university job fair this Friday. We need one more person to work in the company's booth.

W1 Let me see... Friday... Don't we have some out-of-town clients visiting us that morning?

M Oh, thanks for reminding me. I guess we should find someone to go to the fair for us.

W1 Why don't we ask Diana? She's been with the company for a while and should be able to handle any questions attendees ask.

M Good idea. Hey, Diana, are you available to participate in a job fair this Friday?

W2 Well, the only problem is that I have a project status report that needs to be handed in by Friday.

M I'll tell you what—why don't I check the project schedules for next week and make sure you get an extra couple of days for the paper?

50 What does the man ask Jennifer to do?
(A) Sign up for a university class
(B) Visit a client out of town
(C) Work at a business function
(D) Interview a job candidate

51 What is the man supposed to do on Friday?
(A) Go on a business trip
(B) Visit a university
(C) Finish a report
(D) Meet with some clients

52 What does the man offer to do for Diana?
(A) Rearrange some schedules
(B) Organize an event
(C) Work overtime
(D) Volunteer for a project

Questions 53-55 refer to the following conversation.

W Hello. This is Carmen Ayers from the Sales Department. My colleague suggested that I contact the company's travel agency because I'm organizing a one-month multi-stop sales trip on the west coast. I'd like some assistance planning the most cost-effective route and reserving hotels.

M Sure, we actually have an agent in the San Francisco office who books all of the company's west coast travel arrangements. She comes highly recommended by other employees who regularly travel out there. I suggest you speak to her.

W Oh, that's great. Could you give me her contact information? I want to get in touch right away as the trip is quickly approaching. Staying within the allotted budget is extremely important, and prices will go up as the date gets closer.

53 Why is the woman calling?
(A) To ask for driving directions
(B) To get relocation assistance
(C) To request help planning a trip
(D) To change an itinerary

54 What does the man suggest the woman do?
(A) Book a trip online
(B) Cancel a trip
(C) Speak to another agent
(D) Call back another time

55 What does the woman say is important to her?
(A) Not going over her budget
(B) Arriving on time for an appointment
(C) Finding a comfortable hotel
(D) Minimizing travel time

Questions 56-58 refer to the following conversation.

W Keystone Property Management Group. How can I help you?

M Hi, I own a small home here in Melbourne, Australia. I'm interested in renting it out. I've just accepted a job offer in Europe for two years.

W Sure, that's what we specialize in. Have you ever rented out your home before?

M No, I have no experience being a landlord. I don't have time to interview potential tenants. And if something goes wrong—if something breaks or needs to be replaced—Europe is pretty far away.

W Don't worry. We can handle all of that. Now, tell me, how much are you thinking about charging for rent?

M That's something I was hoping you could help me decide. What do you recommend?

56 What kind of service does the woman's company provide?
(A) Construction and remodeling
(B) Financial counseling
(C) Residential property management
(D) International shipping

57 Why does the man say, "Europe is pretty far away"?
(A) To express concern
(B) To show excitement
(C) To turn down an offer
(D) To get a price estimate

58 What will the speakers most likely discuss next?
(A) A delivery location
(B) A rental price
(C) Detailed measurements
(D) Personnel requirements

Questions 59-61 refer to the following conversation.

W Lucas, Mr. Wiley from Blue Ridge Custom Homes just called about the Wiggins project. He wants to know when the engineering calculations will be finished so he can order the steel beams.

M They're almost done. I'm just double-checking the final figures right now. I should have them ready by tomorrow afternoon. Would you like me to return his call and let him know?

W Actually, he said he'll be in an important meeting for the rest of the afternoon, so it's best to send him an e-mail. I'll give you his address.

M Okay. After I send him the e-mail, I'll call you.

W Great. We can focus on a new project starting next week then.

59 Why did Mr. Wiley call?
(A) To order some materials
(B) To schedule a meeting
(C) To cancel an appointment
(D) To check on the status of a work

60 What does the man say he is doing right now?
(A) Reconfirming some information
(B) Making a telephone call
(C) Leaving for the day
(D) Revising some plans

61 What does the woman suggest the man do?
(A) Finish a project
(B) Deliver some drawings
(C) E-mail Mr. Wiley
(D) Call a supplier

Questions 62-64 refer to the following conversation and schedule.

M I'm so glad we have the afternoon free during this conference. I read in a travel magazine that there are tours of Nottaway Plantation. You know, it is the oldest plantation in Louisiana and also one of the biggest.

W I hope we can get tickets.

M Right, but don't forget that we have a lunch appointment with the rest of our team members at one.

W Thank you for reminding me. Okay, let's look at Nottaway Plantation's Web site on my phone. Hmm... It looks like we should be able to take the tour at this time. There are still five tickets left.

M That should work. Let's get two of them right away.

W Good idea.

62 What do the speakers plan to tour?
(A) A historic site
(B) A government building
(C) A cooking school
(D) An ancient palace

63 What does the man remind the woman about?
(A) Attending a presentation
(B) Eating lunch with colleagues
(C) Coming back for a reception
(D) Bringing photo identification

64 Look at the graphic. When will the speakers go on a tour?
(A) 10:00 A.M.
(B) 11:30 A.M.
(C) 1:00 P.M.
(D) 2:30 P.M.

Questions 65-67 refer to the following conversation and list.

W How's the brochure for High Time Travel coming along? The client called and asked for an update.

M I'm almost done. I've created a cover as well as the sections for its popular travel destinations. However, the photography sites I know had a fairly limited selection available.

W Have you tried getimage.com yet? Our company just paid for a membership for a couple of months. That means you can access its photography database. I think it has one of the world's biggest collections of stock photos.

M Wow, that's great! I heard its database is huge.

W When you get to the site, you should browse by category. I'm sure you'll find what you need there.

65 What project is the man working on?
(A) Designing a brochure
(B) Organizing a sports competition
(C) Revising a portfolio
(D) Planning an itinerary

66 Look at the graphic. Which category will the man most likely search?
(A) Category 1
(B) Category 2
(C) Category 3
(D) Category 4

67 Why does the woman recommend using getimage.com?
(A) Photographs are available for free.
(B) Photographs come in various sizes.
(C) It was recommended by professionals.
(D) It offers a large selection of photographs.

Questions 68-70 refer to the following conversation and list.

W Hi. I purchased a Hollywood bedframe from your store, and I'm trying to put it together at home. But I don't think all the parts I need were included in the package.

M Oh, I'm really sorry. Which parts are you missing?

W I'm missing some of the plates. I think there were supposed to be eight of this type, but I only received six of them.

M If you come to the store, you can pick up a package of eight of them at the customer service desk. We'll just need your receipt as proof of purchase.

W Okay, I'll try to stop by this afternoon.

68 What does the woman say she is trying to do?
(A) Repair an appliance
(B) Return a defective item
(C) Get a discount from a store
(D) Assemble some furniture

69 Look at the graphic. What is the woman missing?
(A) Corner plates
(B) Mending plates
(C) T plates
(D) Universal plates

70 What is the woman asked to bring with her?
(A) The original package
(B) An instruction manual
(C) A store receipt
(D) A product warranty

Part 4

Questions 71-73 refer to the following radio broadcast.

And now for a look at the local weather forecast. There is a heat advisory in effect for Wednesday and Thursday of this week. Temperatures are expected to reach a scorching thirty seven degrees Celsius. This certainly will not help with the drought we have been experiencing. The city government has issued water restrictions for washing cars and watering lawns until further notice. Strict fines will be imposed on anyone caught violating this policy. Fortunately, it looks as if temperatures will cool down a bit this weekend. On Saturday and Sunday, we should only see high temperatures reach thirty degrees Celsius, so you may want to save any outdoor activities for the weekend. Coming up next is the evening traffic report for the tri-city area.

71 According to the report, what is unusual about the weather this week?
(A) The high temperatures
(B) The low temperatures
(C) The heavy rain
(D) The strong winds

72 What has the government issued due to the weather conditions?
(A) A cold wave watch
(B) Water restrictions
(C) A state of emergency
(D) Food rations

73 When will the weather be better for outdoor activities?
(A) On Wednesday
(B) On Thursday
(C) On Friday
(D) On Saturday

Questions 74-76 refer to the following talk.

Good morning and welcome to the Bickerstaff residence. My name is Hillary Cummings, and I will be your tour guide today. The Bickerstaff residence was home to the famous Hollywood actress Sandra Bickerstaff for nearly thirty years. Ms. Bickerstaff moved into this house in 1966 at the age of thirty-one, just after her award-winning performance in *Diamonds Are Forever*. She lived here until she lost her battle with cancer in 1994. The house was designed by famous architect Paul Lehman, and everything has been preserved just the way it was when Ms. Bickerstaff lived here. As we tour the house, you will notice the unusual artwork and furniture in all of the rooms. Ms. Bickerstaff loved to collect these exotic items from her extravagant trips around the world. Now, please follow me as we enter the large living room on your right.

74 What is the speaker doing?
(A) Explaining a registration process
(B) Apologizing for a delay
(C) Giving an overview of a tour
(D) Complimenting the product quality

75 Who is Paul Lehman?
(A) An actor
(B) A tour guide
(C) An art collector
(D) An architect

76 What will the listeners most likely do next?
(A) Meet Ms. Bickerstaff
(B) Proceed to a living room
(C) Stop by a gift shop
(D) Gather around an entrance

Questions 77-79 refer to the following announcement.

Attention, shoppers. Thank you for shopping at Price Club. The store will be closing in approximately thirty minutes. So please proceed to the nearest cashier to make a purchase. And be sure to check out our clearance rack, where you can save up to seventy-five percent off the regular price on your way out. The clearance section is located on the first floor next to the main entrance. And don't forget to visit us again this Saturday, when we release our new fall collection, which includes both men's and women's clothing. As always, we offer great prices on your favorites. We appreciate your shopping with us.

77 What does the store sell?
(A) Clothing
(B) Electronics
(C) Food
(D) Books

78 Why does the speaker say, "The store will be closing in approximately 30 minutes"?
(A) The store should start checking inventory.
(B) The special discount will last for half an hour.
(C) Customers need to pay for their purchases soon.
(D) Customers should return products they do not want.

79 Where has a clearance display been placed?
(A) Next to the manager's office
(B) In a rear corner
(C) On the second floor
(D) Near the main entrance

Questions 80-82 refer to the following excerpt from a meeting.

I apologize for the short notice of this meeting, but I just received our final numbers for the year from the main office in London. I'd like to bring the details of the report to your attention today before the office closes for the Christmas holiday tomorrow. Unfortunately, it looks as though our profits this year are going to be slightly less than the goal we set. I know the poor economy has slowed our business somewhat, but we have to find ways to compete in the marketplace. So in the coming year, I'd like to put an emphasis on reducing costs. Let's make a goal of reducing our overhead by ten percent next year. I'd like all of you to think of some cost-cutting ideas over the holiday, and we'll get together in the first week of January to discuss your new ideas. I wish you and your families a happy holiday.

80 What does the speaker say will happen tomorrow?
(A) An office will be closed.
(B) A corporate executive will visit.
(C) A sales meeting will be held.
(D) A company will file for bankruptcy.

81 What does the report say?
(A) Sales have increased.
(B) Costs have decreased.
(C) Profits are less than expected.
(D) A company has met its goals.

82 What does the speaker request?
(A) Details about convention participants
(B) A completed report for the board
(C) Suggestions for reducing costs
(D) A revised marketing strategy

Questions 83-85 refer to the following voice mail message.

Hello. This message is for Ms. Ashley Stotesbury. This is Penelope Lopez calling from National Bank and Trust. We've received your online mortgage application, and I'd like to speak with you personally about the many benefits of financing your home with National Bank and Trust. I would also like you to know that we are currently offering a special discount on closing costs for all new loans issued this month. This offer will only be available until the end of the month, which is only two weeks from now. So I encourage you to call back as soon as you can. I want to ensure that you are able to take advantage of these great savings. Again, this is Penelope Lopez from National Bank and Trust. And you can reach me at 555-9730. Thank you.

83 What type of business is the speaker calling from?
(A) An insurance firm
(B) A fitness club
(C) A telecom company
(D) A financial institution

84 Why is the speaker calling?
(A) To verify some information
(B) To discuss the benefits offered
(C) To quote the mortgage interest rates
(D) To schedule an appointment

85 According to the speaker, why should Ms. Stotesbury call back right away?
(A) An offer will expire soon.
(B) A position is still available.
(C) An application deadline has passed.
(D) An account has been closed.

Questions 86-88 refer to the following excerpt from a meeting.

I want us to meet briefly before we interview the two candidates for the sales manager position. The four of us will be conducting a panel interview with each candidate individually. Rita Solomon will be interviewed first at 10 A.M. and will be followed by John Jeffries at 1 P.M. As you can see from her résumé, Ms. Solomon has been a sales representative for Riley Pharmaceuticals for the past seven years. Mr. Jeffries, as some of you may know, has worked here at Fisher Meds as an assistant marketing manager for three years. During the interview, please take turns asking the prepared questions that we came up with in the predetermined order. We'll meet at four o'clock today. Then, we can compare notes and make our final decision. Now, does anyone have any questions before we meet with Ms. Solomon?

86 Why has the speaker arranged the meeting?
(A) To introduce a new sales manager
(B) To discuss an interview format
(C) To provide feedback on a project
(D) To prepare for a sales meeting

87 What are the listeners asked to do?
(A) Ask assigned questions
(B) Complete a sales report
(C) Create portfolios for an interview
(D) Apply for a position

88 What does the speaker mean when he says, "We'll meet at four o'clock today"?
(A) He has to take care of some urgent businesses now.
(B) The majority of the people are available then.
(C) They need to conduct additional interviews.
(D) A final decision will be delayed until later.

Questions 89-91 refer to the following talk.

Welcome to our workshop on presentation skills. Your company has asked us to help you improve the effectiveness of your sales presentations. You can increase your selling power by making better presentations. First, we'll be covering strategies to create memorable contents that will work for you. Second, we'll teach you how to deliver those contents to different types of audiences. Lastly, you'll learn how to handle questions and get positive feedback. Today, you'll want to practice these skills as much as possible. That's why we didn't schedule a lunch break long enough for you to go out. But as you all know, there are some vending machines at the end of the hallway.

89 What is the purpose of the talk?
(A) To go over sales performance
(B) To describe a factory layout
(C) To explain a workshop schedule
(D) To announce the winner of a competition

90 Who most likely is the speaker?
(A) A plant supervisor
(B) A repair technician
(C) A financial consultant
(D) A professional instructor

91 What does the speaker imply when she says, "there are some vending machines at the end of the hallway"?
(A) The listeners should fix them before lunch.
(B) The listeners should meet there.
(C) The listeners are advised to buy food from them.
(D) The listeners need to move them to another location.

Questions 92-94 refer to the following talk.

Good morning, everyone. I'd like to begin the weekly meeting by introducing the newest addition to our staff, Nina Choi. She has been hired as a production analyst with our manufacturing division. Nina comes to us from Nycom Industries, where she held a similar position. She spent the last three years helping Nycom improve the efficiency of its overseas production facilities. As you all know, we are now redesigning our factories in China in an effort to reduce costs and to increase efficiency in the coming months. We believe that Nina's experience will be very valuable to us and help make the process run smoothly.

92 What is the main purpose of the talk?
(A) To announce the opening of a factory
(B) To introduce a new employee
(C) To explain a new procedure
(D) To discuss details of a production process

93 What does the speaker mention about Ms. Choi?
(A) She studied manufacturing processes in college.
(B) She has worked for the company for three years.
(C) She can speak several foreign languages.
(D) She has experience doing a similar job.

94 What is the company trying to do now?
(A) Launch a new product line
(B) Relocate their headquarters to China
(C) Translate a manual into other languages
(D) Redesign some facilities overseas

Questions 95-97 refer to the following telephone message and directory.

Good morning, Ms. Kim. This is Alan from Acer Gardening. I'm looking forward to meeting with you tomorrow. I've been giving your landscaping project a lot of thought, and I've come up with some solid ideas for improving the property around your company. Since this will be your first time visiting our company, I want to make sure you don't have any problems getting to our office. When you enter the Harford Building, you'll need to visit the security desk and pick up a visitor badge. Then, you'll need to take one of the elevators. The elevators don't stop at every floor. Please take elevator G and get off on the first floor it stops at. Our firm will be on the right when you exit the elevator.

95 What will most likely be discussed at the meeting tomorrow?
(A) An open position
(B) A home renovation
(C) A business acquisition
(D) A landscaping project

96 What should the listener do at the security desk?
(A) Pick up a visitor pass
(B) Get a parking permit
(C) Contact the person in charge
(D) Ask for a floor map

97 Look at the graphic. On which floor is the speaker's office located?
(A) 2nd floor (B) 5th floor
(C) 11th floor (D) 18th floor

Questions 98-100 refer to the following excerpt from a meeting and chart.

To wrap up this morning's sales meeting, let's look at the second quarter results. As you probably know, due to the rise of new incoming electronics makers in the marketplace, we knew those sales figures would be lower than usual. However, this five percent growth rate is very disappointing. We definitely want an increase of more than five percent a quarter. So to improve sales in this category, management has decided to lower the price for the rest of the year. The price cut will go into effect immediately everywhere our products are sold.

98 Who most likely are the listeners?
(A) Stockholders
(B) Product designers
(C) Sales associates
(D) Accounting clerks

99 Look at the graphic. Which category is the speaker concerned about?
(A) Vacuum Cleaners
(B) Coffee Makers
(C) Refrigerators
(D) Washers and Dryers

100 What has the company decided to do?
(A) Research competitors
(B) Reduce prices
(C) Hire a consultant
(D) Launch a new advertising campaign

books.english.co.kr

ANSWER SHEET

수험번호							No.
성명	한글						
	영자						

TEST 01 (Part 1~4)

NO.	ANSWER				NO.	ANSWER				NO.	ANSWER				NO.	ANSWER				NO.	ANSWER			
	A	B	C	D		A	B	C	D		A	B	C	D		A	B	C	D		A	B	C	D
1	Ⓐ	Ⓑ	Ⓒ	Ⓓ	21	Ⓐ	Ⓑ	Ⓒ		41	Ⓐ	Ⓑ	Ⓒ	Ⓓ	61	Ⓐ	Ⓑ	Ⓒ	Ⓓ	81	Ⓐ	Ⓑ	Ⓒ	Ⓓ
2	Ⓐ	Ⓑ	Ⓒ	Ⓓ	22	Ⓐ	Ⓑ	Ⓒ		42	Ⓐ	Ⓑ	Ⓒ	Ⓓ	62	Ⓐ	Ⓑ	Ⓒ	Ⓓ	82	Ⓐ	Ⓑ	Ⓒ	Ⓓ
3	Ⓐ	Ⓑ	Ⓒ	Ⓓ	23	Ⓐ	Ⓑ	Ⓒ		43	Ⓐ	Ⓑ	Ⓒ	Ⓓ	63	Ⓐ	Ⓑ	Ⓒ	Ⓓ	83	Ⓐ	Ⓑ	Ⓒ	Ⓓ
4	Ⓐ	Ⓑ	Ⓒ	Ⓓ	24	Ⓐ	Ⓑ	Ⓒ		44	Ⓐ	Ⓑ	Ⓒ	Ⓓ	64	Ⓐ	Ⓑ	Ⓒ	Ⓓ	84	Ⓐ	Ⓑ	Ⓒ	Ⓓ
5	Ⓐ	Ⓑ	Ⓒ	Ⓓ	25	Ⓐ	Ⓑ	Ⓒ		45	Ⓐ	Ⓑ	Ⓒ	Ⓓ	65	Ⓐ	Ⓑ	Ⓒ	Ⓓ	85	Ⓐ	Ⓑ	Ⓒ	Ⓓ
6	Ⓐ	Ⓑ	Ⓒ	Ⓓ	26	Ⓐ	Ⓑ	Ⓒ		46	Ⓐ	Ⓑ	Ⓒ	Ⓓ	66	Ⓐ	Ⓑ	Ⓒ	Ⓓ	86	Ⓐ	Ⓑ	Ⓒ	Ⓓ
7	Ⓐ	Ⓑ	Ⓒ		27	Ⓐ	Ⓑ	Ⓒ		47	Ⓐ	Ⓑ	Ⓒ	Ⓓ	67	Ⓐ	Ⓑ	Ⓒ	Ⓓ	87	Ⓐ	Ⓑ	Ⓒ	Ⓓ
8	Ⓐ	Ⓑ	Ⓒ		28	Ⓐ	Ⓑ	Ⓒ		48	Ⓐ	Ⓑ	Ⓒ	Ⓓ	68	Ⓐ	Ⓑ	Ⓒ	Ⓓ	88	Ⓐ	Ⓑ	Ⓒ	Ⓓ
9	Ⓐ	Ⓑ	Ⓒ		29	Ⓐ	Ⓑ	Ⓒ		49	Ⓐ	Ⓑ	Ⓒ	Ⓓ	69	Ⓐ	Ⓑ	Ⓒ	Ⓓ	89	Ⓐ	Ⓑ	Ⓒ	Ⓓ
10	Ⓐ	Ⓑ	Ⓒ		30	Ⓐ	Ⓑ	Ⓒ		50	Ⓐ	Ⓑ	Ⓒ	Ⓓ	70	Ⓐ	Ⓑ	Ⓒ	Ⓓ	90	Ⓐ	Ⓑ	Ⓒ	Ⓓ
11	Ⓐ	Ⓑ	Ⓒ		31	Ⓐ	Ⓑ	Ⓒ		51	Ⓐ	Ⓑ	Ⓒ	Ⓓ	71	Ⓐ	Ⓑ	Ⓒ	Ⓓ	91	Ⓐ	Ⓑ	Ⓒ	Ⓓ
12	Ⓐ	Ⓑ	Ⓒ		32	Ⓐ	Ⓑ	Ⓒ	Ⓓ	52	Ⓐ	Ⓑ	Ⓒ	Ⓓ	72	Ⓐ	Ⓑ	Ⓒ	Ⓓ	92	Ⓐ	Ⓑ	Ⓒ	Ⓓ
13	Ⓐ	Ⓑ	Ⓒ		33	Ⓐ	Ⓑ	Ⓒ	Ⓓ	53	Ⓐ	Ⓑ	Ⓒ	Ⓓ	73	Ⓐ	Ⓑ	Ⓒ	Ⓓ	93	Ⓐ	Ⓑ	Ⓒ	Ⓓ
14	Ⓐ	Ⓑ	Ⓒ		34	Ⓐ	Ⓑ	Ⓒ	Ⓓ	54	Ⓐ	Ⓑ	Ⓒ	Ⓓ	74	Ⓐ	Ⓑ	Ⓒ	Ⓓ	94	Ⓐ	Ⓑ	Ⓒ	Ⓓ
15	Ⓐ	Ⓑ	Ⓒ		35	Ⓐ	Ⓑ	Ⓒ	Ⓓ	55	Ⓐ	Ⓑ	Ⓒ	Ⓓ	75	Ⓐ	Ⓑ	Ⓒ	Ⓓ	95	Ⓐ	Ⓑ	Ⓒ	Ⓓ
16	Ⓐ	Ⓑ	Ⓒ		36	Ⓐ	Ⓑ	Ⓒ	Ⓓ	56	Ⓐ	Ⓑ	Ⓒ	Ⓓ	76	Ⓐ	Ⓑ	Ⓒ	Ⓓ	96	Ⓐ	Ⓑ	Ⓒ	Ⓓ
17	Ⓐ	Ⓑ	Ⓒ		37	Ⓐ	Ⓑ	Ⓒ	Ⓓ	57	Ⓐ	Ⓑ	Ⓒ	Ⓓ	77	Ⓐ	Ⓑ	Ⓒ	Ⓓ	97	Ⓐ	Ⓑ	Ⓒ	Ⓓ
18	Ⓐ	Ⓑ	Ⓒ		38	Ⓐ	Ⓑ	Ⓒ	Ⓓ	58	Ⓐ	Ⓑ	Ⓒ	Ⓓ	78	Ⓐ	Ⓑ	Ⓒ	Ⓓ	98	Ⓐ	Ⓑ	Ⓒ	Ⓓ
19	Ⓐ	Ⓑ	Ⓒ		39	Ⓐ	Ⓑ	Ⓒ	Ⓓ	59	Ⓐ	Ⓑ	Ⓒ	Ⓓ	79	Ⓐ	Ⓑ	Ⓒ	Ⓓ	99	Ⓐ	Ⓑ	Ⓒ	Ⓓ
20	Ⓐ	Ⓑ	Ⓒ		40	Ⓐ	Ⓑ	Ⓒ	Ⓓ	60	Ⓐ	Ⓑ	Ⓒ	Ⓓ	80	Ⓐ	Ⓑ	Ⓒ	Ⓓ	100	Ⓐ	Ⓑ	Ⓒ	Ⓓ

ANSWER SHEET

수험번호							No.
성명	한글						
	영자						

TEST 02 (Part 1~4)

NO.	ANSWER				NO.	ANSWER				NO.	ANSWER				NO.	ANSWER				NO.	ANSWER			
	A	B	C	D		A	B	C	D		A	B	C	D		A	B	C	D		A	B	C	D
1	Ⓐ	Ⓑ	Ⓒ	Ⓓ	21	Ⓐ	Ⓑ	Ⓒ		41	Ⓐ	Ⓑ	Ⓒ	Ⓓ	61	Ⓐ	Ⓑ	Ⓒ	Ⓓ	81	Ⓐ	Ⓑ	Ⓒ	Ⓓ
2	Ⓐ	Ⓑ	Ⓒ	Ⓓ	22	Ⓐ	Ⓑ	Ⓒ		42	Ⓐ	Ⓑ	Ⓒ	Ⓓ	62	Ⓐ	Ⓑ	Ⓒ	Ⓓ	82	Ⓐ	Ⓑ	Ⓒ	Ⓓ
3	Ⓐ	Ⓑ	Ⓒ	Ⓓ	23	Ⓐ	Ⓑ	Ⓒ		43	Ⓐ	Ⓑ	Ⓒ	Ⓓ	63	Ⓐ	Ⓑ	Ⓒ	Ⓓ	83	Ⓐ	Ⓑ	Ⓒ	Ⓓ
4	Ⓐ	Ⓑ	Ⓒ	Ⓓ	24	Ⓐ	Ⓑ	Ⓒ		44	Ⓐ	Ⓑ	Ⓒ	Ⓓ	64	Ⓐ	Ⓑ	Ⓒ	Ⓓ	84	Ⓐ	Ⓑ	Ⓒ	Ⓓ
5	Ⓐ	Ⓑ	Ⓒ	Ⓓ	25	Ⓐ	Ⓑ	Ⓒ		45	Ⓐ	Ⓑ	Ⓒ	Ⓓ	65	Ⓐ	Ⓑ	Ⓒ	Ⓓ	85	Ⓐ	Ⓑ	Ⓒ	Ⓓ
6	Ⓐ	Ⓑ	Ⓒ	Ⓓ	26	Ⓐ	Ⓑ	Ⓒ		46	Ⓐ	Ⓑ	Ⓒ	Ⓓ	66	Ⓐ	Ⓑ	Ⓒ	Ⓓ	86	Ⓐ	Ⓑ	Ⓒ	Ⓓ
7	Ⓐ	Ⓑ	Ⓒ		27	Ⓐ	Ⓑ	Ⓒ		47	Ⓐ	Ⓑ	Ⓒ	Ⓓ	67	Ⓐ	Ⓑ	Ⓒ	Ⓓ	87	Ⓐ	Ⓑ	Ⓒ	Ⓓ
8	Ⓐ	Ⓑ	Ⓒ		28	Ⓐ	Ⓑ	Ⓒ		48	Ⓐ	Ⓑ	Ⓒ	Ⓓ	68	Ⓐ	Ⓑ	Ⓒ	Ⓓ	88	Ⓐ	Ⓑ	Ⓒ	Ⓓ
9	Ⓐ	Ⓑ	Ⓒ		29	Ⓐ	Ⓑ	Ⓒ		49	Ⓐ	Ⓑ	Ⓒ	Ⓓ	69	Ⓐ	Ⓑ	Ⓒ	Ⓓ	89	Ⓐ	Ⓑ	Ⓒ	Ⓓ
10	Ⓐ	Ⓑ	Ⓒ		30	Ⓐ	Ⓑ	Ⓒ		50	Ⓐ	Ⓑ	Ⓒ	Ⓓ	70	Ⓐ	Ⓑ	Ⓒ	Ⓓ	90	Ⓐ	Ⓑ	Ⓒ	Ⓓ
11	Ⓐ	Ⓑ	Ⓒ		31	Ⓐ	Ⓑ	Ⓒ		51	Ⓐ	Ⓑ	Ⓒ	Ⓓ	71	Ⓐ	Ⓑ	Ⓒ	Ⓓ	91	Ⓐ	Ⓑ	Ⓒ	Ⓓ
12	Ⓐ	Ⓑ	Ⓒ		32	Ⓐ	Ⓑ	Ⓒ	Ⓓ	52	Ⓐ	Ⓑ	Ⓒ	Ⓓ	72	Ⓐ	Ⓑ	Ⓒ	Ⓓ	92	Ⓐ	Ⓑ	Ⓒ	Ⓓ
13	Ⓐ	Ⓑ	Ⓒ		33	Ⓐ	Ⓑ	Ⓒ	Ⓓ	53	Ⓐ	Ⓑ	Ⓒ	Ⓓ	73	Ⓐ	Ⓑ	Ⓒ	Ⓓ	93	Ⓐ	Ⓑ	Ⓒ	Ⓓ
14	Ⓐ	Ⓑ	Ⓒ		34	Ⓐ	Ⓑ	Ⓒ	Ⓓ	54	Ⓐ	Ⓑ	Ⓒ	Ⓓ	74	Ⓐ	Ⓑ	Ⓒ	Ⓓ	94	Ⓐ	Ⓑ	Ⓒ	Ⓓ
15	Ⓐ	Ⓑ	Ⓒ		35	Ⓐ	Ⓑ	Ⓒ	Ⓓ	55	Ⓐ	Ⓑ	Ⓒ	Ⓓ	75	Ⓐ	Ⓑ	Ⓒ	Ⓓ	95	Ⓐ	Ⓑ	Ⓒ	Ⓓ
16	Ⓐ	Ⓑ	Ⓒ		36	Ⓐ	Ⓑ	Ⓒ	Ⓓ	56	Ⓐ	Ⓑ	Ⓒ	Ⓓ	76	Ⓐ	Ⓑ	Ⓒ	Ⓓ	96	Ⓐ	Ⓑ	Ⓒ	Ⓓ
17	Ⓐ	Ⓑ	Ⓒ		37	Ⓐ	Ⓑ	Ⓒ	Ⓓ	57	Ⓐ	Ⓑ	Ⓒ	Ⓓ	77	Ⓐ	Ⓑ	Ⓒ	Ⓓ	97	Ⓐ	Ⓑ	Ⓒ	Ⓓ
18	Ⓐ	Ⓑ	Ⓒ		38	Ⓐ	Ⓑ	Ⓒ	Ⓓ	58	Ⓐ	Ⓑ	Ⓒ	Ⓓ	78	Ⓐ	Ⓑ	Ⓒ	Ⓓ	98	Ⓐ	Ⓑ	Ⓒ	Ⓓ
19	Ⓐ	Ⓑ	Ⓒ		39	Ⓐ	Ⓑ	Ⓒ	Ⓓ	59	Ⓐ	Ⓑ	Ⓒ	Ⓓ	79	Ⓐ	Ⓑ	Ⓒ	Ⓓ	99	Ⓐ	Ⓑ	Ⓒ	Ⓓ
20	Ⓐ	Ⓑ	Ⓒ		40	Ⓐ	Ⓑ	Ⓒ	Ⓓ	60	Ⓐ	Ⓑ	Ⓒ	Ⓓ	80	Ⓐ	Ⓑ	Ⓒ	Ⓓ	100	Ⓐ	Ⓑ	Ⓒ	Ⓓ

ANSWER SHEET

수험번호						
성명	한글					
	영자					

No.

TEST 03 (Part 1~4)

NO.	ANSWER A B C D	NO.	ANSWER A B C D	NO.	ANSWER A B C D	NO.	ANSWER A B C D	NO.	ANSWER A B C D
1	Ⓐ Ⓑ Ⓒ Ⓓ	21	Ⓐ Ⓑ Ⓒ	41	Ⓐ Ⓑ Ⓒ Ⓓ	61	Ⓐ Ⓑ Ⓒ Ⓓ	81	Ⓐ Ⓑ Ⓒ Ⓓ
2	Ⓐ Ⓑ Ⓒ Ⓓ	22	Ⓐ Ⓑ Ⓒ	42	Ⓐ Ⓑ Ⓒ Ⓓ	62	Ⓐ Ⓑ Ⓒ Ⓓ	82	Ⓐ Ⓑ Ⓒ Ⓓ
3	Ⓐ Ⓑ Ⓒ Ⓓ	23	Ⓐ Ⓑ Ⓒ	43	Ⓐ Ⓑ Ⓒ Ⓓ	63	Ⓐ Ⓑ Ⓒ Ⓓ	83	Ⓐ Ⓑ Ⓒ Ⓓ
4	Ⓐ Ⓑ Ⓒ Ⓓ	24	Ⓐ Ⓑ Ⓒ	44	Ⓐ Ⓑ Ⓒ Ⓓ	64	Ⓐ Ⓑ Ⓒ Ⓓ	84	Ⓐ Ⓑ Ⓒ Ⓓ
5	Ⓐ Ⓑ Ⓒ Ⓓ	25	Ⓐ Ⓑ Ⓒ	45	Ⓐ Ⓑ Ⓒ Ⓓ	65	Ⓐ Ⓑ Ⓒ Ⓓ	85	Ⓐ Ⓑ Ⓒ Ⓓ
6	Ⓐ Ⓑ Ⓒ Ⓓ	26	Ⓐ Ⓑ Ⓒ	46	Ⓐ Ⓑ Ⓒ Ⓓ	66	Ⓐ Ⓑ Ⓒ Ⓓ	86	Ⓐ Ⓑ Ⓒ Ⓓ
7	Ⓐ Ⓑ Ⓒ	27	Ⓐ Ⓑ Ⓒ	47	Ⓐ Ⓑ Ⓒ Ⓓ	67	Ⓐ Ⓑ Ⓒ Ⓓ	87	Ⓐ Ⓑ Ⓒ Ⓓ
8	Ⓐ Ⓑ Ⓒ	28	Ⓐ Ⓑ Ⓒ	48	Ⓐ Ⓑ Ⓒ Ⓓ	68	Ⓐ Ⓑ Ⓒ Ⓓ	88	Ⓐ Ⓑ Ⓒ Ⓓ
9	Ⓐ Ⓑ Ⓒ	29	Ⓐ Ⓑ Ⓒ	49	Ⓐ Ⓑ Ⓒ Ⓓ	69	Ⓐ Ⓑ Ⓒ Ⓓ	89	Ⓐ Ⓑ Ⓒ Ⓓ
10	Ⓐ Ⓑ Ⓒ	30	Ⓐ Ⓑ Ⓒ	50	Ⓐ Ⓑ Ⓒ Ⓓ	70	Ⓐ Ⓑ Ⓒ Ⓓ	90	Ⓐ Ⓑ Ⓒ Ⓓ
11	Ⓐ Ⓑ Ⓒ	31	Ⓐ Ⓑ Ⓒ	51	Ⓐ Ⓑ Ⓒ Ⓓ	71	Ⓐ Ⓑ Ⓒ Ⓓ	91	Ⓐ Ⓑ Ⓒ Ⓓ
12	Ⓐ Ⓑ Ⓒ	32	Ⓐ Ⓑ Ⓒ Ⓓ	52	Ⓐ Ⓑ Ⓒ Ⓓ	72	Ⓐ Ⓑ Ⓒ Ⓓ	92	Ⓐ Ⓑ Ⓒ Ⓓ
13	Ⓐ Ⓑ Ⓒ	33	Ⓐ Ⓑ Ⓒ Ⓓ	53	Ⓐ Ⓑ Ⓒ Ⓓ	73	Ⓐ Ⓑ Ⓒ Ⓓ	93	Ⓐ Ⓑ Ⓒ Ⓓ
14	Ⓐ Ⓑ Ⓒ	34	Ⓐ Ⓑ Ⓒ Ⓓ	54	Ⓐ Ⓑ Ⓒ Ⓓ	74	Ⓐ Ⓑ Ⓒ Ⓓ	94	Ⓐ Ⓑ Ⓒ Ⓓ
15	Ⓐ Ⓑ Ⓒ	35	Ⓐ Ⓑ Ⓒ Ⓓ	55	Ⓐ Ⓑ Ⓒ Ⓓ	75	Ⓐ Ⓑ Ⓒ Ⓓ	95	Ⓐ Ⓑ Ⓒ Ⓓ
16	Ⓐ Ⓑ Ⓒ	36	Ⓐ Ⓑ Ⓒ Ⓓ	56	Ⓐ Ⓑ Ⓒ Ⓓ	76	Ⓐ Ⓑ Ⓒ Ⓓ	96	Ⓐ Ⓑ Ⓒ Ⓓ
17	Ⓐ Ⓑ Ⓒ	37	Ⓐ Ⓑ Ⓒ Ⓓ	57	Ⓐ Ⓑ Ⓒ Ⓓ	77	Ⓐ Ⓑ Ⓒ Ⓓ	97	Ⓐ Ⓑ Ⓒ Ⓓ
18	Ⓐ Ⓑ Ⓒ	38	Ⓐ Ⓑ Ⓒ Ⓓ	58	Ⓐ Ⓑ Ⓒ Ⓓ	78	Ⓐ Ⓑ Ⓒ Ⓓ	98	Ⓐ Ⓑ Ⓒ Ⓓ
19	Ⓐ Ⓑ Ⓒ	39	Ⓐ Ⓑ Ⓒ Ⓓ	59	Ⓐ Ⓑ Ⓒ Ⓓ	79	Ⓐ Ⓑ Ⓒ Ⓓ	99	Ⓐ Ⓑ Ⓒ Ⓓ
20	Ⓐ Ⓑ Ⓒ	40	Ⓐ Ⓑ Ⓒ Ⓓ	60	Ⓐ Ⓑ Ⓒ Ⓓ	80	Ⓐ Ⓑ Ⓒ Ⓓ	100	Ⓐ Ⓑ Ⓒ Ⓓ

ANSWER SHEET

수험번호						
성명	한글					
	영자					

No.

TEST 04 (Part 1~4)

NO.	ANSWER A B C D	NO.	ANSWER A B C D	NO.	ANSWER A B C D	NO.	ANSWER A B C D	NO.	ANSWER A B C D
1	Ⓐ Ⓑ Ⓒ Ⓓ	21	Ⓐ Ⓑ Ⓒ	41	Ⓐ Ⓑ Ⓒ Ⓓ	61	Ⓐ Ⓑ Ⓒ Ⓓ	81	Ⓐ Ⓑ Ⓒ Ⓓ
2	Ⓐ Ⓑ Ⓒ Ⓓ	22	Ⓐ Ⓑ Ⓒ	42	Ⓐ Ⓑ Ⓒ Ⓓ	62	Ⓐ Ⓑ Ⓒ Ⓓ	82	Ⓐ Ⓑ Ⓒ Ⓓ
3	Ⓐ Ⓑ Ⓒ Ⓓ	23	Ⓐ Ⓑ Ⓒ	43	Ⓐ Ⓑ Ⓒ Ⓓ	63	Ⓐ Ⓑ Ⓒ Ⓓ	83	Ⓐ Ⓑ Ⓒ Ⓓ
4	Ⓐ Ⓑ Ⓒ Ⓓ	24	Ⓐ Ⓑ Ⓒ	44	Ⓐ Ⓑ Ⓒ Ⓓ	64	Ⓐ Ⓑ Ⓒ Ⓓ	84	Ⓐ Ⓑ Ⓒ Ⓓ
5	Ⓐ Ⓑ Ⓒ Ⓓ	25	Ⓐ Ⓑ Ⓒ	45	Ⓐ Ⓑ Ⓒ Ⓓ	65	Ⓐ Ⓑ Ⓒ Ⓓ	85	Ⓐ Ⓑ Ⓒ Ⓓ
6	Ⓐ Ⓑ Ⓒ Ⓓ	26	Ⓐ Ⓑ Ⓒ	46	Ⓐ Ⓑ Ⓒ Ⓓ	66	Ⓐ Ⓑ Ⓒ Ⓓ	86	Ⓐ Ⓑ Ⓒ Ⓓ
7	Ⓐ Ⓑ Ⓒ	27	Ⓐ Ⓑ Ⓒ	47	Ⓐ Ⓑ Ⓒ Ⓓ	67	Ⓐ Ⓑ Ⓒ Ⓓ	87	Ⓐ Ⓑ Ⓒ Ⓓ
8	Ⓐ Ⓑ Ⓒ	28	Ⓐ Ⓑ Ⓒ	48	Ⓐ Ⓑ Ⓒ Ⓓ	68	Ⓐ Ⓑ Ⓒ Ⓓ	88	Ⓐ Ⓑ Ⓒ Ⓓ
9	Ⓐ Ⓑ Ⓒ	29	Ⓐ Ⓑ Ⓒ	49	Ⓐ Ⓑ Ⓒ Ⓓ	69	Ⓐ Ⓑ Ⓒ Ⓓ	89	Ⓐ Ⓑ Ⓒ Ⓓ
10	Ⓐ Ⓑ Ⓒ	30	Ⓐ Ⓑ Ⓒ	50	Ⓐ Ⓑ Ⓒ Ⓓ	70	Ⓐ Ⓑ Ⓒ Ⓓ	90	Ⓐ Ⓑ Ⓒ Ⓓ
11	Ⓐ Ⓑ Ⓒ	31	Ⓐ Ⓑ Ⓒ	51	Ⓐ Ⓑ Ⓒ Ⓓ	71	Ⓐ Ⓑ Ⓒ Ⓓ	91	Ⓐ Ⓑ Ⓒ Ⓓ
12	Ⓐ Ⓑ Ⓒ	32	Ⓐ Ⓑ Ⓒ Ⓓ	52	Ⓐ Ⓑ Ⓒ Ⓓ	72	Ⓐ Ⓑ Ⓒ Ⓓ	92	Ⓐ Ⓑ Ⓒ Ⓓ
13	Ⓐ Ⓑ Ⓒ	33	Ⓐ Ⓑ Ⓒ Ⓓ	53	Ⓐ Ⓑ Ⓒ Ⓓ	73	Ⓐ Ⓑ Ⓒ Ⓓ	93	Ⓐ Ⓑ Ⓒ Ⓓ
14	Ⓐ Ⓑ Ⓒ	34	Ⓐ Ⓑ Ⓒ Ⓓ	54	Ⓐ Ⓑ Ⓒ Ⓓ	74	Ⓐ Ⓑ Ⓒ Ⓓ	94	Ⓐ Ⓑ Ⓒ Ⓓ
15	Ⓐ Ⓑ Ⓒ	35	Ⓐ Ⓑ Ⓒ Ⓓ	55	Ⓐ Ⓑ Ⓒ Ⓓ	75	Ⓐ Ⓑ Ⓒ Ⓓ	95	Ⓐ Ⓑ Ⓒ Ⓓ
16	Ⓐ Ⓑ Ⓒ	36	Ⓐ Ⓑ Ⓒ Ⓓ	56	Ⓐ Ⓑ Ⓒ Ⓓ	76	Ⓐ Ⓑ Ⓒ Ⓓ	96	Ⓐ Ⓑ Ⓒ Ⓓ
17	Ⓐ Ⓑ Ⓒ	37	Ⓐ Ⓑ Ⓒ Ⓓ	57	Ⓐ Ⓑ Ⓒ Ⓓ	77	Ⓐ Ⓑ Ⓒ Ⓓ	97	Ⓐ Ⓑ Ⓒ Ⓓ
18	Ⓐ Ⓑ Ⓒ	38	Ⓐ Ⓑ Ⓒ Ⓓ	58	Ⓐ Ⓑ Ⓒ Ⓓ	78	Ⓐ Ⓑ Ⓒ Ⓓ	98	Ⓐ Ⓑ Ⓒ Ⓓ
19	Ⓐ Ⓑ Ⓒ	39	Ⓐ Ⓑ Ⓒ Ⓓ	59	Ⓐ Ⓑ Ⓒ Ⓓ	79	Ⓐ Ⓑ Ⓒ Ⓓ	99	Ⓐ Ⓑ Ⓒ Ⓓ
20	Ⓐ Ⓑ Ⓒ	40	Ⓐ Ⓑ Ⓒ Ⓓ	60	Ⓐ Ⓑ Ⓒ Ⓓ	80	Ⓐ Ⓑ Ⓒ Ⓓ	100	Ⓐ Ⓑ Ⓒ Ⓓ

ANSWER SHEET

수험번호							No.
성명	한글						
	영자						

TEST 05 (Part 1~4)

NO.	ANSWER				NO.	ANSWER				NO.	ANSWER				NO.	ANSWER				NO.	ANSWER			
	A	B	C	D		A	B	C	D		A	B	C	D		A	B	C	D		A	B	C	D
1	Ⓐ	Ⓑ	Ⓒ	Ⓓ	21	Ⓐ	Ⓑ	Ⓒ		41	Ⓐ	Ⓑ	Ⓒ	Ⓓ	61	Ⓐ	Ⓑ	Ⓒ	Ⓓ	81	Ⓐ	Ⓑ	Ⓒ	Ⓓ
2	Ⓐ	Ⓑ	Ⓒ	Ⓓ	22	Ⓐ	Ⓑ	Ⓒ		42	Ⓐ	Ⓑ	Ⓒ	Ⓓ	62	Ⓐ	Ⓑ	Ⓒ	Ⓓ	82	Ⓐ	Ⓑ	Ⓒ	Ⓓ
3	Ⓐ	Ⓑ	Ⓒ	Ⓓ	23	Ⓐ	Ⓑ	Ⓒ		43	Ⓐ	Ⓑ	Ⓒ	Ⓓ	63	Ⓐ	Ⓑ	Ⓒ	Ⓓ	83	Ⓐ	Ⓑ	Ⓒ	Ⓓ
4	Ⓐ	Ⓑ	Ⓒ	Ⓓ	24	Ⓐ	Ⓑ	Ⓒ		44	Ⓐ	Ⓑ	Ⓒ	Ⓓ	64	Ⓐ	Ⓑ	Ⓒ	Ⓓ	84	Ⓐ	Ⓑ	Ⓒ	Ⓓ
5	Ⓐ	Ⓑ	Ⓒ	Ⓓ	25	Ⓐ	Ⓑ	Ⓒ		45	Ⓐ	Ⓑ	Ⓒ	Ⓓ	65	Ⓐ	Ⓑ	Ⓒ	Ⓓ	85	Ⓐ	Ⓑ	Ⓒ	Ⓓ
6	Ⓐ	Ⓑ	Ⓒ	Ⓓ	26	Ⓐ	Ⓑ	Ⓒ		46	Ⓐ	Ⓑ	Ⓒ	Ⓓ	66	Ⓐ	Ⓑ	Ⓒ	Ⓓ	86	Ⓐ	Ⓑ	Ⓒ	Ⓓ
7	Ⓐ	Ⓑ	Ⓒ		27	Ⓐ	Ⓑ	Ⓒ		47	Ⓐ	Ⓑ	Ⓒ	Ⓓ	67	Ⓐ	Ⓑ	Ⓒ	Ⓓ	87	Ⓐ	Ⓑ	Ⓒ	Ⓓ
8	Ⓐ	Ⓑ	Ⓒ		28	Ⓐ	Ⓑ	Ⓒ		48	Ⓐ	Ⓑ	Ⓒ	Ⓓ	68	Ⓐ	Ⓑ	Ⓒ	Ⓓ	88	Ⓐ	Ⓑ	Ⓒ	Ⓓ
9	Ⓐ	Ⓑ	Ⓒ		29	Ⓐ	Ⓑ	Ⓒ		49	Ⓐ	Ⓑ	Ⓒ	Ⓓ	69	Ⓐ	Ⓑ	Ⓒ	Ⓓ	89	Ⓐ	Ⓑ	Ⓒ	Ⓓ
10	Ⓐ	Ⓑ	Ⓒ		30	Ⓐ	Ⓑ	Ⓒ		50	Ⓐ	Ⓑ	Ⓒ	Ⓓ	70	Ⓐ	Ⓑ	Ⓒ	Ⓓ	90	Ⓐ	Ⓑ	Ⓒ	Ⓓ
11	Ⓐ	Ⓑ	Ⓒ		31	Ⓐ	Ⓑ	Ⓒ		51	Ⓐ	Ⓑ	Ⓒ	Ⓓ	71	Ⓐ	Ⓑ	Ⓒ	Ⓓ	91	Ⓐ	Ⓑ	Ⓒ	Ⓓ
12	Ⓐ	Ⓑ	Ⓒ		32	Ⓐ	Ⓑ	Ⓒ	Ⓓ	52	Ⓐ	Ⓑ	Ⓒ	Ⓓ	72	Ⓐ	Ⓑ	Ⓒ	Ⓓ	92	Ⓐ	Ⓑ	Ⓒ	Ⓓ
13	Ⓐ	Ⓑ	Ⓒ		33	Ⓐ	Ⓑ	Ⓒ	Ⓓ	53	Ⓐ	Ⓑ	Ⓒ	Ⓓ	73	Ⓐ	Ⓑ	Ⓒ	Ⓓ	93	Ⓐ	Ⓑ	Ⓒ	Ⓓ
14	Ⓐ	Ⓑ	Ⓒ		34	Ⓐ	Ⓑ	Ⓒ	Ⓓ	54	Ⓐ	Ⓑ	Ⓒ	Ⓓ	74	Ⓐ	Ⓑ	Ⓒ	Ⓓ	94	Ⓐ	Ⓑ	Ⓒ	Ⓓ
15	Ⓐ	Ⓑ	Ⓒ		35	Ⓐ	Ⓑ	Ⓒ	Ⓓ	55	Ⓐ	Ⓑ	Ⓒ	Ⓓ	75	Ⓐ	Ⓑ	Ⓒ	Ⓓ	95	Ⓐ	Ⓑ	Ⓒ	Ⓓ
16	Ⓐ	Ⓑ	Ⓒ		36	Ⓐ	Ⓑ	Ⓒ	Ⓓ	56	Ⓐ	Ⓑ	Ⓒ	Ⓓ	76	Ⓐ	Ⓑ	Ⓒ	Ⓓ	96	Ⓐ	Ⓑ	Ⓒ	Ⓓ
17	Ⓐ	Ⓑ	Ⓒ		37	Ⓐ	Ⓑ	Ⓒ	Ⓓ	57	Ⓐ	Ⓑ	Ⓒ	Ⓓ	77	Ⓐ	Ⓑ	Ⓒ	Ⓓ	97	Ⓐ	Ⓑ	Ⓒ	Ⓓ
18	Ⓐ	Ⓑ	Ⓒ		38	Ⓐ	Ⓑ	Ⓒ	Ⓓ	58	Ⓐ	Ⓑ	Ⓒ	Ⓓ	78	Ⓐ	Ⓑ	Ⓒ	Ⓓ	98	Ⓐ	Ⓑ	Ⓒ	Ⓓ
19	Ⓐ	Ⓑ	Ⓒ		39	Ⓐ	Ⓑ	Ⓒ	Ⓓ	59	Ⓐ	Ⓑ	Ⓒ	Ⓓ	79	Ⓐ	Ⓑ	Ⓒ	Ⓓ	99	Ⓐ	Ⓑ	Ⓒ	Ⓓ
20	Ⓐ	Ⓑ	Ⓒ		40	Ⓐ	Ⓑ	Ⓒ	Ⓓ	60	Ⓐ	Ⓑ	Ⓒ	Ⓓ	80	Ⓐ	Ⓑ	Ⓒ	Ⓓ	100	Ⓐ	Ⓑ	Ⓒ	Ⓓ

ANSWER SHEET

수험번호							No.
성명	한글						
	영자						

TEST 06 (Part 1~4)

NO.	ANSWER				NO.	ANSWER				NO.	ANSWER				NO.	ANSWER				NO.	ANSWER			
	A	B	C	D		A	B	C	D		A	B	C	D		A	B	C	D		A	B	C	D
1	Ⓐ	Ⓑ	Ⓒ	Ⓓ	21	Ⓐ	Ⓑ	Ⓒ		41	Ⓐ	Ⓑ	Ⓒ	Ⓓ	61	Ⓐ	Ⓑ	Ⓒ	Ⓓ	81	Ⓐ	Ⓑ	Ⓒ	Ⓓ
2	Ⓐ	Ⓑ	Ⓒ	Ⓓ	22	Ⓐ	Ⓑ	Ⓒ		42	Ⓐ	Ⓑ	Ⓒ	Ⓓ	62	Ⓐ	Ⓑ	Ⓒ	Ⓓ	82	Ⓐ	Ⓑ	Ⓒ	Ⓓ
3	Ⓐ	Ⓑ	Ⓒ	Ⓓ	23	Ⓐ	Ⓑ	Ⓒ		43	Ⓐ	Ⓑ	Ⓒ	Ⓓ	63	Ⓐ	Ⓑ	Ⓒ	Ⓓ	83	Ⓐ	Ⓑ	Ⓒ	Ⓓ
4	Ⓐ	Ⓑ	Ⓒ	Ⓓ	24	Ⓐ	Ⓑ	Ⓒ		44	Ⓐ	Ⓑ	Ⓒ	Ⓓ	64	Ⓐ	Ⓑ	Ⓒ	Ⓓ	84	Ⓐ	Ⓑ	Ⓒ	Ⓓ
5	Ⓐ	Ⓑ	Ⓒ	Ⓓ	25	Ⓐ	Ⓑ	Ⓒ		45	Ⓐ	Ⓑ	Ⓒ	Ⓓ	65	Ⓐ	Ⓑ	Ⓒ	Ⓓ	85	Ⓐ	Ⓑ	Ⓒ	Ⓓ
6	Ⓐ	Ⓑ	Ⓒ	Ⓓ	26	Ⓐ	Ⓑ	Ⓒ		46	Ⓐ	Ⓑ	Ⓒ	Ⓓ	66	Ⓐ	Ⓑ	Ⓒ	Ⓓ	86	Ⓐ	Ⓑ	Ⓒ	Ⓓ
7	Ⓐ	Ⓑ	Ⓒ		27	Ⓐ	Ⓑ	Ⓒ		47	Ⓐ	Ⓑ	Ⓒ	Ⓓ	67	Ⓐ	Ⓑ	Ⓒ	Ⓓ	87	Ⓐ	Ⓑ	Ⓒ	Ⓓ
8	Ⓐ	Ⓑ	Ⓒ		28	Ⓐ	Ⓑ	Ⓒ		48	Ⓐ	Ⓑ	Ⓒ	Ⓓ	68	Ⓐ	Ⓑ	Ⓒ	Ⓓ	88	Ⓐ	Ⓑ	Ⓒ	Ⓓ
9	Ⓐ	Ⓑ	Ⓒ		29	Ⓐ	Ⓑ	Ⓒ		49	Ⓐ	Ⓑ	Ⓒ	Ⓓ	69	Ⓐ	Ⓑ	Ⓒ	Ⓓ	89	Ⓐ	Ⓑ	Ⓒ	Ⓓ
10	Ⓐ	Ⓑ	Ⓒ		30	Ⓐ	Ⓑ	Ⓒ		50	Ⓐ	Ⓑ	Ⓒ	Ⓓ	70	Ⓐ	Ⓑ	Ⓒ	Ⓓ	90	Ⓐ	Ⓑ	Ⓒ	Ⓓ
11	Ⓐ	Ⓑ	Ⓒ		31	Ⓐ	Ⓑ	Ⓒ		51	Ⓐ	Ⓑ	Ⓒ	Ⓓ	71	Ⓐ	Ⓑ	Ⓒ	Ⓓ	91	Ⓐ	Ⓑ	Ⓒ	Ⓓ
12	Ⓐ	Ⓑ	Ⓒ		32	Ⓐ	Ⓑ	Ⓒ	Ⓓ	52	Ⓐ	Ⓑ	Ⓒ	Ⓓ	72	Ⓐ	Ⓑ	Ⓒ	Ⓓ	92	Ⓐ	Ⓑ	Ⓒ	Ⓓ
13	Ⓐ	Ⓑ	Ⓒ		33	Ⓐ	Ⓑ	Ⓒ	Ⓓ	53	Ⓐ	Ⓑ	Ⓒ	Ⓓ	73	Ⓐ	Ⓑ	Ⓒ	Ⓓ	93	Ⓐ	Ⓑ	Ⓒ	Ⓓ
14	Ⓐ	Ⓑ	Ⓒ		34	Ⓐ	Ⓑ	Ⓒ	Ⓓ	54	Ⓐ	Ⓑ	Ⓒ	Ⓓ	74	Ⓐ	Ⓑ	Ⓒ	Ⓓ	94	Ⓐ	Ⓑ	Ⓒ	Ⓓ
15	Ⓐ	Ⓑ	Ⓒ		35	Ⓐ	Ⓑ	Ⓒ	Ⓓ	55	Ⓐ	Ⓑ	Ⓒ	Ⓓ	75	Ⓐ	Ⓑ	Ⓒ	Ⓓ	95	Ⓐ	Ⓑ	Ⓒ	Ⓓ
16	Ⓐ	Ⓑ	Ⓒ		36	Ⓐ	Ⓑ	Ⓒ	Ⓓ	56	Ⓐ	Ⓑ	Ⓒ	Ⓓ	76	Ⓐ	Ⓑ	Ⓒ	Ⓓ	96	Ⓐ	Ⓑ	Ⓒ	Ⓓ
17	Ⓐ	Ⓑ	Ⓒ		37	Ⓐ	Ⓑ	Ⓒ	Ⓓ	57	Ⓐ	Ⓑ	Ⓒ	Ⓓ	77	Ⓐ	Ⓑ	Ⓒ	Ⓓ	97	Ⓐ	Ⓑ	Ⓒ	Ⓓ
18	Ⓐ	Ⓑ	Ⓒ		38	Ⓐ	Ⓑ	Ⓒ	Ⓓ	58	Ⓐ	Ⓑ	Ⓒ	Ⓓ	78	Ⓐ	Ⓑ	Ⓒ	Ⓓ	98	Ⓐ	Ⓑ	Ⓒ	Ⓓ
19	Ⓐ	Ⓑ	Ⓒ		39	Ⓐ	Ⓑ	Ⓒ	Ⓓ	59	Ⓐ	Ⓑ	Ⓒ	Ⓓ	79	Ⓐ	Ⓑ	Ⓒ	Ⓓ	99	Ⓐ	Ⓑ	Ⓒ	Ⓓ
20	Ⓐ	Ⓑ	Ⓒ		40	Ⓐ	Ⓑ	Ⓒ	Ⓓ	60	Ⓐ	Ⓑ	Ⓒ	Ⓓ	80	Ⓐ	Ⓑ	Ⓒ	Ⓓ	100	Ⓐ	Ⓑ	Ⓒ	Ⓓ

ANSWER SHEET

수험번호						
성명	한글					
	영자					

No.

TEST 07 (Part 1~4)

NO.	ANSWER				NO.	ANSWER				NO.	ANSWER				NO.	ANSWER				NO.	ANSWER			
	A	B	C	D		A	B	C	D		A	B	C	D		A	B	C	D		A	B	C	D
1	Ⓐ	Ⓑ	Ⓒ	Ⓓ	21	Ⓐ	Ⓑ	Ⓒ		41	Ⓐ	Ⓑ	Ⓒ	Ⓓ	61	Ⓐ	Ⓑ	Ⓒ	Ⓓ	81	Ⓐ	Ⓑ	Ⓒ	Ⓓ
2	Ⓐ	Ⓑ	Ⓒ	Ⓓ	22	Ⓐ	Ⓑ	Ⓒ		42	Ⓐ	Ⓑ	Ⓒ	Ⓓ	62	Ⓐ	Ⓑ	Ⓒ	Ⓓ	82	Ⓐ	Ⓑ	Ⓒ	Ⓓ
3	Ⓐ	Ⓑ	Ⓒ	Ⓓ	23	Ⓐ	Ⓑ	Ⓒ		43	Ⓐ	Ⓑ	Ⓒ	Ⓓ	63	Ⓐ	Ⓑ	Ⓒ	Ⓓ	83	Ⓐ	Ⓑ	Ⓒ	Ⓓ
4	Ⓐ	Ⓑ	Ⓒ	Ⓓ	24	Ⓐ	Ⓑ	Ⓒ		44	Ⓐ	Ⓑ	Ⓒ	Ⓓ	64	Ⓐ	Ⓑ	Ⓒ	Ⓓ	84	Ⓐ	Ⓑ	Ⓒ	Ⓓ
5	Ⓐ	Ⓑ	Ⓒ	Ⓓ	25	Ⓐ	Ⓑ	Ⓒ		45	Ⓐ	Ⓑ	Ⓒ	Ⓓ	65	Ⓐ	Ⓑ	Ⓒ	Ⓓ	85	Ⓐ	Ⓑ	Ⓒ	Ⓓ
6	Ⓐ	Ⓑ	Ⓒ	Ⓓ	26	Ⓐ	Ⓑ	Ⓒ		46	Ⓐ	Ⓑ	Ⓒ	Ⓓ	66	Ⓐ	Ⓑ	Ⓒ	Ⓓ	86	Ⓐ	Ⓑ	Ⓒ	Ⓓ
7	Ⓐ	Ⓑ	Ⓒ		27	Ⓐ	Ⓑ	Ⓒ		47	Ⓐ	Ⓑ	Ⓒ	Ⓓ	67	Ⓐ	Ⓑ	Ⓒ	Ⓓ	87	Ⓐ	Ⓑ	Ⓒ	Ⓓ
8	Ⓐ	Ⓑ	Ⓒ		28	Ⓐ	Ⓑ	Ⓒ		48	Ⓐ	Ⓑ	Ⓒ	Ⓓ	68	Ⓐ	Ⓑ	Ⓒ	Ⓓ	88	Ⓐ	Ⓑ	Ⓒ	Ⓓ
9	Ⓐ	Ⓑ	Ⓒ		29	Ⓐ	Ⓑ	Ⓒ		49	Ⓐ	Ⓑ	Ⓒ	Ⓓ	69	Ⓐ	Ⓑ	Ⓒ	Ⓓ	89	Ⓐ	Ⓑ	Ⓒ	Ⓓ
10	Ⓐ	Ⓑ	Ⓒ		30	Ⓐ	Ⓑ	Ⓒ		50	Ⓐ	Ⓑ	Ⓒ	Ⓓ	70	Ⓐ	Ⓑ	Ⓒ	Ⓓ	90	Ⓐ	Ⓑ	Ⓒ	Ⓓ
11	Ⓐ	Ⓑ	Ⓒ		31	Ⓐ	Ⓑ	Ⓒ		51	Ⓐ	Ⓑ	Ⓒ	Ⓓ	71	Ⓐ	Ⓑ	Ⓒ	Ⓓ	91	Ⓐ	Ⓑ	Ⓒ	Ⓓ
12	Ⓐ	Ⓑ	Ⓒ		32	Ⓐ	Ⓑ	Ⓒ	Ⓓ	52	Ⓐ	Ⓑ	Ⓒ	Ⓓ	72	Ⓐ	Ⓑ	Ⓒ	Ⓓ	92	Ⓐ	Ⓑ	Ⓒ	Ⓓ
13	Ⓐ	Ⓑ	Ⓒ		33	Ⓐ	Ⓑ	Ⓒ	Ⓓ	53	Ⓐ	Ⓑ	Ⓒ	Ⓓ	73	Ⓐ	Ⓑ	Ⓒ	Ⓓ	93	Ⓐ	Ⓑ	Ⓒ	Ⓓ
14	Ⓐ	Ⓑ	Ⓒ		34	Ⓐ	Ⓑ	Ⓒ	Ⓓ	54	Ⓐ	Ⓑ	Ⓒ	Ⓓ	74	Ⓐ	Ⓑ	Ⓒ	Ⓓ	94	Ⓐ	Ⓑ	Ⓒ	Ⓓ
15	Ⓐ	Ⓑ	Ⓒ		35	Ⓐ	Ⓑ	Ⓒ	Ⓓ	55	Ⓐ	Ⓑ	Ⓒ	Ⓓ	75	Ⓐ	Ⓑ	Ⓒ	Ⓓ	95	Ⓐ	Ⓑ	Ⓒ	Ⓓ
16	Ⓐ	Ⓑ	Ⓒ		36	Ⓐ	Ⓑ	Ⓒ	Ⓓ	56	Ⓐ	Ⓑ	Ⓒ	Ⓓ	76	Ⓐ	Ⓑ	Ⓒ	Ⓓ	96	Ⓐ	Ⓑ	Ⓒ	Ⓓ
17	Ⓐ	Ⓑ	Ⓒ		37	Ⓐ	Ⓑ	Ⓒ	Ⓓ	57	Ⓐ	Ⓑ	Ⓒ	Ⓓ	77	Ⓐ	Ⓑ	Ⓒ	Ⓓ	97	Ⓐ	Ⓑ	Ⓒ	Ⓓ
18	Ⓐ	Ⓑ	Ⓒ		38	Ⓐ	Ⓑ	Ⓒ	Ⓓ	58	Ⓐ	Ⓑ	Ⓒ	Ⓓ	78	Ⓐ	Ⓑ	Ⓒ	Ⓓ	98	Ⓐ	Ⓑ	Ⓒ	Ⓓ
19	Ⓐ	Ⓑ	Ⓒ		39	Ⓐ	Ⓑ	Ⓒ	Ⓓ	59	Ⓐ	Ⓑ	Ⓒ	Ⓓ	79	Ⓐ	Ⓑ	Ⓒ	Ⓓ	99	Ⓐ	Ⓑ	Ⓒ	Ⓓ
20	Ⓐ	Ⓑ	Ⓒ		40	Ⓐ	Ⓑ	Ⓒ	Ⓓ	60	Ⓐ	Ⓑ	Ⓒ	Ⓓ	80	Ⓐ	Ⓑ	Ⓒ	Ⓓ	100	Ⓐ	Ⓑ	Ⓒ	Ⓓ

ANSWER SHEET

수험번호						
성명	한글					
	영자					

No.

TEST 08 (Part 1~4)

NO.	ANSWER				NO.	ANSWER				NO.	ANSWER				NO.	ANSWER				NO.	ANSWER			
	A	B	C	D		A	B	C	D		A	B	C	D		A	B	C	D		A	B	C	D
1	Ⓐ	Ⓑ	Ⓒ	Ⓓ	21	Ⓐ	Ⓑ	Ⓒ		41	Ⓐ	Ⓑ	Ⓒ	Ⓓ	61	Ⓐ	Ⓑ	Ⓒ	Ⓓ	81	Ⓐ	Ⓑ	Ⓒ	Ⓓ
2	Ⓐ	Ⓑ	Ⓒ	Ⓓ	22	Ⓐ	Ⓑ	Ⓒ		42	Ⓐ	Ⓑ	Ⓒ	Ⓓ	62	Ⓐ	Ⓑ	Ⓒ	Ⓓ	82	Ⓐ	Ⓑ	Ⓒ	Ⓓ
3	Ⓐ	Ⓑ	Ⓒ	Ⓓ	23	Ⓐ	Ⓑ	Ⓒ		43	Ⓐ	Ⓑ	Ⓒ	Ⓓ	63	Ⓐ	Ⓑ	Ⓒ	Ⓓ	83	Ⓐ	Ⓑ	Ⓒ	Ⓓ
4	Ⓐ	Ⓑ	Ⓒ	Ⓓ	24	Ⓐ	Ⓑ	Ⓒ		44	Ⓐ	Ⓑ	Ⓒ	Ⓓ	64	Ⓐ	Ⓑ	Ⓒ	Ⓓ	84	Ⓐ	Ⓑ	Ⓒ	Ⓓ
5	Ⓐ	Ⓑ	Ⓒ	Ⓓ	25	Ⓐ	Ⓑ	Ⓒ		45	Ⓐ	Ⓑ	Ⓒ	Ⓓ	65	Ⓐ	Ⓑ	Ⓒ	Ⓓ	85	Ⓐ	Ⓑ	Ⓒ	Ⓓ
6	Ⓐ	Ⓑ	Ⓒ	Ⓓ	26	Ⓐ	Ⓑ	Ⓒ		46	Ⓐ	Ⓑ	Ⓒ	Ⓓ	66	Ⓐ	Ⓑ	Ⓒ	Ⓓ	86	Ⓐ	Ⓑ	Ⓒ	Ⓓ
7	Ⓐ	Ⓑ	Ⓒ		27	Ⓐ	Ⓑ	Ⓒ		47	Ⓐ	Ⓑ	Ⓒ	Ⓓ	67	Ⓐ	Ⓑ	Ⓒ	Ⓓ	87	Ⓐ	Ⓑ	Ⓒ	Ⓓ
8	Ⓐ	Ⓑ	Ⓒ		28	Ⓐ	Ⓑ	Ⓒ		48	Ⓐ	Ⓑ	Ⓒ	Ⓓ	68	Ⓐ	Ⓑ	Ⓒ	Ⓓ	88	Ⓐ	Ⓑ	Ⓒ	Ⓓ
9	Ⓐ	Ⓑ	Ⓒ		29	Ⓐ	Ⓑ	Ⓒ		49	Ⓐ	Ⓑ	Ⓒ	Ⓓ	69	Ⓐ	Ⓑ	Ⓒ	Ⓓ	89	Ⓐ	Ⓑ	Ⓒ	Ⓓ
10	Ⓐ	Ⓑ	Ⓒ		30	Ⓐ	Ⓑ	Ⓒ		50	Ⓐ	Ⓑ	Ⓒ	Ⓓ	70	Ⓐ	Ⓑ	Ⓒ	Ⓓ	90	Ⓐ	Ⓑ	Ⓒ	Ⓓ
11	Ⓐ	Ⓑ	Ⓒ		31	Ⓐ	Ⓑ	Ⓒ		51	Ⓐ	Ⓑ	Ⓒ	Ⓓ	71	Ⓐ	Ⓑ	Ⓒ	Ⓓ	91	Ⓐ	Ⓑ	Ⓒ	Ⓓ
12	Ⓐ	Ⓑ	Ⓒ		32	Ⓐ	Ⓑ	Ⓒ	Ⓓ	52	Ⓐ	Ⓑ	Ⓒ	Ⓓ	72	Ⓐ	Ⓑ	Ⓒ	Ⓓ	92	Ⓐ	Ⓑ	Ⓒ	Ⓓ
13	Ⓐ	Ⓑ	Ⓒ		33	Ⓐ	Ⓑ	Ⓒ	Ⓓ	53	Ⓐ	Ⓑ	Ⓒ	Ⓓ	73	Ⓐ	Ⓑ	Ⓒ	Ⓓ	93	Ⓐ	Ⓑ	Ⓒ	Ⓓ
14	Ⓐ	Ⓑ	Ⓒ		34	Ⓐ	Ⓑ	Ⓒ	Ⓓ	54	Ⓐ	Ⓑ	Ⓒ	Ⓓ	74	Ⓐ	Ⓑ	Ⓒ	Ⓓ	94	Ⓐ	Ⓑ	Ⓒ	Ⓓ
15	Ⓐ	Ⓑ	Ⓒ		35	Ⓐ	Ⓑ	Ⓒ	Ⓓ	55	Ⓐ	Ⓑ	Ⓒ	Ⓓ	75	Ⓐ	Ⓑ	Ⓒ	Ⓓ	95	Ⓐ	Ⓑ	Ⓒ	Ⓓ
16	Ⓐ	Ⓑ	Ⓒ		36	Ⓐ	Ⓑ	Ⓒ	Ⓓ	56	Ⓐ	Ⓑ	Ⓒ	Ⓓ	76	Ⓐ	Ⓑ	Ⓒ	Ⓓ	96	Ⓐ	Ⓑ	Ⓒ	Ⓓ
17	Ⓐ	Ⓑ	Ⓒ		37	Ⓐ	Ⓑ	Ⓒ	Ⓓ	57	Ⓐ	Ⓑ	Ⓒ	Ⓓ	77	Ⓐ	Ⓑ	Ⓒ	Ⓓ	97	Ⓐ	Ⓑ	Ⓒ	Ⓓ
18	Ⓐ	Ⓑ	Ⓒ		38	Ⓐ	Ⓑ	Ⓒ	Ⓓ	58	Ⓐ	Ⓑ	Ⓒ	Ⓓ	78	Ⓐ	Ⓑ	Ⓒ	Ⓓ	98	Ⓐ	Ⓑ	Ⓒ	Ⓓ
19	Ⓐ	Ⓑ	Ⓒ		39	Ⓐ	Ⓑ	Ⓒ	Ⓓ	59	Ⓐ	Ⓑ	Ⓒ	Ⓓ	79	Ⓐ	Ⓑ	Ⓒ	Ⓓ	99	Ⓐ	Ⓑ	Ⓒ	Ⓓ
20	Ⓐ	Ⓑ	Ⓒ		40	Ⓐ	Ⓑ	Ⓒ	Ⓓ	60	Ⓐ	Ⓑ	Ⓒ	Ⓓ	80	Ⓐ	Ⓑ	Ⓒ	Ⓓ	100	Ⓐ	Ⓑ	Ⓒ	Ⓓ

ANSWER SHEET

수험번호						No.
성명	한글					
	영자					

TEST 09 (Part 1~4)

NO.	ANSWER				NO.	ANSWER				NO.	ANSWER				NO.	ANSWER				NO.	ANSWER			
	A	B	C	D		A	B	C	D		A	B	C	D		A	B	C	D		A	B	C	D
1	Ⓐ	Ⓑ	Ⓒ	Ⓓ	21	Ⓐ	Ⓑ	Ⓒ		41	Ⓐ	Ⓑ	Ⓒ	Ⓓ	61	Ⓐ	Ⓑ	Ⓒ	Ⓓ	81	Ⓐ	Ⓑ	Ⓒ	Ⓓ
2	Ⓐ	Ⓑ	Ⓒ	Ⓓ	22	Ⓐ	Ⓑ	Ⓒ		42	Ⓐ	Ⓑ	Ⓒ	Ⓓ	62	Ⓐ	Ⓑ	Ⓒ	Ⓓ	82	Ⓐ	Ⓑ	Ⓒ	Ⓓ
3	Ⓐ	Ⓑ	Ⓒ	Ⓓ	23	Ⓐ	Ⓑ	Ⓒ		43	Ⓐ	Ⓑ	Ⓒ	Ⓓ	63	Ⓐ	Ⓑ	Ⓒ	Ⓓ	83	Ⓐ	Ⓑ	Ⓒ	Ⓓ
4	Ⓐ	Ⓑ	Ⓒ	Ⓓ	24	Ⓐ	Ⓑ	Ⓒ		44	Ⓐ	Ⓑ	Ⓒ	Ⓓ	64	Ⓐ	Ⓑ	Ⓒ	Ⓓ	84	Ⓐ	Ⓑ	Ⓒ	Ⓓ
5	Ⓐ	Ⓑ	Ⓒ	Ⓓ	25	Ⓐ	Ⓑ	Ⓒ		45	Ⓐ	Ⓑ	Ⓒ	Ⓓ	65	Ⓐ	Ⓑ	Ⓒ	Ⓓ	85	Ⓐ	Ⓑ	Ⓒ	Ⓓ
6	Ⓐ	Ⓑ	Ⓒ	Ⓓ	26	Ⓐ	Ⓑ	Ⓒ		46	Ⓐ	Ⓑ	Ⓒ	Ⓓ	66	Ⓐ	Ⓑ	Ⓒ	Ⓓ	86	Ⓐ	Ⓑ	Ⓒ	Ⓓ
7	Ⓐ	Ⓑ	Ⓒ		27	Ⓐ	Ⓑ	Ⓒ		47	Ⓐ	Ⓑ	Ⓒ	Ⓓ	67	Ⓐ	Ⓑ	Ⓒ	Ⓓ	87	Ⓐ	Ⓑ	Ⓒ	Ⓓ
8	Ⓐ	Ⓑ	Ⓒ		28	Ⓐ	Ⓑ	Ⓒ		48	Ⓐ	Ⓑ	Ⓒ	Ⓓ	68	Ⓐ	Ⓑ	Ⓒ	Ⓓ	88	Ⓐ	Ⓑ	Ⓒ	Ⓓ
9	Ⓐ	Ⓑ	Ⓒ		29	Ⓐ	Ⓑ	Ⓒ		49	Ⓐ	Ⓑ	Ⓒ	Ⓓ	69	Ⓐ	Ⓑ	Ⓒ	Ⓓ	89	Ⓐ	Ⓑ	Ⓒ	Ⓓ
10	Ⓐ	Ⓑ	Ⓒ		30	Ⓐ	Ⓑ	Ⓒ		50	Ⓐ	Ⓑ	Ⓒ	Ⓓ	70	Ⓐ	Ⓑ	Ⓒ	Ⓓ	90	Ⓐ	Ⓑ	Ⓒ	Ⓓ
11	Ⓐ	Ⓑ	Ⓒ		31	Ⓐ	Ⓑ	Ⓒ		51	Ⓐ	Ⓑ	Ⓒ	Ⓓ	71	Ⓐ	Ⓑ	Ⓒ	Ⓓ	91	Ⓐ	Ⓑ	Ⓒ	Ⓓ
12	Ⓐ	Ⓑ	Ⓒ		32	Ⓐ	Ⓑ	Ⓒ	Ⓓ	52	Ⓐ	Ⓑ	Ⓒ	Ⓓ	72	Ⓐ	Ⓑ	Ⓒ	Ⓓ	92	Ⓐ	Ⓑ	Ⓒ	Ⓓ
13	Ⓐ	Ⓑ	Ⓒ		33	Ⓐ	Ⓑ	Ⓒ	Ⓓ	53	Ⓐ	Ⓑ	Ⓒ	Ⓓ	73	Ⓐ	Ⓑ	Ⓒ	Ⓓ	93	Ⓐ	Ⓑ	Ⓒ	Ⓓ
14	Ⓐ	Ⓑ	Ⓒ		34	Ⓐ	Ⓑ	Ⓒ	Ⓓ	54	Ⓐ	Ⓑ	Ⓒ	Ⓓ	74	Ⓐ	Ⓑ	Ⓒ	Ⓓ	94	Ⓐ	Ⓑ	Ⓒ	Ⓓ
15	Ⓐ	Ⓑ	Ⓒ		35	Ⓐ	Ⓑ	Ⓒ	Ⓓ	55	Ⓐ	Ⓑ	Ⓒ	Ⓓ	75	Ⓐ	Ⓑ	Ⓒ	Ⓓ	95	Ⓐ	Ⓑ	Ⓒ	Ⓓ
16	Ⓐ	Ⓑ	Ⓒ		36	Ⓐ	Ⓑ	Ⓒ	Ⓓ	56	Ⓐ	Ⓑ	Ⓒ	Ⓓ	76	Ⓐ	Ⓑ	Ⓒ	Ⓓ	96	Ⓐ	Ⓑ	Ⓒ	Ⓓ
17	Ⓐ	Ⓑ	Ⓒ		37	Ⓐ	Ⓑ	Ⓒ	Ⓓ	57	Ⓐ	Ⓑ	Ⓒ	Ⓓ	77	Ⓐ	Ⓑ	Ⓒ	Ⓓ	97	Ⓐ	Ⓑ	Ⓒ	Ⓓ
18	Ⓐ	Ⓑ	Ⓒ		38	Ⓐ	Ⓑ	Ⓒ	Ⓓ	58	Ⓐ	Ⓑ	Ⓒ	Ⓓ	78	Ⓐ	Ⓑ	Ⓒ	Ⓓ	98	Ⓐ	Ⓑ	Ⓒ	Ⓓ
19	Ⓐ	Ⓑ	Ⓒ		39	Ⓐ	Ⓑ	Ⓒ	Ⓓ	59	Ⓐ	Ⓑ	Ⓒ	Ⓓ	79	Ⓐ	Ⓑ	Ⓒ	Ⓓ	99	Ⓐ	Ⓑ	Ⓒ	Ⓓ
20	Ⓐ	Ⓑ	Ⓒ		40	Ⓐ	Ⓑ	Ⓒ	Ⓓ	60	Ⓐ	Ⓑ	Ⓒ	Ⓓ	80	Ⓐ	Ⓑ	Ⓒ	Ⓓ	100	Ⓐ	Ⓑ	Ⓒ	Ⓓ

ANSWER SHEET

수험번호						No.
성명	한글					
	영자					

TEST 10 (Part 1~4)

NO.	ANSWER				NO.	ANSWER				NO.	ANSWER				NO.	ANSWER				NO.	ANSWER			
	A	B	C	D		A	B	C	D		A	B	C	D		A	B	C	D		A	B	C	D
1	Ⓐ	Ⓑ	Ⓒ	Ⓓ	21	Ⓐ	Ⓑ	Ⓒ		41	Ⓐ	Ⓑ	Ⓒ	Ⓓ	61	Ⓐ	Ⓑ	Ⓒ	Ⓓ	81	Ⓐ	Ⓑ	Ⓒ	Ⓓ
2	Ⓐ	Ⓑ	Ⓒ	Ⓓ	22	Ⓐ	Ⓑ	Ⓒ		42	Ⓐ	Ⓑ	Ⓒ	Ⓓ	62	Ⓐ	Ⓑ	Ⓒ	Ⓓ	82	Ⓐ	Ⓑ	Ⓒ	Ⓓ
3	Ⓐ	Ⓑ	Ⓒ	Ⓓ	23	Ⓐ	Ⓑ	Ⓒ		43	Ⓐ	Ⓑ	Ⓒ	Ⓓ	63	Ⓐ	Ⓑ	Ⓒ	Ⓓ	83	Ⓐ	Ⓑ	Ⓒ	Ⓓ
4	Ⓐ	Ⓑ	Ⓒ	Ⓓ	24	Ⓐ	Ⓑ	Ⓒ		44	Ⓐ	Ⓑ	Ⓒ	Ⓓ	64	Ⓐ	Ⓑ	Ⓒ	Ⓓ	84	Ⓐ	Ⓑ	Ⓒ	Ⓓ
5	Ⓐ	Ⓑ	Ⓒ	Ⓓ	25	Ⓐ	Ⓑ	Ⓒ		45	Ⓐ	Ⓑ	Ⓒ	Ⓓ	65	Ⓐ	Ⓑ	Ⓒ	Ⓓ	85	Ⓐ	Ⓑ	Ⓒ	Ⓓ
6	Ⓐ	Ⓑ	Ⓒ	Ⓓ	26	Ⓐ	Ⓑ	Ⓒ		46	Ⓐ	Ⓑ	Ⓒ	Ⓓ	66	Ⓐ	Ⓑ	Ⓒ	Ⓓ	86	Ⓐ	Ⓑ	Ⓒ	Ⓓ
7	Ⓐ	Ⓑ	Ⓒ		27	Ⓐ	Ⓑ	Ⓒ		47	Ⓐ	Ⓑ	Ⓒ	Ⓓ	67	Ⓐ	Ⓑ	Ⓒ	Ⓓ	87	Ⓐ	Ⓑ	Ⓒ	Ⓓ
8	Ⓐ	Ⓑ	Ⓒ		28	Ⓐ	Ⓑ	Ⓒ		48	Ⓐ	Ⓑ	Ⓒ	Ⓓ	68	Ⓐ	Ⓑ	Ⓒ	Ⓓ	88	Ⓐ	Ⓑ	Ⓒ	Ⓓ
9	Ⓐ	Ⓑ	Ⓒ		29	Ⓐ	Ⓑ	Ⓒ		49	Ⓐ	Ⓑ	Ⓒ	Ⓓ	69	Ⓐ	Ⓑ	Ⓒ	Ⓓ	89	Ⓐ	Ⓑ	Ⓒ	Ⓓ
10	Ⓐ	Ⓑ	Ⓒ		30	Ⓐ	Ⓑ	Ⓒ		50	Ⓐ	Ⓑ	Ⓒ	Ⓓ	70	Ⓐ	Ⓑ	Ⓒ	Ⓓ	90	Ⓐ	Ⓑ	Ⓒ	Ⓓ
11	Ⓐ	Ⓑ	Ⓒ		31	Ⓐ	Ⓑ	Ⓒ		51	Ⓐ	Ⓑ	Ⓒ	Ⓓ	71	Ⓐ	Ⓑ	Ⓒ	Ⓓ	91	Ⓐ	Ⓑ	Ⓒ	Ⓓ
12	Ⓐ	Ⓑ	Ⓒ		32	Ⓐ	Ⓑ	Ⓒ	Ⓓ	52	Ⓐ	Ⓑ	Ⓒ	Ⓓ	72	Ⓐ	Ⓑ	Ⓒ	Ⓓ	92	Ⓐ	Ⓑ	Ⓒ	Ⓓ
13	Ⓐ	Ⓑ	Ⓒ		33	Ⓐ	Ⓑ	Ⓒ	Ⓓ	53	Ⓐ	Ⓑ	Ⓒ	Ⓓ	73	Ⓐ	Ⓑ	Ⓒ	Ⓓ	93	Ⓐ	Ⓑ	Ⓒ	Ⓓ
14	Ⓐ	Ⓑ	Ⓒ		34	Ⓐ	Ⓑ	Ⓒ	Ⓓ	54	Ⓐ	Ⓑ	Ⓒ	Ⓓ	74	Ⓐ	Ⓑ	Ⓒ	Ⓓ	94	Ⓐ	Ⓑ	Ⓒ	Ⓓ
15	Ⓐ	Ⓑ	Ⓒ		35	Ⓐ	Ⓑ	Ⓒ	Ⓓ	55	Ⓐ	Ⓑ	Ⓒ	Ⓓ	75	Ⓐ	Ⓑ	Ⓒ	Ⓓ	95	Ⓐ	Ⓑ	Ⓒ	Ⓓ
16	Ⓐ	Ⓑ	Ⓒ		36	Ⓐ	Ⓑ	Ⓒ	Ⓓ	56	Ⓐ	Ⓑ	Ⓒ	Ⓓ	76	Ⓐ	Ⓑ	Ⓒ	Ⓓ	96	Ⓐ	Ⓑ	Ⓒ	Ⓓ
17	Ⓐ	Ⓑ	Ⓒ		37	Ⓐ	Ⓑ	Ⓒ	Ⓓ	57	Ⓐ	Ⓑ	Ⓒ	Ⓓ	77	Ⓐ	Ⓑ	Ⓒ	Ⓓ	97	Ⓐ	Ⓑ	Ⓒ	Ⓓ
18	Ⓐ	Ⓑ	Ⓒ		38	Ⓐ	Ⓑ	Ⓒ	Ⓓ	58	Ⓐ	Ⓑ	Ⓒ	Ⓓ	78	Ⓐ	Ⓑ	Ⓒ	Ⓓ	98	Ⓐ	Ⓑ	Ⓒ	Ⓓ
19	Ⓐ	Ⓑ	Ⓒ		39	Ⓐ	Ⓑ	Ⓒ	Ⓓ	59	Ⓐ	Ⓑ	Ⓒ	Ⓓ	79	Ⓐ	Ⓑ	Ⓒ	Ⓓ	99	Ⓐ	Ⓑ	Ⓒ	Ⓓ
20	Ⓐ	Ⓑ	Ⓒ		40	Ⓐ	Ⓑ	Ⓒ	Ⓓ	60	Ⓐ	Ⓑ	Ⓒ	Ⓓ	80	Ⓐ	Ⓑ	Ⓒ	Ⓓ	100	Ⓐ	Ⓑ	Ⓒ	Ⓓ

books.english.co.kr

■■ 점수 환산표

LISTENING Raw Score (맞은 개수)	LISTENING Scaled Score (환산 점수)
96-100	475-495
91-95	435-495
86-90	405-475
81-85	370-450
76-80	345-420
71-75	320-390
66-70	290-360
61-65	265-335
56-60	235-310
51-55	210-280
46-50	180-255
41-45	155-230
36-40	125-205
31-35	105-175
26-30	85-145
21-25	60-115
16-20	30-90
11-15	5-70
6-10	5-60
1-5	5-50
0	5-35

READING Raw Score (맞은 개수)	READING Scaled Score (환산 점수)
96-100	460-495
91-95	425-490
86-90	395-465
81-85	370-440
76-80	335-415
71-75	310-390
66-70	280-365
61-65	250-335
56-60	220-305
51-55	195-270
46-50	165-240
41-45	140-215
36-40	115-180
31-35	95-145
26-30	75-120
21-25	60-95
16-20	45-75
11-15	30-55
6-10	10-40
1-5	5-30
0	5-15

※ 절대적인 기준이 아니므로 실제 토익 시험과 다소 차이가 있을 수 있습니다.